Logic
and design

To the bellman

Logic
and design

**in art, science
& mathematics**

Krome Barratt

Design Press

First U.S. Edition, First Printing

Copyright © 1980 by Krome Barratt

Printed in England

Library of Congress Cataloging-in-Publication Data

Barratt, Krome, 1924–
  Logic and design.

  Bibliography: p.
  Includes index.
  1. Design. I. Title.
NK1510.B29 1989   745.4   89–7720
ISBN 0–8306–4012–6

Author and publisher wish to thank the following for permission to
reproduce:

Geographia Limited (Crown Copyright Reserved) – map, page 83;
Graphische Sammlung Albertina, Vienna – Dürer drawing, page 83;
Lund Humphries Publishers Limited – quotation from *Paul Klee
Notebooks*, page 282; Vauxhall Motors – drawing, page 304.

Design Press offers posters and The Cropper, a device for cropping
artwork, for sale. For information, contact Mail-order Department.
Design Press books are available at special discounts for bulk
purchases for sales promotions, fund raisers, or premiums. For
details contact Special Sales Manager. Questions regarding the
content of this book should be addressed to:

Design Press
Division of TAB BOOKS Inc.
10 East 21st Street, Suite 1101
New York, NY 10010

Contents

Preface

This is not a book to be read like a novel. Nor is it a conventional textbook, although it is hoped that the information offered will be of practical value to designers in science, technology and the arts.

The book is conceived as a series of events that are interrelated and sometimes grouped. Each statement is reduced to a minimum so as to invite contemplation of the text in association with the drawings and captions. Although like most books it is prepared in sequential order, the flow of ideas is forward and backward. The many parts are interdependent and, as so often in life, one needs to read through to the end before starting at the beginning.

The statements are intentionally brief to encourage the reader's participation. Consequently they are often open to challenge. But this is not unwelcome. Each event will have served its purpose if it provides food for thought. In this respect my favourite quotation is one ascribed to Thomas Cooper, who is said to have asked in 1974:

'What is green and has got wheels?'
To which the reply was:
'Grass. I lied about the wheels.'

Our awesome universe proclaims a mighty sense of humour at every turn. Its many lies, as revealed through our senses, are less provocative than the truth. For, as contemporary science has discovered in nuclear physics, events, particles, objects, things are merely punctuations of rates of change. Nothing is necessarily what it seems. The most solid of rocks is more than 90 per cent empty space. The smallest man is, like Gulliver, a giant among ants.

This gathering of general information into unusual combinations is an attempt to provoke feelings on the meaning and purpose and means of design. The objective is, therefore, to open the doors of the mind, even imitating Mr Cooper by producing a dogma that invites the reader's protest.

You will think for yourself in any case and if, in the fullness of time, you come to enjoy the wisdom of the bellman, then our purpose will be served.

KB

Acknowledgements

I wish to take advantage of this public place to give thanks to those generous minds, throughout the ages, whose explorations are recorded in paint and stone, in number, writing and sound. For it is they who give intellectual continuity, dignity and courage to the human species. They are bellmen all.

The achievements of design logic in science and technology are obvious, yet I suspect that creative art and ideas also rely upon a sixth sense that is born of excellence in the other five. Therefore it is hoped that your travels about my whiteboard may help to realize a few dreams.

In the production of the first edition I must thank Julian Castle and James Burrell for producing from my sketches many of the technical drawings. Without their timely aid I would be drawing still.

The section Mapping the Macrocosm (pp. 97–102) was partially inspired in recollection by an article by J. J. Callahan in *Scientific American* Vol. 235/2, 1976 entitled 'The Curvature of Space in a Finite Universe'.

In preparing this second edition I am grateful for the help and encouragement of Peter Rich, Nell Burgaud, Stuart Russell and Pearl Atkinson. But in particular I wish to record my eternal gratitude to my beloved wife, Adelaide, for her courage, loyalty and meticulous caring, in addition to help with this book, during a testing period of our lives.

KB

Introduction

The whiteboard

Our knowledge of the physical universe has more than doubled during the last 25 years. Such a proliferation, not only of information but of the sources of information, should remind us of the Teacher who, equipped with a large box of chalks, recorded on a spotless, new blackboard every stage in the history of knowledge from Archimedes and Hipparchus to Reimann, Einstein and their miriad successors – without the use of a duster.

Progressively, the blackboard changed to a whiteboard, with here and there a quiver of greys at its edges. In the fullness of time, these peripheral ripples and turbulences, suggesting an occasional symbol or phrase, were the only obvious clues to the riches that lay buried in the layers of chalk.

In the absence of the Teacher, it is not difficult to imagine the plight of his students when presented with the whiteboard of knowledge; for it is our plight. As we attempt to decipher the topmost ripples and dig deeper into the layers of chalk, we must use our every faculty and make common cause with all explorers whose curiosity is spurred by the enigma of the board.

For our studies are revealing a majestic cosmic drama, from para-psychology and biology to particle physics, astronomy and beyond. As our information increases it has become more difficult to interrelate the many parts and, for convenience sake and in acknowledgement of our limitations, we are prone to compartmentalise them until they become separate kingdoms, denying the very unity from which they sprang.

But thoughts must start somewhere. Though they can rarely start from the beginning. Most times our first clues are in some intermediate stage of the whiteboard's history and it is these that we must interrelate, albeit temporarily, as a base from which we can explore in many directions. Gradually we learn to argue ourselves full circle upon the board; many times over to question our initial observations and assumptions, voyage upon voyage, layer after layer, progressively adjusting our datum as we dig deeper.

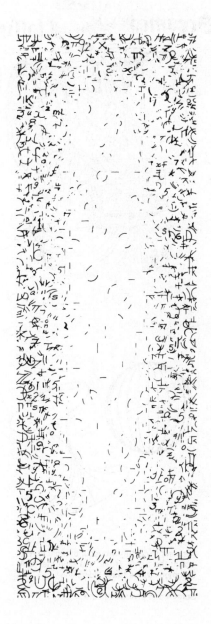

Oceanica Classis

That is the purpose of this book. To journey about the vast ocean of the whiteboard, with here and there a brief plunge beneath the surface. Not in any way to attempt to establish a datum. Nor yet to offer a chart for subsequent voyages. But to explore a variety of basic observations that may lead us nearer to a beginning, and confirming meanwhile that in challenging our imagination the exercise of *design and creativity* has common cause in art, technology and science.

Presence and beauty

For design is about the making of *things*: things that are memorable and have *presence* in the world of the mind. It makes demand upon our ability both to consolidate information as knowledge and to deploy it imaginatively to creative purpose in the pursuit of fresh information. The formulation of models, and their subsequent criticism, is perhaps our most useful guide in deciphering the knowledge of the whiteboard.

Therefore, as we consider the interrelationship of art, technology and science as a function of design, it may be helpful to be reminded of the advice given by Aristotle:

It is not everything that can be proved, otherwise the chain of proof would be endless. You must begin somewhere, and you must start with things admitted but undemonstrable. These are first principles common to all sciences which are called axioms or common opinions.

The evolutionary nature of knowledge is well illustrated by the geometry summarised by Euclid. Over 2000 years ago he prepared a basis for our everyday mechanical engineering on planet Earth. His 300 and more theorems evolved from a series of apparently simplistic axioms, such as:

A point is that which has no parts: therefore a point occupies nil space.
A straight line is that which lies evenly between its ends: therefore it is the shortest distance.
Parallel lines never meet: therefore the rectilinear grid of our Earthly lives continues unto Eternity.

Today many theorems deduced from the works of Euclid have been queried and sometimes disallowed in alternative geometries. For

A sixteenth century woodcut thought to represent the *Santa Maria*, the ship that took Columbus to the West Indies.

Sphere and pseudo-sphere.

example, the properties of straight parallel lines can be different when drawn on the surface of a sphere or a pseudosphere. Even so, great scholars tend to have influence far beyond their chosen discipline, and this is certainly true of Euclid.

It follows that, if design is about the making of things that are memorable, then it is the business of all people who aspire to creativity and innovation. Artists, technologists, scientists alike: none can proceed without an ability to gather, select and organise their information into a comprehensible form. All may profit from a study of design processes developed in other parallel disciplines for, to quote Professor Morris Kline:

The first rate mathematician depends on the kind of inspiration that we usually associate with the composer of music.

Similarly visualisation, by drawing or by model, is a primary design tool, as important to an engineer as to a portrait painter, a biochemist or an architect. Not only the transmission of ideas but the very ideas themselves are limited by the designer's sensitivity to visual relationships. Understanding is based upon a perception of pattern amidst the ebb and flow of visual stimuli. Sometimes an apparent order can turn out to be illusory; but that is by the way. Comprehension is based upon values that are acceptable at the instant, even if at another time they appear to be random and of no significance.

It is not at all difficult for a landscape painter to discern, amidst the twigs of winter trees, straight lines described against the sky: and these in turn echoed in the hedgerows, their sinews and grasses, seemingly as though a complete spinney, copse or woodland had been programmed by a geometer. Of course that is in fact the case; for this painter, this devotee of straight lines, is finding what he seeks.

Such is the enormity of the whiteboard that it can encompass all the dreams and constructions of mankind.

The making of things, from the simplest to the most complex of crafts, involves method. Skills in problem solving are needed by all who work with their hands, their senses, their brains. Such processes are conditioned by the human state, the whole human experience, and are not the prerogative of a particular field of activity or interest. Recently a group of psychologists have claimed that they can now measure a new born baby's capacity for solving problems . . . and find that the infant's motivation is the sheer joy of solving them.

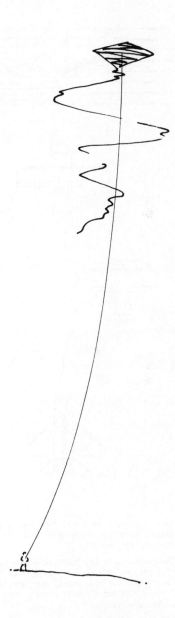

Kites have been flown for hundreds of years.

3

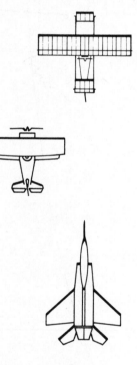

Kites, wings and sails work by creating a vacuum along the sheltered surface. This provides lift to leeward.

The direction of lift of a boat's sails is about 90° to the wind. A deep keel impedes lateral movement of the boat, setting up a triangle of forces to pinch the boat forward, close hauled, to windward.

With the wind over the left, or port, bow the boat on page 5 is on port tack.

If this is indeed the case, it seems that we are programmed to enjoy problem solving. Perhaps that is why scientists are more prone than artists to use the word *beautiful*. It is their description of a simple, all-embracing answer to a series of questions.

Often the construction and innovation of a simple idea may require a complex, multidimensional language. Both Newton's infinitesimal calculus and Turner's infinite sunsets were produced by rare, specialised skills. But the wonder of their discoveries can be enjoyed by all who care to look and admire their beauty, their ultimate simplicity as concepts.

Another beautiful solution to a complex problem is the double helix of DNA, which permits procreation when they separate. As the helices spiral out one from another, each builds a partner from the organic soup that feeds them and when this construction is complete each may divide again.

But the zip fastener, the wheel, the safety match and the aeroplane also solve difficult problems and should claim beauty.

The word beautiful is defined as *eminently satisfying to the senses and the mind*. It seems to be applicable whenever a series of disparate elements are brought together to form a memorable pattern, a cohesive whole, a physical or conceptual unity.

In a living creature millions of cells share a common coding, yet each performs a particular role in a specific location. The thumb of a human hand, for example, is opposed by its four companion fingers, yet they work in unison. Their group activity is mutually pro-survival and thus *harmonic*. None can live alone. A thumb, separated from its parent body, rapidly loses its utility and much of its beauty. Certainly its identity is changed, for it soon ceases to be a thumb.

So it is with the many parts of any complex living organism. The ordering of its varied elements into a unity is such that *the whole is more than the sum of the parts*.

For example, a human being is more than an assembly of hands, arms, legs, body and brain, arranged according to a certain programme. The intimate co-ordination of the parts produces a unity that exists in its own right and acquires *presence*.

It is. It becomes a *thing* and desires a name.

All things deserve names. If they are identifiable, as units, they become memorable and may be used as points of reference. The word 'tree' evokes an image, tree. The word 'cat' evokes the image, cat. The acquisition of a name implies a recognisable form that can be repeated as physical experience or as memory. This is not to suggest that we have names, as verbal language, for our every memorable sensory image. Far from it. It is merely to suggest that each recoverable image stored in our memory banks has a unity and sufficient presence to command a name. And if it can be given a name then it can be symbolised. In effect a name and a symbol perform similar functions, and symbolism can be regarded as a form of visual language.

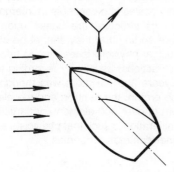

5

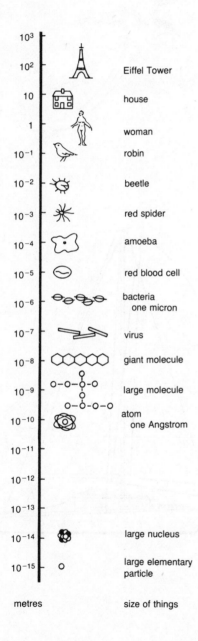

10^3	
10^2	Eiffel Tower
10	house
1	woman
10^{-1}	robin
10^{-2}	beetle
10^{-3}	red spider
10^{-4}	amoeba
10^{-5}	red blood cell
10^{-6}	bacteria one micron
10^{-7}	virus
10^{-8}	giant molecule
10^{-9}	large molecule
10^{-10}	atom one Angstrom
10^{-11}	
10^{-12}	
10^{-13}	
10^{-14}	large nucleus
10^{-15}	large elementary particle
metres	size of things

Elegance

When the elementary parts of a design are organised to contribute efficiently, and therefore without superfluities, to a common bonding programme, their individuality is subordinated to the emergent group identity. The process can be observed in any successful football team. Given sufficient freedom within the group programme and an adequate supply of energy, the parts tend to find their most stable and convenient internal distribution and the identity is intensified. They appear to obey the principles of entropy and by jostling, inflection and deflection, arrange and rearrange themselves into a state of minimum boundary.

When any part undertakes more than one function then the overall efficiency of the organisation is enhanced. Elegance is achieved when a variety of roles is accepted by each part, permitting the whole to operate at several levels of awareness, with interweaving functions inflecting one to another in a state of equilibrium and flux. It is then that an organisation can acquire the hypersensitive qualities that we associate with life, as though its chemistry has condensed space itself into a vibrant cauldron of energy. And when the building process is not revealed, it can acquire just a hint of magic.

It is fascinating to observe that physicists are moving closer to the thought forms of the ancients . . . of the mystics who found magic, the origin of the universe, in number and geometry. As they search beyond our sensory scales into concepts of intergalactic space/time so the models for its structure are based upon the minutest of particles. These are so tiny that they cannot be observed by direct means and the nuclear physicist is learning to tabulate them by the pattern of their interactions, usually by recording the tracks of their collisions. A few years ago the atom was thought to contain only three particles, the proton, the neutron and the electron. Today the behavioural pattern of over 300 elementary particles can be recognised and their proliferation is such that physicists are looking deeper still to find their finer common properties.

The ultimate unity

As science peels away layer beyond layer of the whiteboard the suspicion grows that the original chalk mark, if we can ever reach it, may contain a unity that becomes inexplicable because we are of it and in it. Science is concerned with a description of the world and to achieve this requires an observer and an observed. It is, therefore, incapable of describing unity and is ever in danger of chasing its own tail.

But goodness knows how many layers of knowledge have yet to be removed . . . to quote Albert Einstein:

The most incomprehensible thing about this universe is that it is comprehensible.

There is, of course, a school of thought that does not share Einstein's optimism. However there is accumulating evidence to suggest that in terms of number this universe has been made in the only possible way. This view is based upon the principles of resonance, as understood by a musician, and of a behavioural simplicity that conserves energy.

The conservation of energy and momentum requires that, in an elementary particle interaction, the total energy and momentum are constant. Nothing is gained and nothing is lost during the redistribution.

The conservation of energy leads to a need for symmetry of behaviour – any positive action shall permit an equal and opposite negative action; left hand spin is balanced by right hand spin; matter requires anti-matter; mirror imagery, requiring a fulcrum, a fold or neutral axis is necessary to the equilibrium of the system.

Gifts from God

The interpretation of experimental evidence in terms of such axioms taxes the imagination of scientists as in no previous age. In this twentieth century the vision of our universe produced by astronomy, physics and biology rivals in its sheer innovation the wildest flights of fancy of our artists. Whilst their discourses are couched in the 'proofs' of inductive and deductive reasoning, the promoters of *black holes*, *quarks* and *charm* freely acknowledge that many of their best ideas have 'come out of thin air', in a moment of insight, of inspiration . . . or, as painters remark when a chance dribble of paint looks just right: 'A gift from God.'

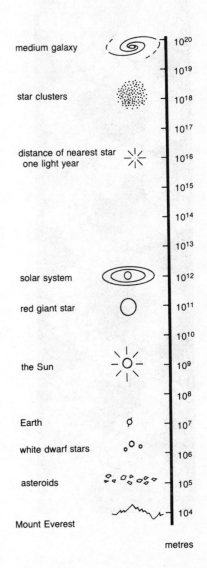

medium galaxy	10^{20}
	10^{19}
star clusters	10^{18}
	10^{17}
distance of nearest star one light year	10^{16}
	10^{15}
	10^{14}
	10^{13}
solar system	10^{12}
red giant star	10^{11}
	10^{10}
the Sun	10^{9}
	10^{8}
Earth	10^{7}
white dwarf stars	10^{6}
asteroids	10^{5}
	10^{4}
Mount Everest	
	metres

The scale of things. Atoms provide us with natural units of length.

Therefore, an exploration of design principles does not deny faculties, jealously guarded by scientist and artist alike, that may be described as intuitive. If the definition of *logic* is *the art of reason*, then it assumes that a study of the means of knowing can augment the power of instantaneous knowingness. Certainly the weight of evidence seems to support this view; for if sequential reasoning rarely reveals the unknown, only scholarship can illuminate it when chance turns it up.

Recognition

Our thoughts evolve in many ways, not all of them understood. One, of particular interest as a design tool, is recognition: the positive comparison of any new experience with information held in a memory bank.

To permit simple comparisons the memory need be only short term. To establish, for example, that three foreign coins are alike requires a memorisation of one while the others are scrutinised. Although the eyes and hands can move rapidly from one to another, absolute simultaneity is not achieved. The transfer of attention from one coin to another involves an act of memory, however brief, superficial and quickly overlaid by the paraphernalia of life.

But a little of the experience may be held in long term memory; its magnitude dependent upon the intensity and on the emotional overtones with which the coins were studied. If the incident occurred, say, during a financial crisis at some distant frontier post, the characteristics of the coins are more likely to loom large in the memory than if they were thrown aside as valueless counters in a party game.

The transfer of an experience from short term to long term memory requires an additional charge of intellectual or emotional energy so that it is raised above the level of the norm. Memory, like life itself, has peaks and troughs and can be likened to a relief sculpture. The most persistent qualities of a long term memory are for most people positive, like the initial touch, shape, form, even smell of one's mother. Instantly recognisable, throughout this life. *Unique to me*.

Unique to me

These are the memories that we cherish, both consciously and unconsciously. They contribute to our personal identity both as individuals and as functioning members of a group, a club, the human race, life itself.

Recognition can occur on all these levels but is most intense when it is personal and apparently unique to the individual. Although several persons may have similar experiences, they will not be the same. There is a demonstrable link between long term memorability and singularity. Repetition blurs the sensitivity to a series of events so that interest is directed to those isolated incidents that break the sequence. If an incident triggers any practical or emotional chords, then it may cross the personal threshold, gain the inner sanctum of feeling, and acquire a hint of unique to me.

Women pay extraordinary prices to be dressed in Paris, to ensure not only that their garments are well designed but also that they are 'original'. Men can be equally extravagant in their choice of a car, giving attention to those ancilliary items that convert a mass-produced vehicle into a personal chariot. There is probably no surer way of holding the affection of a human being, and perhaps any mammal, than by sharing a memory that contributes to its recognition of self, its identity.

The artist is thus motivated to seek a personal language with which to contact us individually. When he succeeds, each member of his audience is offered a personal relationship with the artist. It is this that we can share with others. In the concert hall, in the art gallery, we can savour a sense of *unique to me*, as both individual and group. Perhaps therein also lies the greatest secret of the whiteboard?

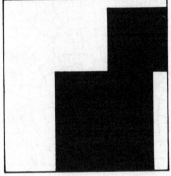

Modern art can be subdivided, for simplicity's sake, into two parallel, yet interactive streams: Expressionism and Constructivism. Both seek to define *presence* and were explored in the work of Jean Arp.

9

Creativity by kit

On this basis any group of people can be regarded as a gathering of individuals. Successful propagandists and advertising executives know this. They sell their product to the person, not to the crowd. Similarly an orator is trained to address all parts of his assembly; he uses eyes, gesture and posture to emphasise emotive phrases. With these he triggers the memory of each member of his audience.

From high theatre to cinema, radio and television, the viewers need to identify with a character, a mood or a situation. In recent years audience participation has interested experimental theatre, even to the point where members of the audience have become the actors.

Similarly painters and sculptors have designed modular kits that permit their audience to complete, with personal variations, a programme prepared by the artist — rather like assembling a jigsaw puzzle in which you make up your own picture.

The idea of *creativity by kit* has a potential market in all fields of design, from pleasure boats to bungalows.

Today technology has made it possible for our products and our processes to be mass organised. The increasing use of automation is tending to accentuate the shortage of *unique to me*. Mass production techniques that are essential to the maintenance of an expanding population, are also, by definition, highly repetitive. But we are learning that it is possible to introduce variety. In the motor car, previously mentioned, market forces have offered the prospective buyer a choice of colour and trim, seat covers, engine power, three, four or five doors, cigar lighters (one or two?), halogen headlights and a multitude of ancilliary items that can express his personality; and all of them mass-produced.

Cracking patterns have an inherent beauty that represents forces in equilibrium. As a pattern of rupture it reveals the weakest points in a surface. If these are strengthened to form a grid structure, then it is immensely strong.

A cracking process usually reveals right angles (sometimes 60°) by following a generative programme from major to subsidiary cracks. Curvature expresses variation in field strength.

These methods can be extended wherever the skilful design of parts can offer sufficiently varied combinations and permutations to provide a little of *unique to me* for every customer. In this way the economic advantages of mass production can be enhanced into a sophisticated means of self expression and self identification for the individual.

The dialogue of designers and customers is through the medium of a complex and sometimes massive industrial technology, involving a series of specialised skills and crafts. Even so, it has similarities to the relationships between fine artists and members of their audience. Most art forms require a contribution from the observer, by persuasion or preparation, whether he is aware of it or not.

The observer's contribution to a fine art dialogue tends to increase as the work becomes non-objective, non-figurative or abstracted in form. Functioning as a trigger, it invites him to indulge his own imaginings, and perhaps to find some attributes of his own identity. The ultimate artist-observer partnership would be ideally an equal one — 50/50.

Paul Klee suggested that a painting was like a mirror . . . .

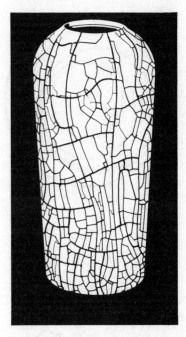

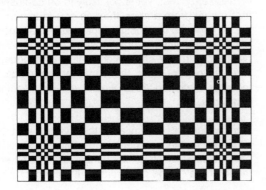

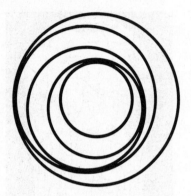

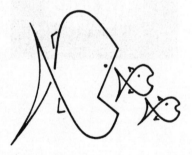

1 Same and similar

The triggered response to signals

Our human antennae or feelers, our fingertips, our eyes, our ears are attuned to the matching of like with like. The response to similarity is immediate: sometimes acutely sensitive to detail, at others concerned only with the broad forms of characterisation.

In the world of sound, music lovers are conscious of fine differences in audio frequency or pitch. This is why a concert orchestra takes such pains to finely tune its instruments to a key frequency before commencing a performance. Alternatively, particularly in the world of vision, we can appreciate a loose fit, using wide tolerances to obtain a group definition.

In the everyday world of colour signalling, responses are conditioned to a few popular hues: red, yellow, blue, green, black, white, purple and, perhaps, orange. These are broad concepts, each embracing a band of frequencies in the colour spectrum. Redness can vary from crimson to scarlet, yet is not likely to be confused with a yellowness that ranges from amber, through egg to lemon. Yet the decorating trades know, to their cost, of the need for a precise colour matching of paints and finishes. Juxtaposition of finishes can reveal very slight differences in hue, chroma and value. Consequently they advise that only wallpapers from the same printer's batch should be hung together. Matching areas of paint, similarly, should be taken from the same mix.

Our judgement of similarity thus varies with the urgency of the situation. At the raw beginning of life, recognition of likenesses is basic to survival. New experiences are compared with memory. Is it friend of foe? Food or predator? If it cannot be identified, beware!

Our basic level of communication, the triggered response to signals, remains the most emotive and impelling tool available to the designer. Recognition of signals and signs is based upon assessments of similarity using simple observations. The object under scrutiny is compared with an observed or preconceived datum. Is it more than or less than; hotter than or colder than; bigger than or smaller than?

Ultimately the response to relative quantities leads to relative qualities and to preferences.

Thus, if in the majority of recorded cases *smaller than's* are less dangerous than *bigger than's*, in the limit there may be no recordings of bigger than's. All the smaller than's having the misfortune to meet a bigger than will have been devoured.

As a matter of general interest developed in Chapter 8, it is this kind of behavioural pattern that can permit an eccentricity, that may be quite minor at the initial stages, ultimately to dictate the whole growth pattern of a population.

In a post Einstein world, ideas about sameness and similarity require a precision that was not necessary in a regular Euclidean space. Einstein wrote at length to explain that no two events can be simultaneous, for a displacement in space is also a displacement in time. Only a photon or some hypothetical object travelling at the speed of light is not conscious of time and is intrinsically timeless.

But our observations are made at velocities well below that of light, so that although the two circles illustrated were produced by the same compass setting, they are not *same*; the circles are *similar*. They are seen to be displaced in space, therefore they are displaced in time. One is to the left of the other. One has slightly more visual importance, significance or weight because they have a hierarchy of position. In this context the term *weight* is frequently used by artists to describe the composite, multi-dimensional significance of a thing, a shape, a group of lines, a brush stroke.

The sensory weight of a unit is affected by its proximity to other units, their centres and their boundaries. Metaphorically, sensorially, every observed particle of energy, whatever its form, has a gravitational field or, better, each seems to bend the space in its vicinity. The significance of any event is not constant; it varies with location, with circumstances. It is *relative*. Therefore, when apparent duplication occurs, there cannot be sameness but only similarity.

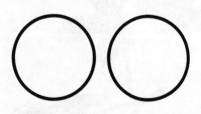

Schemata from *The Three Musicians* by Picasso (1921) oil on canvas. New York Museum of Modern Art.

14

If a musician sounds three brief notes, perhaps repeating middle C upon a piano, the three notes cannot be the same. The first will have surprise, even shock if unexpected. The second note, anticipated or not, will produce some resonance in the listener who is carrying a memory of the first note. Whereas the first note was a sound and, if brief and staccato, not fully comprehended as a note, the second note can be savoured, studied and recorded in its fullness. This applies even more distinctly to a third note, which becomes confirmatory. Timing, the relative length of notes and intervals to the intrinsic time of the audience, perhaps their very heartbeats, will suggest whether the third note is a repeat, an echo or a full stop. By inversion, current experiments in the fine arts are exploring the subdivision of a continuous experience, such as a sustained musical note, a sheet of colour, a 'wrapped' landscape, into the discontinuity of the observer's timescale: his beginning, his middle and his end, which is all one. Ultimately this becomes a passive vehicle for audience participation and is not unrelated to traditional programmes for meditation, both philosophic and religious.

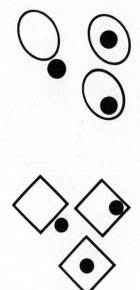

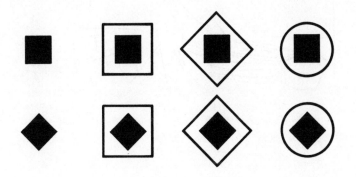

The Great Wall of China is a linear wrapping of a landscape.

15

Paul Cézanne

The painter Cézanne anticipated many of Einstein's findings. When studying apples upon a table, Cézanne observed that an attempt to copy them by any technique, naturalist, realist or impressionist, would fail. Sameness could not be achieved.

Cézanne adapted the impressionist technique to a study of space relationships. This exploration evolved through his lifetime into a quest to *realise his sensations*. He grasped the spacial totality of the scene before him and translated it into paint. Objects, trees, buildings, plains, mountains, clouds, apples, bottles, persons, all were declassified. They served only as the nodal points, edges and planes of a spacial flux.

Cézanne's paintings attempt to penetrate and transcend matter. They inspired *Cubism*; they contributed to the birth of *Expressionism*, during the years that Einstein worked upon his general theory of relativity and Freud was studying dreams.

Nicholas de Staël (1914–55) was one of the many artists influenced by Paul Cézanne.

In the search for self expression each abstract artist of note has found a set of personal forms that could be converted into symbols. These include:

(a) The exploitation of gesture; the energy trapped within a material by its *handling*, as typified in the dribble paintings of 'Tachism'.

(b) Dramatisations of geometric properties, as in early Cubism, Suprematism, Purism, Neo-Plasticism and Constructivism generally.

(c) The juxtaposition of emotive, organic or biomorphic forms, as in Surrealism, Dada and 'Pop' Art.

Expressionism

Expressionism can be broadly defined as an exploration of the emotional, intellectual and thus human response to sensory stimuli. These can be everyday *things*, possessing names, or extraordinary things that demand names. Or the stimuli can be non-figurative, clusters of energy particles, commonly referred to as *abstract*.

Expressionism has been, and remains, a major influence upon the arts of the twentieth century, taking many and varied forms. It sometimes seems that the possibilities are inexhaustable.

When this discourse upon same and similar was put to a well-known painter, she commented that her particular interest was the dis-similarities that can occur between fruits, such as apples, when set upon a table to form a still life. These dissimilarities could become fascinating because of their shared quality of *appleness*, which includes shape, colour, lustre, texture, smell, flavour and much more that she attempted to translate into paint upon canvas. Her form of expressionism has much in common with the mature Matisse, yet is in sharp contrast with the ageing Cézanne. He worked very slowly and the fruits arranged to form his still life would shrivel and wizen long before the painting was completed. So he replaced them with wax models. He was not interested in appleness: his interest was space.

Yet all these painters are expressionist. Despite their very different attitudes towards space, life and apples, they are concerned to express their sensations through the selection of similarities. These can lead, in due course, to the processes of analogy and metaphor discussed in Chapter 15.

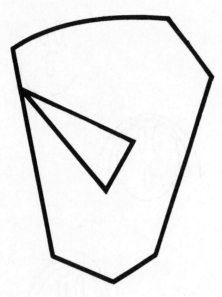

The repetition of similarities

Long traditions have been established upon a harmony of *the same and the similar*. The mind finds security in repetition. A form that is unprepossessing, even ugly, when viewed in isolation, can become acceptable, even likeable, in a repeat pattern. This can happen in one's personal life. A friend who was not particularly attractive at first sight can grow on you.

Of course, familiarity can also breed contempt!

The repetition of similarities is not only a basis of the decorative and popular arts; it also formulates the highest dramatic statements. In theatre, music, architecture, painting, similarity exploits both the short term and the long term memory. The terminology is revealing: repetition, alliteration, rhythm, rhyme, simulation, likeness, impersonation, imitation, parody, semblance, copy, mimicry, emulation, reflection, variation. But there are more: theme, analogy, metaphor, to transcribe, to plagiarise, to fake . . . echo . . . .

Euclidean similarity

The structure of Euclidean geometry, also, is based upon similarity: the properties of points, lines and, of course, similar triangles.

An understanding of plane triangles is essential to the appreciation of more complex structures, areas, volumes and rates of change. It is helpful, therefore, to be reminded of certain properties.

The sum of the internal angles of any triangle resting on a flat plane is 180°. If the triangle were on the external surface of a sphere the total internal angle would exceed 180°. In the following examples, the simplest cases, resting on a flat plane, are considered.

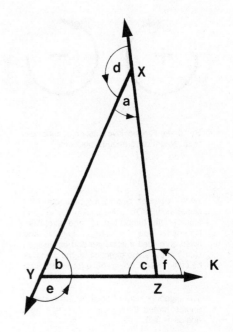

In any triangle XYZ, let a, b and c be internal angles; and d, e and f be external angles.
At each corner internal + external angles = two right angles.
Therefore, $a + b + c + d + e + f = 3 \times 2$ right angles = 6 right angles.   (i)

Consider a man standing at Z, facing towards K. He is required to walk completely around the perimeter of the triangle. Therefore he turns anticlockwise through angle f and walks to X. He turns through angle d and walks to Y. He then turns through angle e and walks to Z. Thus he completes the circuit.

He has turned through a complete revolution and arrives back at Z, facing towards K.

Therefore $f + d + e = 1$ rev = 4 right angles.   (ii)

Referring to equations (i) and (ii),

$a + b + c = 6 - 4$ right angles = 2 right angles.

The sum of the internal angles of any triangle is 2 right angles.
The sum of the external angles of any triangle is $6 - 4$ right angles $= 2 = (2n - 4)$ right angles, where n is the number of sides.

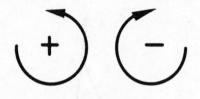

By convention, positive rotation is anticlockwise. Negative rotation is clockwise.

Similarly any plane polygon with n number of corners has n number of sides.

At any corner, internal angle + external angle = 2 right angles.
Total internal + external angles = $2n$ right angles.
Total external angle = 1 rev = 4 right angles.
Therefore, total internal angle = $(2n - 4)$ right angles.

When a person circuits the perimeter of a closed polygon to arrive back at the starting point, he has turned through one revolution. No matter how the polygon wriggles and twists, provided it is closed and he finishes facing in the same direction on the plane as he commenced, he will have turned through one rev.

The algebraic sum of positive and negative angles turned through is 1 rev = 4 right angles = 360°.

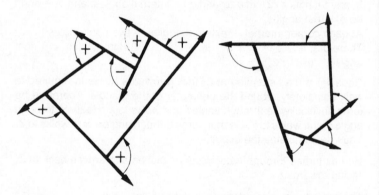

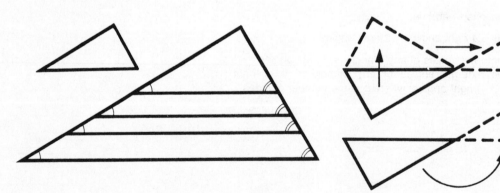

20

Similar triangles have equal angles, taken in order. In the example, the third triangle must be reflected twice to bring its angles into the order of the first two triangles.

Similar triangles can be superimposed so that one angle is common and two sides are shared. The third sides then become parallel.

The corresponding sides of similar triangles are in common ratio:

$$\frac{a}{d} = \frac{b}{e} = \frac{c}{f}$$

by cross multiplication it can be shown that:

$$\frac{a}{b} = \frac{d}{e} \qquad \frac{b}{c} = \frac{e}{f} \qquad \frac{a}{c} = \frac{d}{f}$$

Since all polygons can be assembled from triangles, the properties of similar triangles can be extended throughout geometry.

The right angled triangle has one angle equalling 90°.
Therefore the remaining two angles summate to 90° in plane geometry.
In any triangle, the longest side is opposite the largest angle.
In the right-angled triangle, the longest side is the hypotenuse.

Pythagoras' Theorem for a right angled triangle
In any right angled triangle the square on the hypotenuse equals the sum of the squares on the other two sides.

A neat proof is given by Dr J. Bronowski in his book, *The Ascent of Man*:

By moving two triangles, the original square on the hypotenuse is transformed into two adjacent squares on the sides enclosing the right angle.

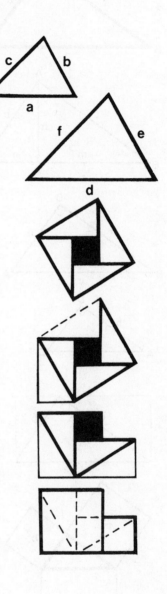

21

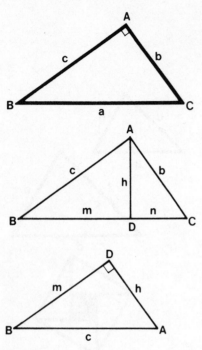

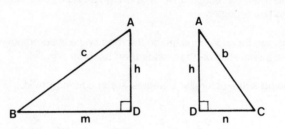

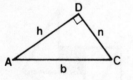

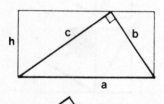

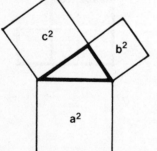

A proof based upon similar triangles

In any right angled triangle ABC, let the angles be labelled A, B and C and their opposite sides be a, b and c.

Orientate the triangle to place the right angle A at the top.
Construct a perpendicular h to the hypotenuse a from A.
Let h cut a at D, so that $m + n = a$.

Three right angled triangles, ABC, DAB and DCA have been formed. If the two smaller triangles are reflected once, they can be seen to be similar to triangle ABC (they have same angles taken in order).

Considering similar triangles DBA and ABC:

$$\frac{c}{m} = \frac{a}{c} \text{ therefore } c^2 = am \quad \text{(i)}$$

Considering similar triangles DAC and ABC:

$$\frac{b}{n} = \frac{a}{b} \text{ therefore } b^2 = an \quad \text{(ii)}$$

hence, adding (i) and (ii):

$$b^2 + c^2 = an + am = a(n + m) = a^2$$

$$\text{therefore } a^2 = b^2 + c^2$$

Another property of a right angled triangle emerges from the above.

The area of a triangle is half that of its containing rectangle, therefore in the right angled triangle ABC:

area of $ABC = bc/2 = ah/2$ hence $bc = ah$

22

Dominant similarities

Humans seem to be more sensitive to similar triangles than to similar angles, with three notable exceptions:

(i)   a complete revolution, 360°, a point
(ii) a half revolution, 180°, a straight line or short length of a constant curve
(iii) a right angle, 90°, a quadrant.

Other angles tend to be grouped as sharp or acute (less than 90°), obtuse (between 90° and 180°) or reflex (more than 180° but less than a rev).

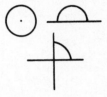

Which is the dissimilar angle?

Unless guided to the contrary, we tend to read acute and obtuse angles as internal angles. In general, internal angles are easier to comprehend than external angles, even though they are usually in partnership, one conditional upon the other (see Chapter 4).

A pentagon has 5 sides

hexagon	6
septagon	7
heptagon	7
octagon	8
nonagon	9
decagon	10
duodecagon	12

The precision of Euclid's similar triangles is selected from a much broader concept: a triangle is a plane figure or polygon having three sides. By this definition all triangles share similarity and the concept, triangle, may even be retained when the corners are truncated and the sides serrated.

Therefore quadrilaterals also have similarity, as four sided polygons. So it is with all shapes that have similarity by definition.

Such awareness of similarity, and therefore of differences, leads to a recognition of repetition, variation, continuity and number.

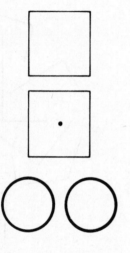

The prime step, from zero to one, belongs to God.

Duplication, from one to two, is emphatically mortal; a discovery of limits; a beginning and an end; a first and last, and an inbetween.

Twin circles have predatory associations. Without content they can be intimidating, even hypnotic.

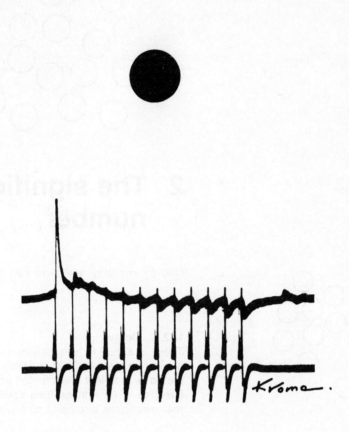

Were it not for number and its nature, nothing that exists would be clear to anybody either in itself or in its relation to other things . . . You can observe the power of number exercising itself not only in the affairs of demons and Gods but in all the acts and the thoughts of men in all handicrafts and music.

Philolaus, School of Pythagoras (*c* 450 BC)

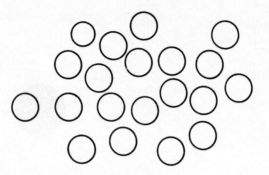

2 The significance of number

Only by inventing new forms can an artist produce art.

Du Purisme, Fernand Léger

1, 2, 3, plenty

There is a tribe in New Guinea even today that has, reputedly, a numbering system of 1, 2, 3, plenty. It is not at all difficult to imagine the advantage that this afforded traders using the decimal system. Even so, if he refrains from counting, the most sophisticated of mathematicians also has a surprisingly limited response to number.

Experimental information is confirming numerical properties which, during the Middle Ages and earlier, were thought to be *magical*.

Using similar visual units, we have an assured numerical response up to a variable threshold in the vicinity of seven or more. Beyond that number a rapid deterioration in accuracy leads into the concept *plenty*. The uncertainty arising can be interpreted as a form of numerical *dazzle* until it evolves into multitude or texture.

At a glance, without counting, how many?

Consider, for example, 19 discs displayed in a random group: the addition or subtraction of one disc will scarcely be noticed. If the distribution is such that no *flow lines* are apparent, then two and even more discs can be removed or added without significant effect. The 19 discs, plus or minus a few, remain *plenty.* The integer threshold into plenty occurs, therefore, where the addition or subtraction of one unit ceases to have precise effect, and for most of us this is in the vicinity of seven.

26

In the series of regular polygons, recognition is by the number of sides and angles. The viseo-tactile rate of change is maximum from triangle to square, diminishing to pentagon, hexagon, septagon, octagon, nonagon.

At this stage it becomes easier to recognise any parallelism that signifies an even number than to judge the actual number of sides. Even allowing for the natural grouping offered by quartering the circle, the number of sides becomes vague at 8+. By the time the number of sides has reached 15 or so, the regular polygon has become a serrated circle.

Grouping procedures
The dazzle of numbers in excess of seven can be mitigated by *grouping procedures*. Each group should contain less than eight units. The number of groups should not exceed seven. For numbers in excess of 49, therefore, it is usually necessary to group the groups. In practice, for high response, it is often necessary to use an optimum number less than seven.

The grouping of groups offers a cognisance of number beyond plenty into multitude. Experimental data are suggesting that this is in the region of 56, varying with the design, the illumination and the grouping procedures adopted.

In summary, therefore, our response to number, without counting or grouping, may be regarded as 0, 1, 2, 3, 4, 5, 6, 7, plenty, multitude.

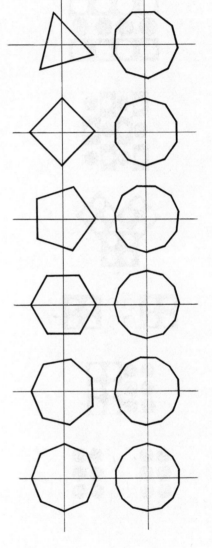

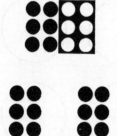

All human measuring systems use grouping procedures.

The metric system is based upon the group, 2 × 5, and multiples of that group.

The duodecimal system was based upon 12, a number that factorises conveniently into 2 × 6, or 2 × 2 × 3, or 4 × 3.

The canvases of the painter Mondrian were for many years gridded into 16 × 16 intervals. The number 16 groups with variety into 4 × 4, or (2 × 3) + (2 × 5).

Any grouping procedure involves conscious repetition. It is based upon the principles of similarity. Comprehension is assisted by the selection of readily memorable repeats, and these should be echoed at each grouping of groups.

The regimentation of groups, like parading soldiers, certainly provides order. However if it is to be read with ease then a *flowpath* should be offered to the eyes, the fingers, the ears, whatever the sensory organ may be. The senses need guidance across the assembly, and although cognition often seems to be instantaneous, its process is sequential, involving a *scanning* along a path that is rarely straight.

A group is a unit comprising several independent elements. Their individuality is essential to the expression of the group. To be read sequentially within the group they need a *hierarchy*.

In a high efficiency group, that would correspond to a living organism or a work of fine art, every member contributes to the group activity, whatever it may be. No member is superfluous or redundant. All are necessary. If any one is removed, the group's efficiency *per member* is reduced. It follows, therefore, that the most efficient group in any context, from industrial worksites to pips on a playing card, is likely to be the smallest number that can effectively do the job in all its aspects.

A grouping of, say, 12 pips is not easy. This is why playing cards have *royals* for numbers 11, 12 and 13.

28

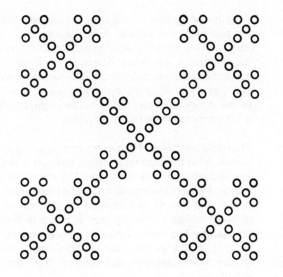

At high levels of efficiency the full contribution of each member of a group is dependent upon every other contribution. Each member fulfils a specific function. In the five-group illustrated, all five spots have an integral function. The group cannot be five if it loses any one of them. All are essential. A hierarchy is needed to assist the reading of the group. The central spot holds a dominant position by suggesting a $(1 + 4 = 5)$ group. By eliminating each spot in turn it can be seen that although all five spots are essential to the fiveness, they have a sequential order. Like a living creature, all parts are essential to its totality, but each makes a different contribution to the whole.

An alternative distribution of the five group equidistant around the circumference of a circle tends to accentuate the central void and renders the number of spots more difficult to read.

In group working conversation is a necessity. If all speak together then a Tower of Babel arises. Left to resolve itself within the group, an intermittent flux of semi-private conversations between sub-groups of two and three persons usually emerges. If each member of a five-group is required to address the other four, then it is necessary to structure the conversation so that they can speak in turn. The sequence thus ordered is a flowpath through the group.

29

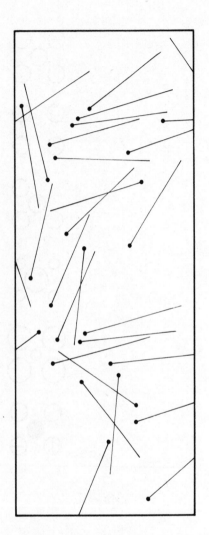

A hierarchic system amongst equals can be established by introducing additional dimensions. A five-group of discs, for example, can vary in colour intensity, applied pattern, size and even shape, so that the hierarchic sequence differs in each dimension. Assuming a constancy of order, five dimensions would be required to give each unit the experience of occupying each position in a hierarchic series. An experience of all possible interrelationships would require a full permutation of 120 dimensions.

The basic principles of numeracy and grouping are simple. Difficulties usually arise from failure to define flowpaths, and thus the hierarchy and sequence of units to be read. The limited human response to the numbers beyond seven (and the next chapter will suggest that seven is rather too high) is balanced by an intense awareness of the smallest integers. This balance is not only critical to the fine arts, from poetry and music, through painting, sculpture, architecture and beyond. It is also essential to those many human activities that require order, precision and decision, from documentation to plant layout.

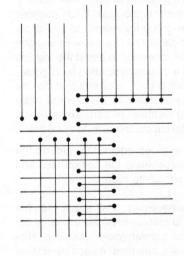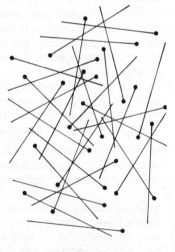

Distributions of 30 pins.

The magic of numbers

Numbers have a magical property. History records their fascination for mankind, their sense of mystery that is, perhaps, an expression of their apparent universality. They have an abstraction that seems independent of all earthly things. A chosen number that is within our human measure has constancy, a superhuman quality that holds true throughout eternity. For example, the number two, is two, is two, is two, is two, is two, is two . . . or so it seems.

We are particularly sensitive to oneness and twoness; odd and even. Their massive difference, a doubling process, is the prime example of integer growth in our material universe. It is a numerical relationship that is instantly recognised by mankind and subordinate only to their origin: Genesis, The Act of Creation, from nothing to one.

This dipolarity seems to be sustained throughout our observations of life to amazing degree, and conditions our attitudes towards *reality*. I suspect that all our numerical concepts are based upon the interaction of three numbers, zero, one and two.

Why do we not see the world in triplets? Odd, even and odder? Or quadruplets? or quintuplets? Perhaps it is to do with our human one-fold symmetry? The twoness of sex, and arms, and eyes and legs? But no. It goes deeper into our origins. The helices of DNA, theoretically, can be either left hand or right hand, but a third hand is not available. An electrical potential can be positive or negative but a third alternative is not yet detected. It is our human paradox that the biologist and the physicist may be in the position of the landscape painter mentioned in the introduction . . . finding what he seeks.

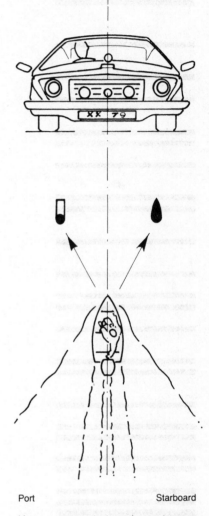

Port   Starboard

Linear movement towards a twoness describes a foldline for symmetry. Symmetry is traditionally associated with even numbers.

Left: Numerical series intelligence tests are usually mixtures of multiplication, addition, division and subtraction, in sequence or opposition. Answers are on page 34.

On another numerical dimension *prime numbers* have long been regarded as mysterious. Prime numbers are integers that cannot be divided by another integer other than one. They continue, ever larger from

1, 2, 3, 5, 7, 11, 13, 17, 19, 23, 31, 37, 41, 43, 47, 53, 59, 61, 67, 71, 73 . . .

They represent a *negative* of the sum of *positive* repeats of smaller prime numbers. For example: $35 = 7 \times 5$; $36 = 2 \times 2 \times 3 \times 3$. 37 is prime; $38 = 2 \times 19$; $39 = 3 \times 13$ etc.
When prime numbers grow into the thousands their distribution becomes so difficult to predict that they have long been regarded as devilish and threatening, as their location appears to become random.

The Ancient Greeks pondered at length upon some wondrous forms of numerical growth which, in the modern world, we have turned to advantage in the construction of space frames and geodesic structures. Some of these are discussed in Chapters 11 and 12.

The simplest numerical order is of *sequential* integers: 0, 1, 2, 3, 4, 5, 6, 7 . . . grow by adding one to each term to assert a *linear* rate of change that is easily comprehended.

Thinking in two dimensions, the *triangular* numbers 0, 1, 3, 6, 10, 15, 21 . . . grow by adding 1, then 2, then 3, 4, 5, 6, 7 . . . The growth accelerates at a constant rate.

Considered in three dimensions, the *tetrahedral* numbers 0, 1, 4, 10, 20, 35, 56, 84, 120 . . . are formed by adding the triangular numbers. This series gives the number of close-packed spheres that are needed to grow a tetrahedron.

In the fourth dimension, a *supertetrahedron* would give the number sequence: 0, 1, 5, 15, 35, 70, 126, 210 . . . by adding the tetrahedral numbers.

It is interesting to note that usually the Greeks did not include the initial zero in their series, preferring to leave it to the Gods. We include it nowadays because our numbers can grow in both positive and negative directions, in opposition. We therefore require a centre of balance, a fulcrum, datum or origin. The use of zero, the adoption of this axiom, renders number independent of philosophy and of the Gods.

The smaller prime numbers in vertical sequence.

In contrast deep superstitions have been associated with *magic polygons*. The most famous are those that require a set of integers to be arranged so that the sum of each natural row, diagonal and column is a constant.

Four such *magic triangles* date from early Greek mathematics:

```
    3              4              1              6
  5 4            3 2            6 4            3 1
 1 6 2          5 1 6          3 2 5          2 5 4
```

Such a distribution of number can be interpreted into, say, colour. A visual structure of five subjectively equal steps from black to white can represent the integer series 1 to 6. When these are arranged according to a magic triangle it can attain a maximum distribution of contrast between adjacent integers within a unified group.

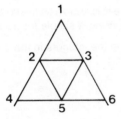

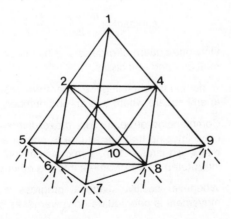

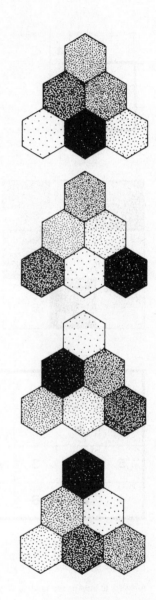

8	1	6	8	1	6	8	1	6
3	5	7	3	5	7	3	5	7
4	9	2	4	9	2	4	9	2
8	1	6	8	1	6	8	1	6
3	5	7	3	5	7	3	5	7
4	9	2	4	9	2	4	9	2
8	1	6	8	1	6	8	1	6
3	5	7	3	5	7	3	5	7
4	9	2	4	9	2	4	9	2

y	1	12	7
11	8	y−1	2
5	10	3	y+2
4	y+1	6	9

The magic square of $x - 20 = y$

Answers to intelligence tests:

(a) 34: Add 16 to 18.
(b) 13: Treble 5 then subtract 2.
(c) 17: Put numbers in ascending series 111359; then add last 3 numbers.

The *magic square* has a long history. The order of a magic square is the number of cells on one side, so that a magic square of order four has $(4 \times 4) = 16$ cells; similarly, a magic square of order five has 25 cells.

The sum of the integers in each row of cells is known as the *constant* of the square and this can be found by using a simple formula:

If the order of the magic square is n, and the integers in the square commence at 1, then the constant equals

$$\frac{n^3 + n}{2}$$

In the example shown, the magic square of order $n = 3$, using the integers 1 to 9, requires a constant as follows:

$$\text{constant} = \frac{n^3 + n}{2} = \frac{3^3 + 3}{2} = \frac{27 + 3}{2} = 15$$

Only one square of order $n = 3$ has been found, if we disregard its rotations and reflections.

A method for obtaining the order three magic square can be applied to any square where n is an odd number, as follows:

Commencing at centre top, move diagonally on the positive slope only. Imagine that the square is one of a repeat pattern of similar magic squares. Then a movement out of the square can be interpreted as a movement into the other side of the square.

Whenever positive diagonal progress is blocked, the alternative movement is one square downwards, as shown in the illustration.

34

2	16	13	3
11	5	8	10
7	9	12	6
14	4	1	15

	2	3	
5			8
9			12
	14	15	

16	2	3	13
5	11	10	8
9	7	6	12
4	14	15	1

To devise a magic square of order four:
Draw the diagonals, then number each square in normal sequence, left to right, top to bottom, but leaving the diagonal squares blank.

Then reverse the procedure, numbering each square from 16 to 1, marking the diagonal squares only.

This method can be adapted to larger squares of even order.

13	8	11	2	13	8	11	2
3	10	5	16	3	10	5	16
6	15	4	9	6	15	4	9
12	1	14	7	12	1	14	7
13	8	11	2	13	8	11	2
3	10	5	16	3	10	5	16
6	15	4	9	6	15	4	9
12	1	14	7	12	1	14	7

11	2
5	16

14	7
11	2

4	9
14	7

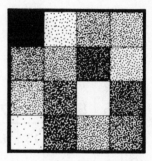

At order four, 880 magic squares are possible, ignoring rotations and reflections. Some of these are *diabolical squares*, which retain their magical quality wherever the block of 16 squares may be selected from a repeating pattern. The diabolical square illustrated was found in an eleventh/twelfth century inscription at Khajuraho, India.

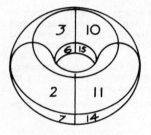

A diabolical square can be printed on to the surface of a torus. It can be transferred on to a hypercube so that the four corners of each plane summate to 34.

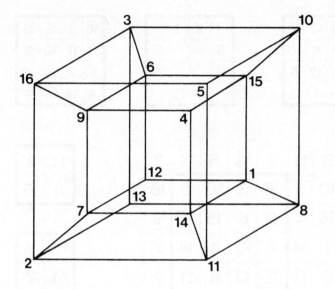

	5	8	1	4	7
9	14	17	10	13	16
2	7	10	3	6	9
0	5	8	1	4	7
6	11	14	7	10	13
3	8	11	4	7	10

A variation on the magic square is this superficially random distribution of numbers.

Yet if any five numbers are selected so that one only appears in any one column, they will add up to 45.

The key is given outside the square, which is generated by adding the vertical and horizontal control numbers at each location.

The fascination of magic polygons of numbers generally rests in their use of simple arithmetic to reveal a multidimensional constancy. To a medieval scholar it must have seemed as though they brought down to Earth the secrets of the Heavens. And even today, we are not free of that sense of wonder that responds to the revelation of multi-dimensional order in variety and variety in order. And when its explanation is not apparent we sense mystery and magic.

The diabolical square was presented as an apparently random distribution of numbers from 1 to 16. The magnitudes were not sensorially apparent when quoted as numbers, and even when expressed as a series of greys most observers might well puzzle upon the method by which the unified yet vigorous distribution was achieved. Numerical structures of this form can be used to provide flowpaths through groups of groups, offering stimulation and variety while building a total comprehension of the series.

In this context, when any *thing* is truly expressive of its multi-dimensional function and structure and reveals the product of skills and sensitivities beyond the norm, then whether it be a painting, a jetliner, a kitchen kettle or a steam locomotive, that expression is likely to acquire a little magic.

It is sometimes said that if Aristotle was the first exponent of scientific observation and collation of information, then Descartes was the first conscious practitioner of scientific method. Certainly his confrontation with mystery was not to deny it or its wonder, but the better to comprehend it. He wrote of his method as follows:

If I have first found out by separate mental operations what the relation is between the magnitudes A and B, then that between B and C, C and D and finally between D and E, that does not entail my seeing what the relation is between A and E, nor can the truths previously learned give me a precise knowledge of it unless I recall them all.

To remedy this I would run them over from time to time, keeping the imagination moving continuously in such a way that while it is intuitively perceiving each fact it simultaneously passes on to the next; and this I would do until I had learned to pass from the first to the last so quickly, that no stage was left to the care of the memory, but I seemed to have the whole in intuition before me at the same time.

The mathematician, scientist and philosopher Descartes described to amazing degree a function of fine art. The above quotation could be attributed to Cézanne, the Cubists and those responsible for much of modern music and plastic design, under the general heading of Constructivism (see Chapter 15).

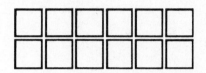

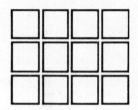

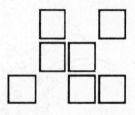

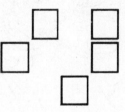

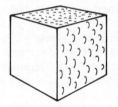

A grid, once established, can have selected units eliminated yet retain its essential structure.

Below left: Differing textures or colours on the faces of a cube can suggest that it is a piece broken from a bigger cube.

3 Rhythm

A repeating beat or flow

Everyone has rhythm. From the pre-natal comfort of a mother's heartbeats to the acts of breathing, eating, sleeping, thinking, walking, running, dancing and sex, we have all got rhythm.

The dictionary defines rhythm as a *repeating beat or flow*.

But this description is inadequate. A clock can tick away until it is no longer heard, for it is no more rhythmic than utter silence . . . until perhaps it stops.

Within limits the human nervous system can switch repetitive or sustained and invariant stimuli out of consciousness. We can savour the continuity of a single note or a repeated cluster, chord, line, colour or space-time grid but they can become rhythmic only as a textural contrast to our intrinsic body rhythms. A texture or multitude can condition our foreground activities, setting their mood and scale, but it cannot in itself claim rhythm.

To become rhythmic, stimuli need to avoid the dazzle of plenty by grouping within our small number threshold. Larger numbers need the grouping of groups and it is this restraint that has led to the familiar lines, verses and melodies of most traditional music.

Our artistic heritage suggests that a repeating beat or flow needs a meaningful variety to make it rhythmic. This can be achieved by a hierarchic system using grouping, accent, amplitude, pitch, timing and the conscious exploitation of the body rhythms of both artist and audience.

Top: Variation on Yin-Yang.

Drawing of Agnes Dürer, by Albert Dürer (Vienna, Albertina).

38

The incidence of accents and rests, permuted through a regular space-time grid, becomes rhythmic in itself as it modifies, defines and enriches the grouping procedure. For example, a traditional American jazz band was subdivided into a front line (melodic) section, usually led by trumpet, and rhythm section, usually based on drums. During an extemporisation it was common practice for the sections to exchange roles midway through a work. The rhythm section could not be truly rhythmic without some accentuation derived from an interpretation of the melody. Similarly, individual instruments could move from melody to harmony to ensemble on like, though simpler, principles to the great concert orchestras of the world.

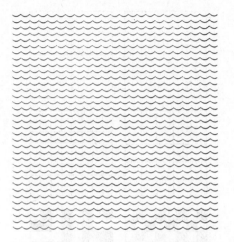

Rhythm and variation
Rhythm can be defined as *a repeating beat or flow in which no two elements are identical*.

As previously discussed, a continuous unwavering note, like the ticking of a clock cannot be rhythmic. It provides an aural multitude in which one moment cannot be differentiated from another, like the texture of a woven fabric.

Groupings of triads. Progressive complexity of accent and timing increases the identity.

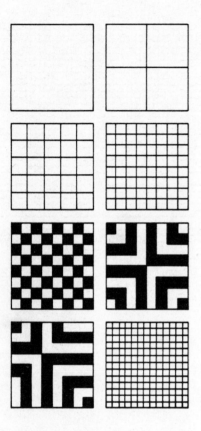

At the other extreme is the concept *oneness*. A single brief sound, anticipated or not, can do no more than excite the ear and alert the mind. If it is very loud or unexpected it may shock the sensory channels and can thus be a tool of the dramatist. But in its solitude it cannot be rhythmic.

As an experiment in audience participation and reaction, it would be helpful if you, dear reader, would maintain a sense of humour while attempting to solve the following anagrams:

Sly ware	Lawyers
Two acorns	
Frail china	
Merit not	
Voices rant on	

A second sound, resembling the first, is confirmatory. Whereas the first sound was information, its repeat can be contemplated, comprehended and detailed into the memory.

A third sound, resembling the first two, is substantive. Resonating with memory of the second sound, it can constitute a primary *rhythm*. Its timing, pitch and amplitude can suggest continuity into a further series of notes, or it can transmit *end of message*.

○　○　○　○　○　○　○

A square is subdivided into:
A comprehensible number of squares.
A bountiful yet comprehensible number.
Plenty of squares, approaching multitude; restrained by checkerboard counter-change; simplified by linear grouping;
dazzle reduced by asymmetry, giving hierarchy;
multitude.

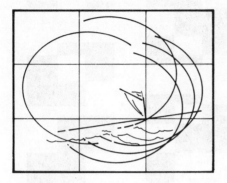

Most traditional paintings and stage sets divide into nine parts, such that the geometric centre also locates the dramatic centre.

The dramatic intensity of the central rectangle can be intensified or relaxed by closing or expanding the centre. Compare the mood of seascapes by Turner and Jan Van de Cappelle with landscapes of the Impressionists.

Below: This abstract is taken from a photomicrograph of an etched polycrystalline specimen of copper. (Published in *Materials Science* by Anderson, Leaver, Alexander and Rawlings.)

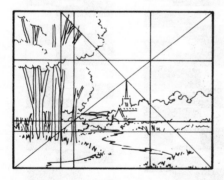

41

Repeats are synchronised at three, four and
five beats to the bar. They are programmed
to overlap so that white on white is white,
black on black is white.

The lower programme has regular accents,
suggesting syncopation.

42

Left: Series of elongated rectangles, accents at multiples of four, five and six; with (below) a similar programme using two, three and minus nine.

Right: In a regular grid, alternating black and white stripes grow and decline at a constant rate . . . AP (see Chapter 5).

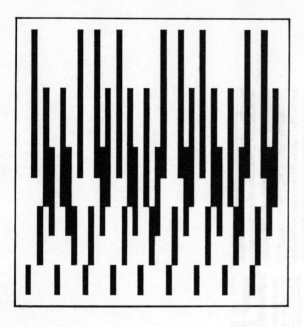

In a regular rectangular grid, linear units are grouped into fives and graded vertically.

The distribution within each group is then permuted to obtain sequential variety. The number order is: 1, 5, 2, 4, 3; 1, 4, 3, 2, 5; 1, 2, 5, 3, 4; and so on, with the one supplying a regular beat.

The principle is extended vertically and horizontally. The vertical distribution is 9(4 + 5), 6, 7, 8, 9.

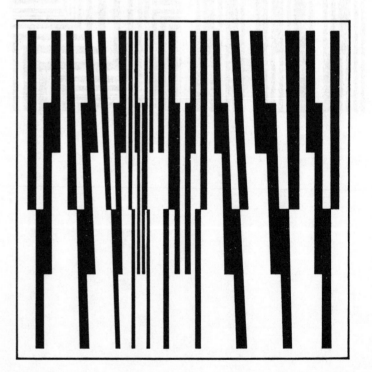

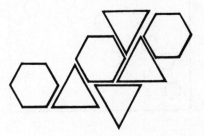

Left: A curvilinear programme on a square grid Idea derived from the work of Bridget Riley.

Above: In a square grid, a random initial distribution is programmed to move diagonally.

45

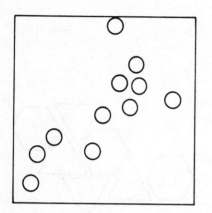

Rhythmically, full comprehension of a group of stimuli is limited numerically, in any one dimension, to the range from three to seven. Most popular music is based upon either three or four beats to the bar. Five-four time is reserved for experts. Six beats to the bar usually resolve into three pairs, as in Latin American music. Seven notes to the bar are usually gripped firmly into a *square*, four beat, grid such as 2, 1, 2, 2. Eight to the bar is probably handled as four pairs.

The rectilinear certitude of four is discussed graphically in later chapters. In music it may be associated with marching, *left, right, left, right*, and has a determined sense of direction. Even when translated into a ballroom dance such as the fox-trot, it tends to be linear with abrupt changes of direction. It is amusing to observe how very often a series of eight beats are interpreted into a phrase made famous by the late Victor Sylvester: 'Slow, slow, quick, quick, slow.' Numerically this can be read as 2, 2, 1, 1, 2.

Three beats to the bar, however, can suggest curvature and lends itself to the spiralling dance of the waltz. At first sight this seems to conflict with the graphic image of a triangle which is the least curvilinear of polygons. However it may be significant that a line of waltz comprises four bars of three beats with heavy emphasis upon beat numbers 1, 4, 7 and 10. Its graphic form may be better interpreted by the 12 sided regular duodecagon, derived from a rotating equilateral triangle.

We are well aware that five is one of nature's, and our, favourite numbers. Its high incidence in both the vegetable and animal kingdoms may have some bearing upon its significance in our cognitive processes. Midway between our rhythmic limits at three and seven, it becomes an optimum number for most human beings.

Continuing, with your goodwill, our experiments with anagrams, you are again requested to solve the following examples, without regard to previous experience, and to note your emotional reaction.

Apt   Pat
Angered
Main race
Maids hips
On mental topic

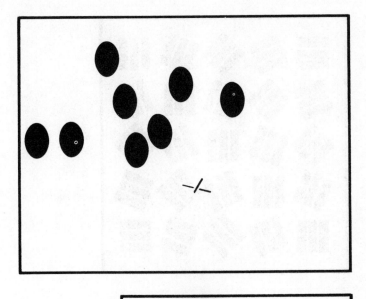

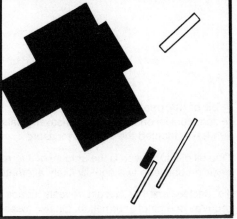

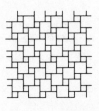

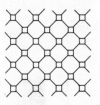

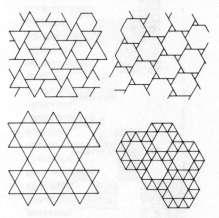

Top left: Diagram showing the distribution of heads and their relationship to the focus in a famous painting by Rembrandt, *Dr Nicholaes Tulp demonstrating the Anatomy of the Arm* (1632).

Left: Schemata of a *Suprematist Composition* (1915) by Kasimir Malevitch.

Above: Accented plane grids move rapidly into multitude and cease to be rhythmic unless given a grouping of groups, a melodic line perhaps? This often requires an additional dimension: texture, tone, colour, emotive signs and symbols.

Right: Clockwise rotation of a square in two dimensions.

Below: Six bits of information.

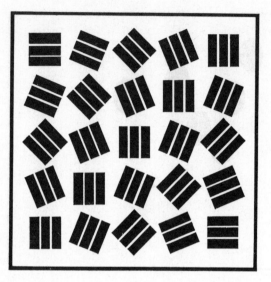

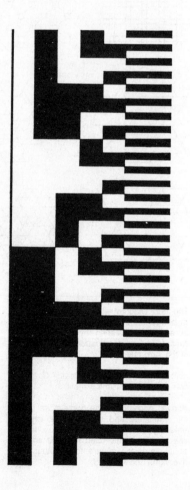

A bit of information

In communications theory, electrical engineers and some psychologists have adopted the *bit* as a measure.

One bit of information is the amount of information needed to make a decision between two equally likely alternatives.

To decide whether a coin reveals heads or tails, on one toss, requires one bit of information. On two tosses of the coin, two bits of information are required, and so on.

The general rule is that every time the number of alternatives is doubled, one bit of information is added. The growth of information, stage by stage, is, therefore, logarithmic to base two. Hence the information carried by a binary digit, which offers two alternatives, 0 and 1, is $\log_2 2 = 1$ bit.

The information carried by a decimal digit is $\log_2 10 = 3.32$ bits.

48

For a short period, most people can memorise up to eight decimal digits or nine binary digits. It would be difficult, therefore, to remember the following binary number containing 24 digits:

1 1 0 0 0 0 0 0 1 0 1 0 0 1 1 1 0 1 1 0 0 1 0 0

Note: a binary number is based on a choice from two alternatives at each stage: on or off; yes or no; one or zero.

Psychologists have explored various ways in which we might recode a series of digits into a more suitable form for the human memory.

One method might be to count alternating groups of ones and zeros thus: 2 ones, 6 zeros, 1 one, 1 zero, 1 one and so on – giving

2 6 1 1 1 2 3 1 2 2 1 2.

This is still difficult to remember. Perhaps it can be grouped further into, say, two hundred and sixty-one, one hundred and twelve, three hundred and twelve and two hundred and twelve?

The Post Office telephone service is convinced that we can remember groups of five decimal digits, therefore the example becomes: 26111 : 23122 : 12

Still difficult?

Hence the search for methods to recode *bits* of information into memorable *chunks*. It is a designer's problem, in any context, to find a recoding that expresses the information in its most memorable form. The above problem could have been recoded decimally as:

3:1 chunks recoding	110	000	001	010	011	101	100	100
	6	0	1	2	3	5	4	4

5:1 chunks recoding	11000	00010	10011	10110	0100
	24	2	19	22	4

Using 4:1 chunks, with *A* representing 0000, the binary number might have been recoded alphabetically as *MAKHGE*.

Equivalent binary and denary (decimal) digits:

01	1
10	2
11	3
100	4 = 2^2
101	5
110	6
111	7
1000	8 = 2^3
1001	9
1010	10
1111	15
10000	16 = 2^4
11110	30
100000	32 = 2^5
1000000	64
10000000	128
100000000	256 = 2^8

Graphic interpretations of:
11000000101001110110100

49

Coding

I TISSO METIM:
ESDES IRA BLETOD,
ISGU ISEINF,
ORMAT IONAN DIDEAS.

From early times forms of coding have been associated with secrecy, privilege, magic and the arts. This may be even truer today when many disciplines are developing a private jargon.

Ironically the creative artist or scientist, the innovator, can also be obliged to invent or extend a language in which to realise his discoveries. And until his ultimate beneficiaries have become familiar with his encoding, his work may be considered unnecessarily abstruse or élitist.

Scientists and artists can be likened to the two faces of a single coin representing humanity, in that one is the obverse of the other. They are interdependent. When one face is up, it rests upon the other.

Yet in their work both artist and scientist share an assumption that the universe is a magnificent cipher to be unravelled by the sensory and thought processes of its progeny. They share the ultimate paradox. Can the cipher decipher itself?

Above: Variations on Yin-Yang, the Chinese symbol for eternity. Yin is female, rain, cloud, mist, space. Yang is male, hill, rock, thing.

Right: Variation on four chords in a circle. Note that the central square is slightly enlarged to emphasise the mass of each truncated disc.

Anagrams

Anagrams date back to the Greek poet Lycophron, circa 260 BC. For centuries they were considered to be a great art form.

Of the first group of anagrams given in this chapter, the solutions to 2, 3 and 4 are not known. The solution to 5 is *conversation*.

Solutions to the second group are:

> *pat*
> *enraged*
> *american*
> *amidships*
> *contemplation*

With the hope that undue distress was not caused by the first group, these anagrams were used to illustrate two basic techniques of dramatisation: *learned helplessness* and *learned confidence*. Comparison of your personal reactions to difficulties arising in the first group with successes in the second group can be instructive. Did you solve *conversation* as readily as you solved *contemplation*? Theory has it that the frustrations of items two, three and four will have impaired your ability to tackle item five, yet will have heightened your ultimate sense of achievement. If indeed you persisted through to a solution at all you are exceptionally determined. Certainly the alternation of learned helplessness and learned confidence can be the very stuff of magic and, thus, of the arts. In the limit, it can interchange order with chaos.

> *Twas brillig, and the slithy toves*
> *Did gyre and gimble in the wabe;*
> *All mimsy were the borogoves,*
> *And the mome raths outgrabe.*
>
> *Beware the Jabberwock, my son!*
> *The jaws that bite, the claws that catch!*
> *Beware the Jubjub bird, and shun*
> *The frumious Bandersnatch!*

From *Alice through the Looking Glass* by Lewis Carroll, 1872

A memorable example of rhythm, with multidimensional *chunks* and not a little recoding.

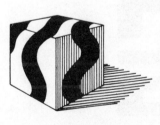

A graphic alphabet can be developed from a group of nine squares.

Visual anagrams can take the forms of camouflage.

4 Positive and negative

Events and intervals

Number, as discussed in Chapter 2, is an awareness of separation, of an independence that is also interdependent. The rational and mystical significance of these properties has been long debated. They form a basis for our major religions.

But their significance is no less in philosophies based upon nuclear physics and cosmic exploration. The big bang theory, the steady state and the oscillation theories on the origin of our universe are all expressions of number.

Twoness, for example, requires that two units have an interval between them ... otherwise they are one. Similarly, *threeness* requires two intervals. Numeracy can thus be regarded as a *splitting* process or, conversely, a coming together to form a series of *n* events separated by *n* − 1 intervals.

Events and intervals can be labelled positive and negative. One is a condition of the other. No intervals ... no multiplicity.

An interval can be *explicit*, when it is complete; or *implicit* when separation is partial, forming a group.

As two stimuli are moved apart the twoness is progressively overwhelmed by the interval and they become isolated unities. An optimum distance, a threshold, exists at which the interval becomes dominant and this varies with circumstances. *Apparent proximity* affects our awareness of number.

The relationship can be inverted. If attention is directed upon the interval, the positive elements change function, serving as limits ... like bookends.

Variations on a theme of C.

52

Dichromatic patterns in crystallography. Three examples of 244 rotations and three of 236 rotations.

Alternating periods of emphasis, from events to intervals then back to events, are a source of emotive energy basic to all music, from Beethoven to Muggsy Spanier, the Orient, Africa and the Occident. It serves all languages, aural, tactile and visual. The good industrial designer works like a musician or a painter to alternate finishes and forms – hard and soft, coarse and smooth, solid and void – constantly using principles of positive and negative with their periodic *inversions*.

A traditional State Coach emphasises the interval, the box. Imagine His Majesty journeying to the Palace in a State Minibus.

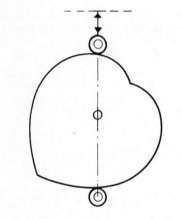

It seems, at this stage in our understanding, that all mankind's concepts are unidimensional. And each dimension has the concept *me* centering it. Any sensation that can be named has only one antithesis. The opposite of hot is cold. There are not two antitheses to hotness, only one: coldness – and *I* am between them. So it is in other dimensions: up and down, in and out, left and right, alive and dead, red and cyan, black and white. The concept *I* is near the centre of a miriad dimensions that generate an apparently complex entity that is *me*.

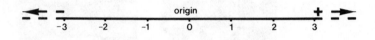

An objective study of a given dimension can be simplified by using the abstract agreed conventions of mathematics. Linear measure from *origin 0* is outwards in both positive and negative directions.

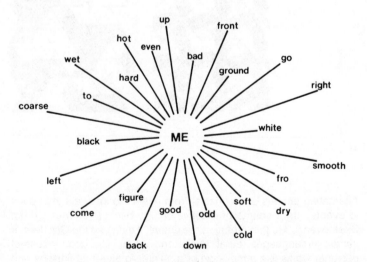

The taming of the *quark*.

The heart form is an excellent example of implicit duality. Presumably this is a reason why scientists have chosen these variations to symbolise the sub-atomic particles within a proton, which are bound together by *charm*.

Used as a *cam*, this curve converts uniform angular motion into uniform linear motion. Based upon the *Spiral of Archimedes*:
 Polar equation, $r = a\theta$; θ in radians.

Hence the two rollers remain equidistant as they move vertically.

Interdependence of positive and negative

If a musician sounds two notes upon an instrument, it can be argued that five events have occurred, including both positive and negative. The silence before; the first note; the interval; the second note; the time after, with attendant memories. The particular importance of *before and after* will be discussed later. They form the stage upon which life is played.

In a post Einstein universe (see Chapter 5), in which scale converges with distance, we live and design, into a *relatively* finite everyday world. Most people seek the apparent security of a defined boundary, environmentally and psychologically, although they may dispute its location.

Within any closed space a positive experience is accompanied by a complementary negative. In the rectangles on page 57 a circle describes the area of a disc and also its envelope. One is a condition of the other. Just as a cup can be simultaneously half empty and half full.

Segregation by differentiation and proximity.

If two parallels are added outside of the first two, the interval between them becomes background.

Dominance

The outline sketch is from a work by Toulouse-Lautrec. He used the space around and between objects to contain the area within them and also to stress the rectilinearity of his canvas. A single frame is used to fix a brief moment in eternity.

It can be said that design in the twentieth century is an exploration of the properties of change. We work with comparative values: positive is a condition of negative; male a condition of female; near a condition of far.

We feel, we see, we judge by differences.

Above: Schemata of a work by Victor Vasareley.

Right: Outline of a lithograph, *The Jockey*, by Toulouse-Lautrec, 1899.

56

Although competition between positive and negative expresses the energy of a rhythm, at any moment the mind requires a dominance of one by the other. A design offering alternating periods of positive-dominant and negative-dominant variations on a theme gains *presence* and subtlety. Town planners seek to balance areas of pierced solids against intermittent voids; buildings against thoroughfares and gardens; internal and external spaces that share a common theme. This leads to *counterchange* and, when two or more complementary themes are used, to *counterpoint*.

Similarly, the architect will decide whether or not a particular fenestration is solid or void dominant. Is it a wall pierced by windows or a framed plane through which life and light may travel freely? Elsewhere in the building complex he will seek opportunity to reverse the relationship and to echo it in plan.

The principle applies in all fields of design and was examplified early in this century by Neo-plasticism (ref: Van Doesburg, Mondrian, de Stijl).

Figure and ground

The need for focusing, both senses and mind, leads to recognition of figure and ground. Insecurity, ambiguity, dazzle arises when positive and negative stimuli compete without the ultimate supremacy of one or the other as *figure*. Normally, dazzle is avoided by emphasis of the positive elements; however too much emphasis can be overpowering.

The degree of dominance should be related to the circumstances. A roadside poster must have spontaneous impact upon a motorist speeding by. An advertisement in a railway carriage can be conversational, even entertaining. A painting on the same subject, to be hung at head office, should invite contemplation and offer a dialogue with the observer.

The circles have similar radii, yet the white disc seems larger.

Schemata of *Seated Woman* by Modigliani emphasises her positive form.

57

In a book, the near white paper is assumed to be ground and the print, which contains the message, is read as figure. The eyes are directed upon the figure, not the ground. Even so, the blandness and repose of areas of blank paper should be as joyous as the more eventful typescript and drawings. The texture and colour of the paper can thus become critical to the quality of the book.

Eyes are designed to respond to light, not to night.

'Only the ever changing is never changing.'

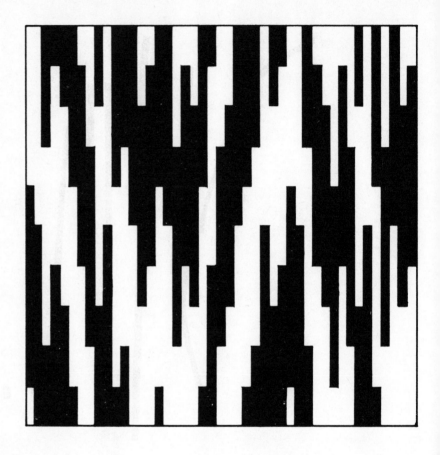

The square is divided into 45 vertical strips.
Each strip is ten units high and divided into
equal lengths of black and white, permuted
to avoid repetition of sequence.

A   B   C

In the three sets of stripes, example *A* is white dominant on a white ground; *B* has equal areas of black and white; *C* is black dominant. Which do you prefer and why?

Theoretically it should be easier to read a white figure on a black ground. Fortunately, in view of the high cost of printing a complete book in negative reversal, it would also fail visually. For continuous reading of white on black, the eyes would adjust to a twilight sensitivity, distending the pupils until they suffer glare in the general environment. The book would become a visual *black hole.*

Under certain circumstances, after nightfall for example, the luminosity of white figure on dark ground can be a safety factor favouring legibility. It has many industrial applications.

The rotating vector

Ideas of space and time are linked, for us at least, by movement or change. We think of time as a positive journey into the future and as a negative movement, via memory, into the past. The apparent inevitability of this process offers immediate challenge to the genius of an H. G. Wells or a Jules Verne. Whatever the direction, the key to our measurement of time is *change*. From earliest times technology and the arts recognised that rotary movement could record for mankind the interdependence and continuity of space and time.

Mathematical and aesthetic convention has it that positive rotation of a positive vector of length $= r = OP$ about an origin O is *anticlockwise*.

Possible reasons for this contradiction with a normal clock are discussed in Chapter 9.

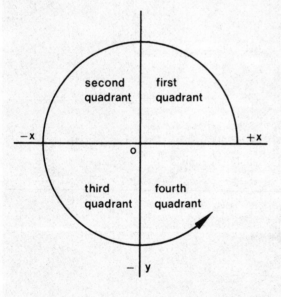
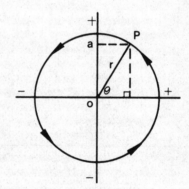

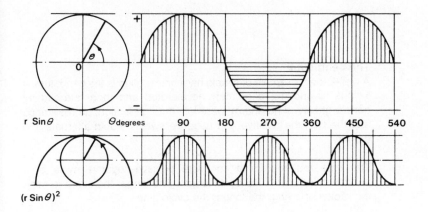

r Sin θ $\theta_{degrees}$ 90   180   270   360   450   540

(r Sin θ)^2

As the vector rotates about O, P describes a circle, radius r. If the vector starts at rest on the positive x axis, let the angle turned through $= \theta$.

Let the height, or amplitude of P (referred to the y axis) $= a$.

Then, at any moment, $a = r \sin \theta$.

As the vector rotates about O, it describes four quadrants to complete one revolution, 1 *rev*.

In the first and second quadrants, a is positive. In quadrants three and four a is negative.

The rate of change of a is maximum when the vector is horizontal and minimum when it is vertical. This is known as *simple harmonic motion* and occurs whenever circular motion is directly translated into linear motion, as in a piston or an electrical generator of alternating current, AC.

One complete rev of the vector can be projected horizontally to form a *wavelength*.

The maximum amplitude, maximum $a = +r$ and $-r$.

Thus half of the wave is positive and half is negative.

Further revolutions duplicate the projected waveform.

If a is squared, the wave becomes completely positive (minus times minus equals plus), the frequency is doubled and the wavelength is halved. It can be seen that the frequency f multiplied by the wavelength equals the angular velocity of the vector. In this diagram this is translated into linear velocity.

The waveform of $a^2 = r^2 \sin^2 \theta$ could be produced by a vector, length $r/2$, rotating about point $+r/2$ on the y axis, at twice the velocity. The diagrams all assume that $r =$ one unit.

If a rotating vector, length $r/2$, is to project the curve a^2 then it should start with 90° *lag*. Hence, when $r = 1$,

$$2 \sin^2 \theta = \sin(2\theta - 90) + 1.$$

The movement of a simple piston describes a sinusoidal wave in time.

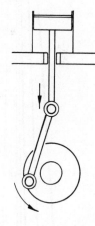

The pendulum

A well-known example of simple harmonic motion is the pendulum. It swings to and fro, alternately accelerated and then retarded by earth's gravity. If no energy were lost through friction, air resistance and the like, the positive and negative swings would alternate into eternity.

The time required for a complete positive-negative cycle of a pendulum is determined by its length. The longer the string forming the radius of swing, the longer the cycle time.

The rate of acceleration is not significantly affected by the weight of the bob. Galileo found that objects of differing weights hit the ground together when dropped from the top of a high tower. Subsequently, Isaac Newton established that gravitational force is inversely proportional to the square of the distance between the centres of gravity of two bodies. It is also directly proportional to their total mass. In the Galileo experiment the mass of the earth is so overwhelmingly large that the dropped objects appeared to be accelerating at the same rate.

At maximum swing in each half cycle the pendulum is momentarily poised, motionless, before commencing to move downwards. The pivoted string demands a circular path for the bob, so that acceleration due to gravity is converted into acceleration due to curvature. The bob tries to fly off into space: *centrifugal* force. The restraining string is stressed by *centripetal* force, pulling the bob radially towards the centre.

The bob reaches maximum velocity at mid-swing and then proceeds to slow down.

The angle θ, through which the pendulum swings, does not affect the frequency. When θ is large the maximum velocity is proportionately high. As θ gets smaller so the maximum velocity is reduced. Therefore, assuming no energy losses, the pendulum will maintain its cyclic frequency whether θ be 1° or 180°. If a rod replaces the string, the pendulum could swing through $\theta = 360°$.

A graph of the position of the bob against time produces a *sine curve*.

64

The bob describes a circular arc with radius R equal to the length of the string. A direct relationship exists between the length of the arc and the angle subtended by it at the centre of the circle, such that:

$$\frac{\text{length of arc}}{\text{perimeter of circle}} = \frac{\theta°}{360°}$$

$$\text{therefore } \frac{\text{arc}}{2\pi R} = \frac{\theta°}{360°}$$

If angle θ is quoted in radians, then arc $= \theta R$.

Note: a radian is the angle subtended at the centre of a circle by an arc length equal to the radius.
Therefore, 2π radians $= 360°$.

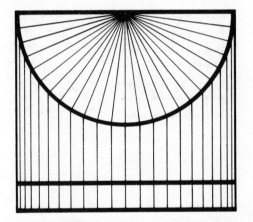

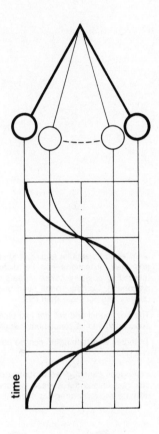

time

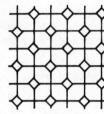

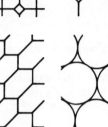

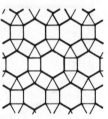
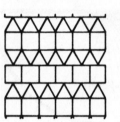

Only regular triangular and rectangular grids and their distentions can be dichromatic (permitting adjacent colour repeats only on diagonals). Complex grids need up to four colours, but not more than four.

The hexagonal grid will not fold unless it is subdivided into its constituent triangles.

Triangles and rectangles can be combined in a grid.

Pentagons cannot close to form a continuous grid unless the surface is curved ... ultimately to form a regular dodecahedron.

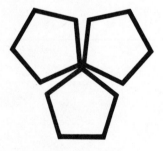

Repeat patterns

The number of uniform spacial grids that can be formed from Euclidean traditional geometry is very limited. In a flat plane repeat patterns of regular polygons can be based only upon triangles and rectangles. They can be squeezed, pulled, dropped, mixed and truncated, but the basic grids will remain triangular or rectangular.

A pentagonal grid curves the surface; an hexagonal grid subdivides into triangles; an octagonal grid is fundamentally square. No regular polygon can repeat on a regular or mixed regular plane grid unless the number of sides factorises into multiples of two and three.

This restraint is taken into the third dimension and therefore applies volumetrically.

66

宋・蹴球紋

Chinese patterns, Sung Dynasty, 960–1279
AD.

The free form counterchange pattern has the
same basic grid as the geometric pattern.

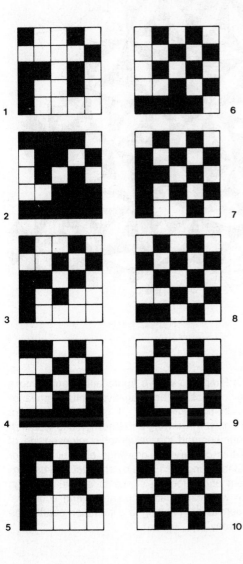

1

2

3

4

5

6

7

8

9

10

This life cycle in positive and negative has the following program:

Diagonal relationships are not considered.
The initial distribution of black and white squares in a squared grid occurs by chance.
Each square dislikes the company of a similar colour in an adjacent square.
At each generation, the four squares immediately adjacent (two or three at the edges of the grid) dictate the required colour for the next generation, by majority vote, simultaneously across the grid.
When the vote is equal the square does not change colour.
The process is repeated, through ten generations in this case, until stability is achieved.

If the programme is adjusted to apply to diagonally adjoining squares only, an impasse occurs at the fourth generation.

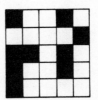

69

A simple elaboration on a 236 grid.

History reveals many attempts to weave figure and ground into a cohesive unity, offering both positive and negative stimuli simultaneously, without dazzle. In the philosophy of Islam a search for reconciliation between Knower, Knowing and Known led to research into the mystique of number and the calligraphic interweaving of subject and object. In this century the drawings of Paul Klee, for example, were succeeded during the 1950s by *abstract expressionist* attempts to fragment and reform a sense of space. Although abstract expressionism was essentially a painters' and sculptors' form, it was widely influential, contributing to a liberation of attitudes in design that persists today.

70

This hexagonal Islamic pattern can be found in North Africa and Spain.

5 Progressions and growth

The true spirit of delight, the exaltation, the sense of being more than Man, which is the touchstone of the highest excellence, is to be found in mathematics as surely as in poetry.

Mysticism and Logic, Bertrand Russell (1917)

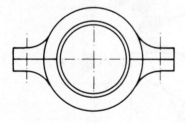

In any engineering project the tolerances, the maximum permissible plus and minus variance from an optimum value, should be stated. For example, the design of a shaft to rotate in a bearing should allow for a film of suitably viscous oil to isolate both their minimum and maximum diameters.

If both diameters have a tolerance of ±0.001 units, the oil film can vary by 0.002 units in thickness.

Tolerances

Normally our assessment of distance is an approximation. Only within our personal space, which varies with activity, does it need to be precise. Beyond that we are usually concerned with similarity and with comparisons of *more than* with *less than*. We have, therefore, a ready response to the ratio 1:1, and the generative expression of their sum, 2:1 and 1:2.

Confidence in our judgement of relationships dwindles as ratios increase from 2:1 to 3:1 and beyond.

We prefer to simplify compound ratios such as 5:2 or 7:3. For example, 9:4 would probably be assessed as slightly more than 2:1.

Irrational ratios are generally beyond the conscious mind, yet research, initiated by Fechner (1801–1887) and continuing today, suggests that we have a subliminal response to a select few, such as √2:1, which are discussed in Chapter 6.

What is precision? Nature is inexhaustably committed to a miriad variations upon any theme. Every manmade product, every sensory relationship, is subject to physical and mental tolerances. Every human being, for example, is a variation within the programme *homo sapiens*. No two are identical yet their humanity is acknowledged within limits that are not easy to define, though most of us have a notion of what they might be. In this respect, the paintings of Picasso, Miró and Bacon are instructive.

The designer attempts to parallel the processes of nature. If his commitment is to the making of a complete pattern, the precision of individual elements becomes subordinate to that objective.

The permissible tolerances in the *parts* are related to the functional efficiency of the *whole*. In a car engine, for example, the permissible tolerances between moving parts are determined by the viscosity of the selected oil under working conditions. The clearances must allow for an oil film that can prevent direct contact between metal parts, either by binding when it is minimal or by juddering and spin-off when it is excessive.

Arithmetic progression

A repetition of differences leads to observations of growth and the ways in which nature expands and contracts. The patterns are many and challenging to the mathematician. Fortunately, they have been resolved into a few basic forms that can serve the designer.

The most readily understood series of magnitudes is the *arithmetic progression*, AP. The series 1 2 3 4 5 6 7 8 9 10 11 12 13 14 15 is an AP with a *base* of 1 and a *common difference* of 1.

Let a = the base and d = the common difference.
An AP is constructed by adding d to the preceding term T.

$$\text{Term}_1 \quad T_2 \quad T_3 \quad T_4 \quad T_n$$
$$a \quad a + d \quad a + 2d \quad a + 3d \quad a + (n - 1)d$$

Other AP's are:

1	3	5	7	9	11	13	15	17	$a = 1$	$d = 2$
2	4	6	8	10	12	14	16	18	$a = 2$	$d = 2$
25	22	19	16	13	10	7	4	1	$a = 25$	$d = -3$

For design purposes, unless the progression continues into negative numbers, the positive base should be numerically less than or equal to d.

The sum of an AP to n terms can be found by formula:

$$S = \frac{n}{2}[2a + (n - 1)d]$$

hence, when $a = 2, d = 3$ and $n = 6$

$$S_6 = 3[4 + (6 - 1)3] = 3[4 + 15] = 57$$

In this simple case the sum can be checked by adding:

$$2 + 5 + 8 + 11 + 14 + 17 = 57$$

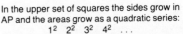

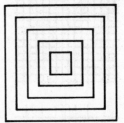

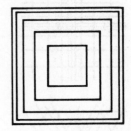

In the upper set of squares the sides grow in AP and the areas grow as a quadratic series:
$$1^2 \quad 2^2 \quad 3^2 \quad 4^2 \quad \ldots$$
In the lower set the areas grow in AP and suggest a curvature of space.

73

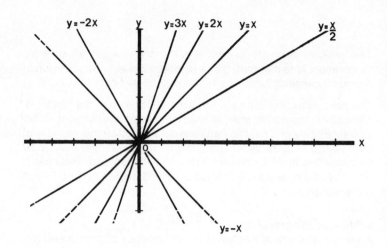

Right: Graphs of $y = mx$ all pass through the origin.

Below: Planar AP grids based upon the series:
1 1 1 1 1 1 1 1 . . . and
the series: 1 2 3 4 5 . . .

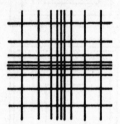

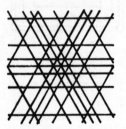

An *AP* grows by *simple interest*. Its rate of change is a constant throughout the series. It adds the same d per term at T_{40} as at T_4.

It can commence at zero and seems independent of man. The constancy of measure ensures that a metre in Australia is similar to a metre in Europe.

Architects need and love an *AP*. Aesthetic and physical economy require the duplication of *modules* from their bricks, masonry, timbers, concrete formwork and exposed aggregates. Interior and industrial designers have similar modular materials: fabrics, tiles, structures, services and furnishings. So it is in all the arts, fine and applied: in the brushstrokes of painters, the drummer's beat and the microns of science we seek an arithmetic scalar system to secure, capture and control a measure of space.

AP's provide the texture of our living space. Our most satisfactory measuring systems are in *AP*: feet and inches, metres, degrees, minutes, pounds, calories, pence. When we deviate from this practice, confusion can arise, as in the decibel system for measuring the amplitude of sound. Decibels are logarithmic. At about the normal noise level of a petrol-engined motor car a reading of 73 dB(A) is twice that of 70 dB(A).

The *arithmetic mean* of two numbers is commonly known as their average. This is found by dividing their sum by two. The three numbers are thus in arithmetic progression, *AP*.
For example: the *AM* of 3 and 27 = 30/2 = 15; giving an *AP* of 3, 15, 27.

Straight line graphs

In a Cartesian graph (named after its originator, Descartes) the x and y axes are normally arithmetic, forming a square grid. Variable values of x are projected vertically from the x axis. Dependent values of y are projected horizontally.

If the equation $y = x$ is plotted upon the grid, a straight line curve emerges: y varies in direct ratio to x.

values of x:	1	2	3	4	5	6	7
values of $y = x$:	1	2	3	4	5	6	7
values of $y = 2x$:	2	4	6	8	10	12	14
values of $y = 3x$:	3	6	9	12	15	18	21

All produce straight line curves of the form $y = mx$, where m is the slope of the curve. Slope is the ratio of vertical compared with horizontal distances.

Any point on the grid can be located by reference to the x and y axes. Always give the x reference first. Introduce the terms latitude and longitude and we have the basis for Descartes's contribution to charting and navigation.

When m is positive, the slope is positive, climbing upwards from left to right. When m is negative, the slope is negative, falling from left to right.

The addition or subtraction of a constant c to the equation has the effect of moving the straight line curve bodily upward or downward by quantity c.
The equation for a straight line graph is therefore $y = mx + c$.

An integer AP produces a serrated straight line graph. The point at which it cuts the y axis is a:

therefore $y = a + dx$

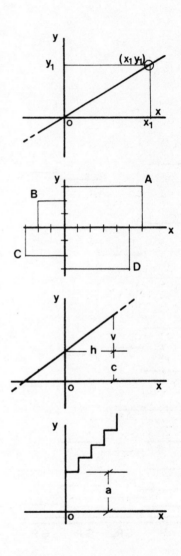

Slope $= m = y_1/x_1 = \tan \theta$

Locations by x and y references (known as ordinates):
A is at $(6, 3)$; B at $(-2, 2)$
C at $(-3, -2)$; D at $(5, -3)$

75

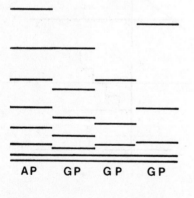

Geometric progression
Nature does not work modestly. It invented splitting and, therefore, duplication. Perhaps, somewhere in the universe, there is life based upon triplication or even quintuplication? The hypothesis raises some challenging practical questions! But, whatever the rate, nature tends to grow by *compound interest*, or geometric progression, GP.

In its simplest form, compound interest is a doubling process:
1 2 4 8 16 32 64 128 256 512 . . . .
This series is known as a geometric progression, GP, having a base, $a = 1$ and a common ratio, $r = 2$.

This is a particularly important GP in that it shares initial terms with the simplest *AP*: 1 2 3 4 5 . . ..

GP's are all of the form:

$Term_1$	T_2	T_3	T_4	T_5	T_6	T_n
a	ar	ar^2	ar^3	ar^4	ar^5	$ar^{(n-1)}$

where a is the base and r is the common ratio.

Other typical GP's are:

1 3 9 27 81 243 729	$a = 1$	$r = 3$
2 6 18 54 162 486 1458	$a = 2$	$r = 3$
3 15 75 375 1875	$a = 3$	$r = 5$

The sum of a GP to n terms can be found by formula:

$$S_n = \frac{a(r^n - 1)}{(r - 1)} = \frac{a(1 - r^n)}{(1 - r)}$$

Thus, when $a = 2, r = 3$ and $n = 5$

$$S_5 = \frac{2(3^5 - 1)}{(3 - 1)} = \frac{2(243 - 1)}{2} = 242$$

In this case, a simple check is to add: 2 + 6 + 18 + 54 + 162.

The additive linear progressions; with a = 1; AP, d= 1; GP's, r = 1.5, 2.0, 2.5.

When *r* exceeds 2, the growth rate rapidly accelerates beyond human measure.

AP   GP   GP   GP

76

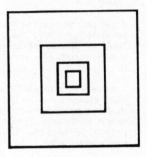

A superimposed series of squares in AP emphasises their flat plane. The growth of area is proportional to the side lengths and, thus, parabolic. However it can also be described as a complex AP. For example, assuming $a = d = 1$:

    sidelengths: 1 2 3 4 5
    areas: 1 4 9 16 25
    growth of side: 1 1 1 1
    growth of area: 3 5 7 9
    hence areas have $a = 1$ and $d = 2$

Superimposed squares in linear GP have an emphatic centre of energy, suggesting a third dimension, depth.

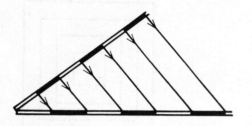

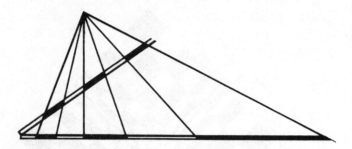

The scale of an AP can be transposed by parallel lines.

A GP can be produced from an AP by radiations from a point. The angle between the AP and GP axes and the relative position of the point control the common ratio in the GP.

The integration of AP and GP scales can be widely observed in nature and is one of the most exciting, and sometimes mystifying, tools of the designer. Dimensions from the projected GP have been used to form the configurations below.

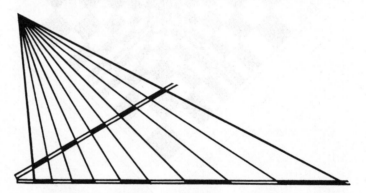

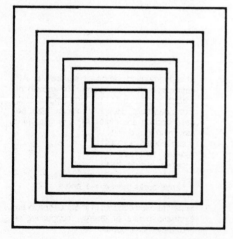

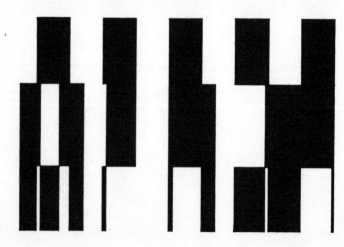

Logarithms

A GP grows by compound interest. Its rate of change grows with its position in the series. It is logarithmic.

The *logarithm* of a number is the power to which a *base* must be raised in order to equal the number. If

$a^x = N$ then $\log_a N = x$, where a is the base.

Because a *GP* develops by multiplication it cannot originate at zero. The philosophic implications are profound. All growth by compound interest, nature's method, requires an initiating investment . . . a *principal*, however small . . . it cannot start at zero.

Plotted on to a Cartesian grid, GP's have a slope at any point that varies with the value of x.

The curves produced have the general equation $y = ar^x$ where r is the common ratio and a is a constant.
Therefore the curve cuts the y axis at a.
Any number raised to the power 0 equals 1.

$$2^0 = 1, 9^0 = 1, 99^0 = 1, n^0 = 1.$$

Therefore a logarithmic curve cannot pass through the origin.
If $y = n^x$, when $x = 0$, $y = n^0 = 1$.

Using log-lin graph paper, GP's can produce straight line curves by plotting log y against x.
The log y axis is cut at log a.
The slope of the curve reveals the value of n.

A *logarithmic scale* is produced by applying a multiplication to a regular arithmetic scale, as in a sliderule.

1	2		4		8		16		32		64		128		256
		3			9				27			81			243
				6		12		24		48		96		192	
	2		3 4 5 6 7 8 10							50		100		200	

Logarithms were not fully understood until the work of Lord Napier (1550–1617). Naperian or natural logarithms contributed to the advance of oceanic navigation during the seventeenth century and culminated in the foundation of the Greenwich Observatory in 1675.

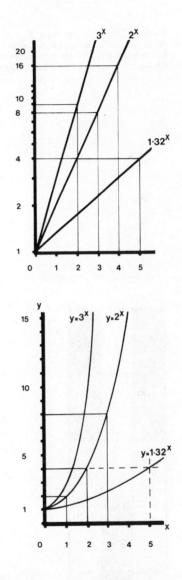

Curves of $y = 1^x$, 1.32^x, 2^x and 3^x plotted on logarithmic and arithmetic scales.

Plotting the y values on to a logarithmic scale straightens a compound interest curve.

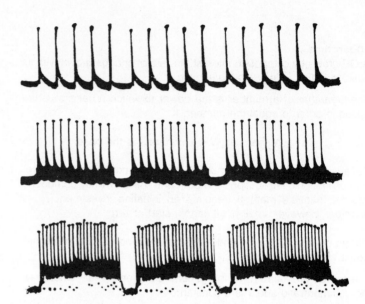

Electrical pulses on the axon of a tactile sensor neuron under increasing pressures. An axon is a thin fibre which protrudes from a living cell to act as an electrical conductor.

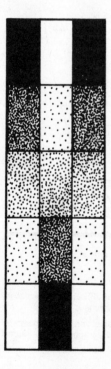

Sensory communications

Sensory communications media are vibratory. Each sense is optimised at its most efficient frequency in terms of function. Sensitivity usually depreciates in geometric progression from that datum.

In hearing, notes audible to the human ear range from about 16 to 16 000, 2^4 to 2^{14} cycles per second (cps). Middle C, easily found on a piano, is 2^8, or 256 cps or Hertz, Hz.

In vision a series of intermediate greys, in visually equal steps from white to black, cannot be obtained by mixing black and white pigments arithmetically. A measure of white pigment will have more effect when mixed with black than mixed with light grey. Starting with black, the quantity of white pigment required to establish each successively lighter grey increases logarithmically. For the very last step, the white must completely overwhelm the last vestiges of black.

Our internal communications are similarly logarithmic. If you press your thumb upon a surface, information is sent via the nervous system to the brain as an alternating electric current at a potential of about 100 millivolts.

If the pressure is increased from one to two to three pounds force per unit area, then the frequency increases in geometric progression. Needless to say, the voltage does not increase, otherwise some delicate fuses would burn.

80

Mendel's theory

The series: 11111111111111111111111111111111111111111111
is an AP with $a = 1$ and $d = 0$; it is also a GP, $a = 1$ and $r = 1$.

Its constancy is comforting, but in life generally there is an urge to multiply. Some form of logarithmic doubling process precipitates every population explosion. This is modified but not negated, by the bisexuality of the higher orders of life on earth. The manner of their diversity, yet continuity through the evolutionary process, was explained by Mendel (1822–1884). He deduced that an inherited characteristic is regulated by two genes, one from each parent. If the genes are different, one will be dominant and the other recessive. This means that when two hybrids are brought together, one offspring in four will be characterised by the recessive genes.

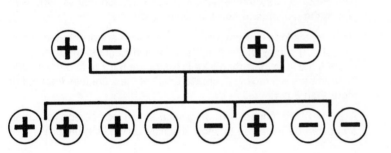

On this basis the next generation should produce 5 + +, 5 − − and 14 positive dominated hybrids.

Pascal's triangle

Pascal's triangle is a well known distribution pattern. It is a system of flowpaths that split and rejoin on a binary principle.

At each location the number of flowpaths available is the sum of two sources in the previous generation.

It can be seen that after the fourth distribution only two chances in sixteen offer a *pure* form. If the outer cups are marked *win* in a pinball machine it is not difficult to calculate the odds favouring the bank.

A mixed choir produces sound between 64 and 1500 cps. About 300 discernable frequencies are available in music. The timbre or particular quality of a note is produced by overtones, as discussed in Chapter 6.

It is now clear that the hybrids form seeds having one or other of two differentiating characters, and of these one half develop again the hybrid form, while the other half yield plants which remain constant and receive the dominance of the recessive characters (respectively) in equal numbers.
Mendel (1866)

Below: Pascal's triangle describes the availability of flowpaths down a hexagonal net.

```
               1
            1  1
          1  2  1
        1  3  3  1
      1  4  6  4  1
    1  5 10 10  5  1
  1  6 15 20 15  6  1
1     6    15    20   15    6    1
```

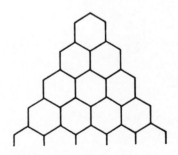

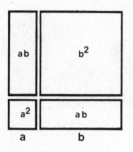

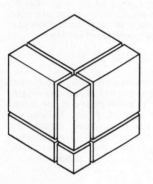

Graphic forms of $(a + b)^2$ and $(a + b)^3$.

Pascal's triangle is a useful mnemonic in the *binomial theorem*:

$$(a + b)^2 = a^2 + 2ab + b^2$$
$$(a - b)^3 = a^3 - 3a^2b + 3ab^2 - b^3$$
$$(a + b)^4 = a^4 + 4a^3b + 6a^2b^2 + 4ab^3 + b^4$$

If b is negative, then plus and minus signs alternate.

Pascal's triangle can be circumscribed by a *distribution curve*, sometimes referred to as a *Gaussian curve*, named after the nineteenth century mathematician, Karl Friedrich Gauss, who was one of the pioneers of non-Euclidean geometry.

Most populations that have an optimum value are distributed in this way. If in a survey of the heights of men in England the average is about 5 ft 8 in, a majority will be in the range 5 ft 7 in to 5 ft 9 in, and the numbers will rapidly decrease until very few are less than 5 ft or more than 6 ft 4 in tall.

A study of the congestion, or ground space per person, of urban areas can be expected to show a similar distribution pattern.

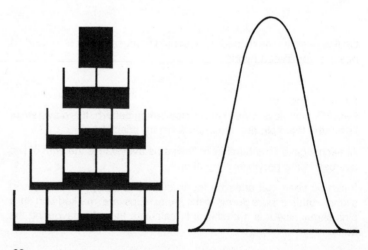

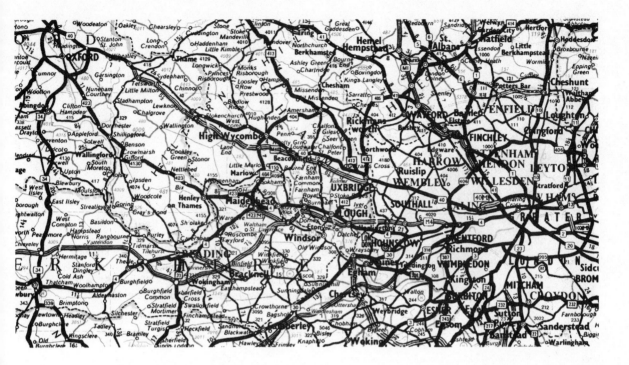

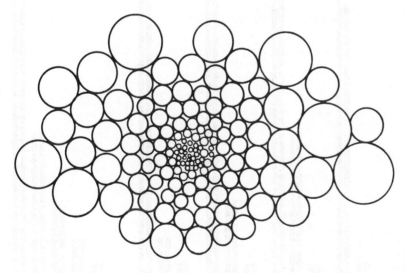

A map of major roads in the vicinity of London is representative of a typical distribution curve.

Of course, when people are permitted more space, they will expand to fill it . . . but this is the behaviour of any fluid energy.

The geometric mean

The geometric mean GM is derived from the GP.

If x, y and z are in GP, to find y when x and z are known:
y is the square root of the product of x and z.
$y = \sqrt{xz}$, eg, the GM of 3 and 27 = $\sqrt{(3 \times 27)} = \sqrt{81} = 9$;
whereas their AM, or average, was found to be 15.

Above: Schematic drawings of the painting *Composition Arithmétique* (1930) by Theo Van Doesburg. The mechanical structure of the work is humanised by slight modification of edges and corners and careful graduation of background tonalities.

The arithmetic, geometric and harmonic means of any two magnitudes are themselves in GP (see Chapter 6). Therefore a GM links both the two base terms and their AM and HM.

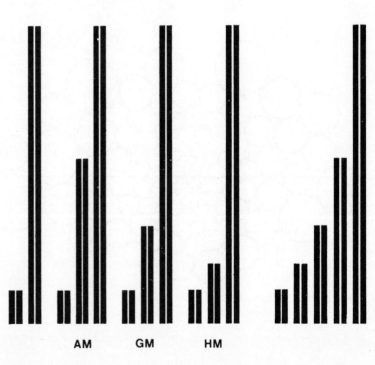

AM   GM   HM

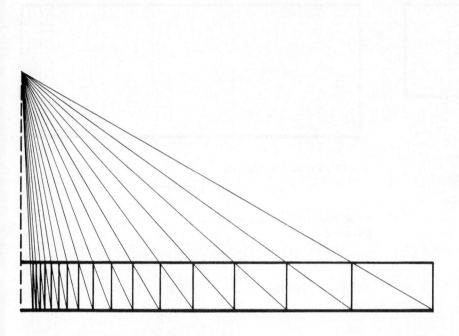

The sum of a convergent GP

The GP's discussed so far have been *divergent*, growing ever larger. GP's can also be *convergent*. This occurs when the common ratio is less than zero.

Hence when $a = 16$ and $r = \frac{1}{2}$, the GP is:

$$16 \ 8 \ 4 \ 2 \ 1 \ \tfrac{1}{2} \ \tfrac{1}{4} \ \tfrac{1}{8} \ \tfrac{1}{16} \ \tfrac{1}{32} \ \tfrac{1}{64} \ \tfrac{1}{128}$$

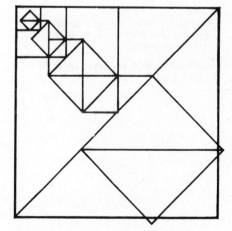

In a convergent series, the terms get ever smaller, approaching zero in quantity. A perplexing paradox arises here, that has made much sport amongst mathematicians. It is that this GP can be classed as an infinite series on the basis that no matter how small the fractions become they never actually reach zero.

Even so, we make the assumption that when r is a fraction, r^n approaches zero as n approaches infinity. For example, when

$$r = \tfrac{1}{2} \ \ r^2 = \tfrac{1}{4} \ \ r^3 = \tfrac{1}{8} \ \ r^8 = \tfrac{1}{256} \text{ etc.}$$

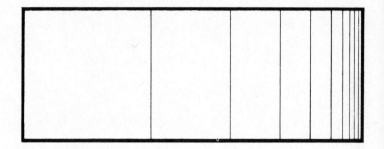

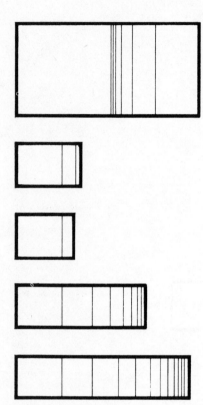

A centre of interest can be suggested by reversing the direction of a convergent series in midflow.

Sums of the infinite, convergent GP's:
$r = \frac{1}{3}, \frac{1}{4}, \frac{2}{3}, \frac{3}{4}$.

In a GP, the sum to n terms

$$S_n \equiv \frac{a(1 - r^n)}{1 - r}$$

if r is fractional, in the *limit* $r^n = 0$
therefore

$$S_\infty = \frac{a}{1 - r}$$

This means that the GP with $a = 1$ and $r = \frac{1}{2}$ has

$$S_\infty = \frac{1}{1 - \frac{1}{2}} = 2$$

The numerical relationship between the common ratio and the sum to infinity in this particular GP is readily understood by the human being.

When $a = 1$ and $r = \frac{1}{2}$, $S_\infty = 2$.

By comparison, when $a = 1$ and $r = \frac{1}{3}$ $S_\infty = \frac{3}{2}$
$a = 1$ $r = \frac{1}{4}$ $S_\infty = \frac{4}{3}$
$a = 1$ $r = \frac{2}{3}$ $S_\infty = 3$
$a = 1$ $r = \frac{3}{4}$ $S_\infty = 4$

As r gets smaller the sum to infinity gets smaller and approaches unity.

The most useful common ratios lie between 0.5 and 1, with their reciprocals.

Ratio 1:2, reciprocal 2:1; in decimals 0.5:1 reciprocal 2:1
1:$\sqrt{2}$, reciprocal $\sqrt{2}$:1; in decimals 0.707:1 reciprocal 1.414:1
1:$\sqrt{3}$, reciprocal $\sqrt{3}$:1,; in decimals 0.577:1 reciprocal 1.732:1

86

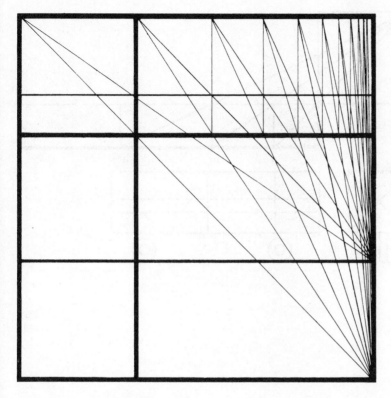

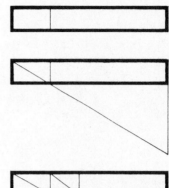

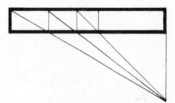

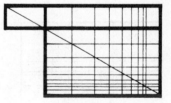

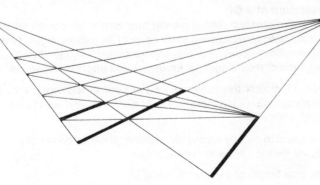

Given base *a* and the sum to infinity of a convergent GP, the series can be formed by diagonals radiating from a control point to form a linear series of rectangles. The control point locates the far corner of a control rectangle.

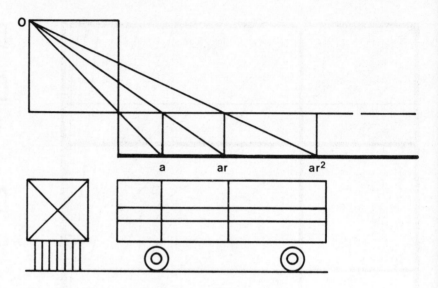

Projection of a GP

When the common ratio is greater than one, a GP can be projected beyond a square between extensions of its parallel sides. Given a and ar, the square and the first rectangle can be drawn. Convergence of their diagonals locates O, the origin of the series.

From O project the diagonal for the second rectangle, with side length ar^2. Successive projection of diagonals and rectangles continues the series.

O is found to occupy a strategic position on the far corner of a control square for the GP series of rectangles.

The side length of the control square is

$$\frac{(a-1)r+1}{r-1}$$

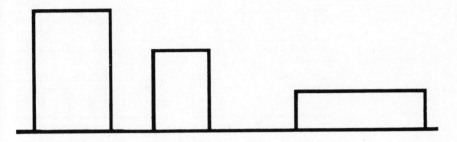

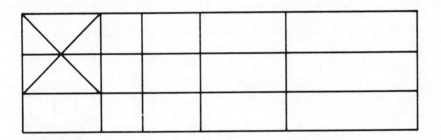

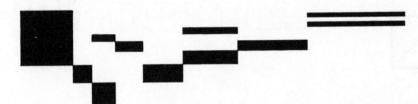

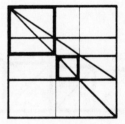

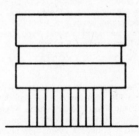

When $a = 1$, the formula simplifies to

$$\frac{1}{r - 1}$$

hence, when $r = 3/2$, side of control square = 2

   $r = 2$, side of control square = 1

   $r = 4/3$, side of control square = 3

Geometrically and, it is suggested, sensorially the control square holds the key to the series.

The projection can be used to form a two or three dimensional grid. This master grid can relate both positive and negative, solid and void, elements.

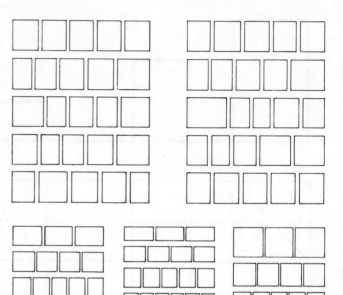

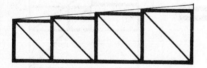

A block of 25 rectangles can be invigorated by *variations on a theme.* A row of similar rectangles is put into AP or GP. These are then permuted to avoid vertical repetition.

For example: 51342
32154
25431

The number of rectangles per row can be put into AP. These may have similar height or similar area or similar shape. Maintained in integer series they form a visual structure that is strongest when they share similar shape.

When the corresponding sides of similar polygons are in GP their areas and volumes are also in GP, with common ratios of r^2 and r^3 respectively.

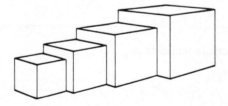

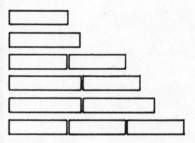

These GP series of cubes, with tarred roofs, are projected in three dimensions by geometric perspective, from a control square. Positive and negative volumes are interdependent.

Combinations, by addition, are the basis of many industrialised building systems. In this example the basic units of lengths four and five can be added to give lengths of 4, 5, 8, 9, 10, 12, onwards. 12 is the *critical number* of this combination of lengths.

AP and GP superimposed within a square.

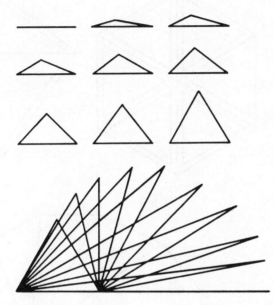

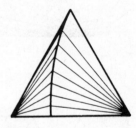

AP and GP triangles

The sides of triangles can be put into AP or GP. The selection of AP triangles ranges from the linear 1, 2, 3 to the equilateral 1, 1, 1 via 2, 3, 4; 3, 4, 5; 4, 5, 6 etc.

The selection of GP triangles ranges from the linear 0.618, 1, 1.618 to the equilateral 1, 1, 1 via 1, 3/2, 9/4; 1, $\sqrt{2}$, 2 etc.

Triangles which have the same base and height have similar areas.

Arrays of AP triangles (the sidelengths are a, $a + d$, $a + 2d$), based on the shortest and longest sides. Similar arrays can be produced by GP triangles, with the common ratio between $r = 1$ and $r = 1.618$.

Bottom: An array of triangles sharing same base and of equal area.

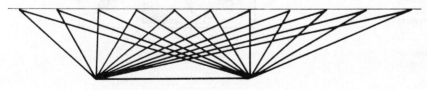

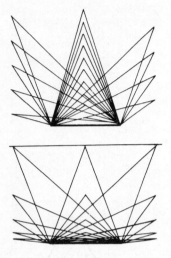

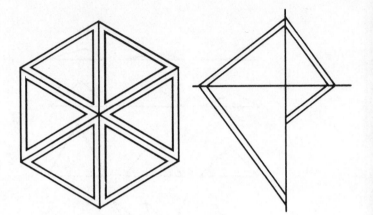

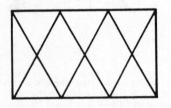

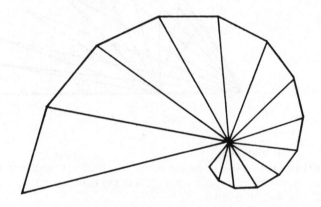

Top: Arrays of triangles sharing a common base and with areas (thus heights) in AP and GP.

Right: Similar GP triangles can also grow to form a spiral.

At least 5000 years ago, while the Egyptians mastered the 3, 4, 5 right angled triangle, the Babylonians used the equilateral triangle to devise circular measure.

Above: The Timaeus Rectangle, based on interweaving equilateral triangles, has a proportion of 1 to $\sqrt{3}$.

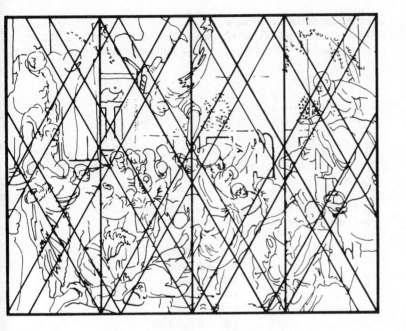

Within the equilateral triangle, parallels decrease with a common ratio of 0.75.

It became a major tool of the Renaissance, providing a stable and generous finite space, as shown in the broad structure of *The Miracle of St Mark* by Tintoretto (Venice, *c* 1580). It also offers strong right angles at key points. Such merits were urged on the Cubists, about 1910, by Corbusier.

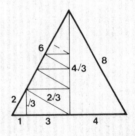

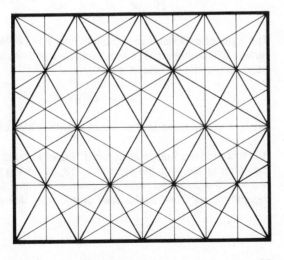

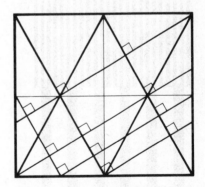

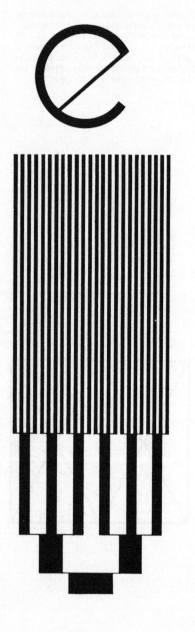

The exponential function, e

Another form of growth can be based upon *factorial numbers*. These are signified in mathematics by an exclamation mark, ! thus:

$$1! = 1 \qquad\qquad\qquad = \quad 1$$
$$2! = 1 \times 2 \qquad\qquad = \quad 2$$
$$3! = 1 \times 2 \times 3 \qquad\qquad = \quad 6$$
$$4! = 1 \times 2 \times 3 \times 4 \qquad = \quad 24$$
$$5! = 1 \times 2 \times 3 \times 4 \times 5 \qquad = 120, \text{ etc.}$$

The rate of growth in a factorial number series accelerates very rapidly.

This means that the reciprocal series of factorial numbers converges ever more rapidly:

$$1/1! = 1.0000$$
$$1/2! = 0.5000$$
$$1/3! = 0.1667$$
$$1/4! = 0.0417$$
$$1/5! = 0.0083$$
$$1/6! = 0.0014 \text{ etc.}$$

The reciprocal series can be summated to a required accuracy:

$$1 + \frac{1}{1!} + \frac{1}{2!} + \frac{1}{3!} + \frac{1}{4!} + \frac{1}{5!} + \frac{1}{6!} = 2.718 \text{ approx}$$

The symbol *e* is used to represent this number which has some remarkable properties. The most important of these is that, when it is used as a common ratio in a GP:

$$e^0 \; e^1 \; e^2 \; e^3 \; e^x,$$

where *x* is any number, the rate of growth is also e^x.

It is this property that enabled Lord Napier to build a set of *natural logarithm* tables, with the base of 2.718, by adding tiny elements to provide the required rate of change at any point. Common logarithms, with their useful base of ten, were developed later.

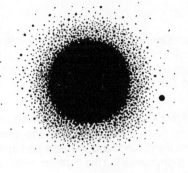

Quasars are thought to be the most distant objects observed by man. Each emits the energy of a hundred large galaxies at distances exceeding two billion light years, as it races from us at incredible speed.

Mapping the macrocosm

The study of progressions and growth is basic to scientific exploration of our universe, from the tiny particles of nuclear physics to the awesome spectacle of modern astronomy. Quite recently computation of the distribution of matter in the galaxy M87, in the constellation of Virgo, has revealed the probability of a black hole at its centre. It has 5000 million times the mass of the sun.

Black holes are believed to be the remnants of huge stars which collapsed when their nuclear fuel ran out. The compacted mass concentrates the gravitational field so that nothing, not even light, can escape. It then proceeds to grow as more and more material is sucked in. By definition, a black hole cannot be observed directly but its presence can be detected by the influence of its outer gravitational field upon the behaviour of observable radiating bodies.

In recent years science has discovered a fantastic universe. Our galaxy is in the form of a spiral and has one hundred billion stars. To cross it on a photon of light would take 100 000 years; yet it is only of average size as galaxies go. Each light year represents the distance travelled by light in one year at a velocity in a vacuum of 186 282 miles per second. This means that our tiny speck of a *catherine wheel*, one of a minor cluster of galaxies isolated in space, has a diameter of 600 000 000 000 000 000 miles.

Since 1920, when Edwin Hubble first described the nature of galaxies, telescopes have found over one hundred million. One million have been counted in the bowl of the Great Dipper alone. As they probe ever deeper into space, radio light and x-ray scanners peer back into the past to reveal possibilities of awesome beauty.

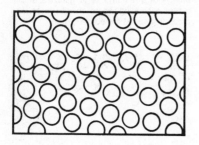

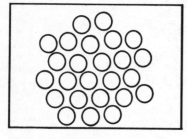

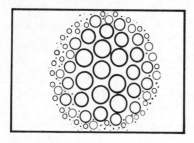

In 1905 Einstein was 26 years of age and working in the patent office in Berne when his first theory of relativity resolved an age-old dispute concerning the dimensions of our physical universe. He made a simple geometric explanation possible.

By the late seventeenth century, Leibnitz in Germany and Newton in England had inherited the scientific discoveries of Descartes and Galileo. Rembrandt and Vermeer had completed their masterpieces in the Netherlands but the rhythmic order of J. S. Bach and Canaletto had yet to come.

Quite independently, within a few years, Leibnitz and Newton each invented the infinitesimal calculus. Their mathematics were similar yet their philosophic conclusions were opposed. They remained so for over two hundred years – until Einstein.

Both had accepted that space is Euclidean, with three straight dimensions at right angles to each other and of infinite length. But they differed upon the location of *matter* within that space.

Newton argued that the distribution of what we would now call the galactic system was finite and inhomogenous. Matter was clustered into only part of infinite space and thus, like any finite body, it had a centre and a boundary. Newton also believed that the universe requires a controlling power, God, to order it. Only He can be infinite, therefore the universe must be something less than infinite . . . finite.

Leibnitz, however, rejected the finite universe precisely because it has a centre and a boundary. Such a universe, he argued, must have an inside and an outside. What happens outside? But even more unacceptable was an inhomogeneity in which not all galaxies have neighbours on all sides. Some unsatisfactory mathematics occur at the edges of such a universe.

In 1854 a German mathematician, Bernhard Riemann gave his now famous lecture suggesting that geometry and physics are inseparable: *that the presence of matter determines the structure of space*. The physicist has long acknowledged the importance of this statement but its full implications for the aesthete remain unresolved and largely motivate books such as this.

Graphic interpretations of three universes:
The homogeneous, continuous universe of Leibnitz;
The finite inhomogeneous universe of Newton;
Einstein's variable, relative space.

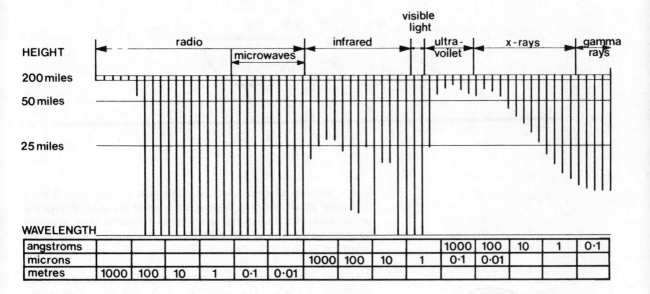

HEIGHT — radio — microwaves — infrared — visible light — ultra-voilet — x-rays — gamma rays

angstroms									1000	100	10	1	0·1
microns						1000	100	10	1	0·1	0·01		
metres	1000	100	10	1	0·1	0·01							

Riemann's lecture revealed that the theories of both Leibnitz and Newton had been based on a false assumption that space existed as an infinite Euclidean matrix, as a geometric abstraction independent of matter.

Half a century later Einstein showed how to interpret gravitation, a property of matter, as being a curvature of space. The presence of a lump of matter has the effect of compressing space and influences the paths of moving bodies. A simplistic view of Einstein's work can be derived by consideration of the problem in one dimension only.

The Earth's atmosphere shields us from most interstellar radiation. Significant electromagnetic penetration to the Earth's surface occurs in the radio and light bands.
10^{10} Angstroms = 1 metre.
10^{10} is mathematical shorthand for the number one followed by ten noughts.

In the model (*below*) Einstein suggested that the long stick joining two of the galaxies represents a similar distance to the nine short sticks. This requires a spacial plasticity that is non-Euclidean.

99

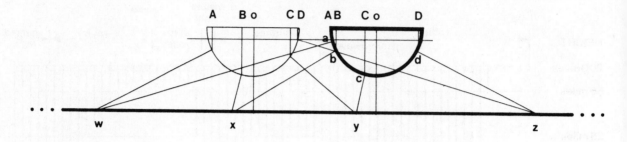

In the diagram Leibnitz's infinite dimension is represented by a horizontal band extending beyond the limits of the page. Above it a semicircle is provided so that all points on the infinite dimension can be mapped on to the circumference of the semicircle, by radial projection to centre O.

Points on the semicircle can then be projected vertically on to its horizontal diameter. The points W, X, Y and Z on the infinite dimension are projected to a, b, c and d on the semicircle and then to A, B, C and D on the finite diameter which can thus map infinity within its limits. This introduces a convergence of scale with distance. Scalar relationships are affected by the position of the semicircle. The observed relationships differ when datum O is above W or X, Y or Z. Such inflexion of space occurs both locally and in the macrocosm.

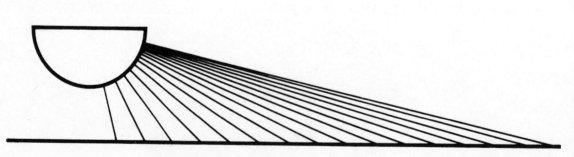

100

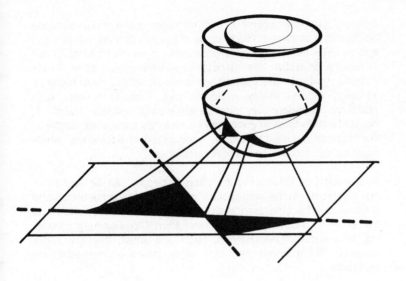

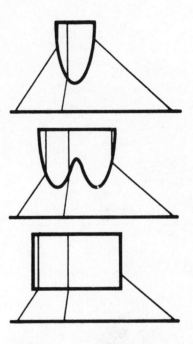

Linear mappings through forms other than a semi-circle can cause fluctuating rates of change of scale. The saddle can be used to amplify the scale in the middle distance. The rectangle provided the finite geometry of the Renaissance, true to the limits of its baseline.

In our everyday world Euclidean geometry and Newtonian mechanics offer very practical and invariant approximations. Our physical dimensions are dominated by the overwhelming mass of our galaxy, our sun, this Earth. However, recent experience has revealed the importance of a flexible space in astronomy and nuclear physics. It is likely to be of comparable significance in the sensitive world of the mind.

The semicircle is a two dimensional figure. Therefore the expression of an infinite dimension within a finite length was accomplished by projecting the mapping through a second dimension. If a similar solution is applied to an infinite plane, then it can be mapped through the surface of a hemisphere on to a disc. Mathematically, three dimensions are needed to map an infinite two dimensional plane.

Similarly, the application of a *fourth mathematical dimension* permits a mapping of an infinite volume. In each case an additional dimension is needed to perform the mapping.

The choice of a semicircle as a vehicle for the primary mapping was instinctive. Could it be to do with symmetry? A mapping could be obtained through any two dimensional closed form.

A simple, practical application of *convergent space* is now common practice on motorways. The marking of transverse lines, visually and also as slight humps, in convergent series gives the motorist a false sense of acceleration. His instinct is to slow his vehicle down. This is a useful device on the approaches to junctions and other hazards; however, with familiarity, motorists may learn to counter such measures. Therefore they must be applied with subtlety. The planting of roadside trees in convergent series has attractions. Traffic in the opposite direction would be encouraged to accelerate, which might be desirable in certain circumstances?

This method of influencing the pace of people can be applied in many contexts. In the approaches to a market place the shops and stalls should become progressively narrower and packed towards the centre, thus slowing the customers down. Close packing, clustering, is a natural phenomenon, large and small, throughout our universe. But it brings into play other forces of implosion and explosion.

Of such is *beauty*!

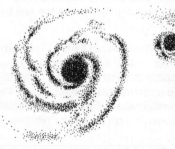

Right: One of the two arms of the whirlpool galaxy reaches out to a nearby, smaller galaxy.

102

6 Dynamic and harmonic series

As in music . . . the man who understands every note will the more readily comprehend the whole.

Charles Darwin

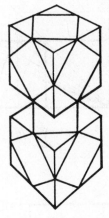

Dynamic rectangles

It is possible to conceive a myriad variations upon a theme of AP's and GP's. They can be combined to sit one atop the other; they can be set in opposition so that one diverges as the other converges; they can alternate and they can oscillate. A common difference or ratio can be programmed so that it is no longer common, or constant, but becomes an AP or GP in its own right. But when such programmes become so complex that their pattern and scale is beyond the normal limits of our sensory response systems, then we need some form of recoding or deciphering technique. We have to think about them and subject them to the processes of reason. They have thus become the familiar subject matter for 'intelligence tests'.

However certain forms of change to which we are acutely sensitive are not simple AP's and GP's, yet are related to them. Most of these were devised or discovered (according to the point of view) by geometricians. Their classical drawing instrument, the compass, was used to rotate a straight line, a radius, from one dimension to another.

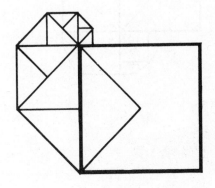

The act of drawing an arc is a dynamic act. It records a transfer of energy from one dimension to another and can be used to interrelate the properties of lines, areas and volumes, usually via their energetic diagonals.

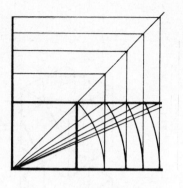

$1 \quad \sqrt{2} \quad \sqrt{3} \sqrt{4} \sqrt{5}$

A square of side length 1 has a diagonal length = $\sqrt{2}$. Two parallel sides of the square are extended indefinitely. The diagram shows the diagonal rotated to form a $\sqrt{2}$:1 rectangle within the parallels. The diagonal of this rectangle is $\sqrt{3}$. Rotation of successive diagonals forms a dynamic series of rectangles from a shared datum. Their dimensions are in the *dynamic series* 1: $1\sqrt{2} \ \sqrt{3} \ \sqrt{4} \ \sqrt{5} \ \sqrt{6} \ \sqrt{7} \ldots$

The rate of increase of sidelength gets ever smaller; even so, it is an infinite series.

This dynamic series, projected in two dimensions, offers a series of squares with areas of 1 2 3 4 5 6 7 . . . square units.

Alternating positive and negative rotation, to the *x* and *y* axes, produces an intermittent series of dynamic rectangles. Rearrangement brings the centre of energy to the centre of the pattern.

Rotating each diagonal into the next quadrant produces a spiralling series of dynamic rectangles.

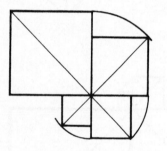

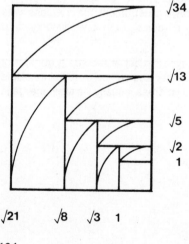

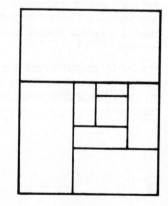

$\sqrt{34}$

$\sqrt{13}$

$\sqrt{5}$

$\sqrt{2}$
1

$\sqrt{21} \qquad \sqrt{8} \quad \sqrt{3} \quad 1$

104

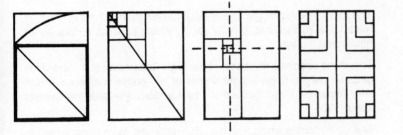

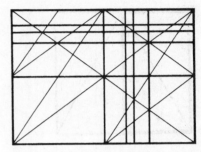

Some dynamic rectangles have special properties.

The *root two rectangle* doubles in area, by symmetry, along fold lines, as in standard 'A' paper sizes. It is the only rectangle possessing this property. Aesthetically, it offers a generous feeling of area, with a strong axis. Its internal geometry has been favoured by architects and landscape painters. It is one of six bisecting, diagonal planes of a cube. It *whirls* with its own complement to provide a centre of energy at one third of the sidelengths.

Note: similar rectangles, sharing a corner, also share a diagonal.

Below: Dynamic series can be generated between lines that are not straight and develop unique characteristics.

Below left: $a^2 = b^2 + c^2$ – Pythagoras' Theorem for a right angled triangle – reveals that the linear structure of a rectangular prism is in dynamic series.

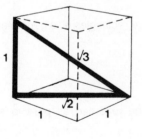

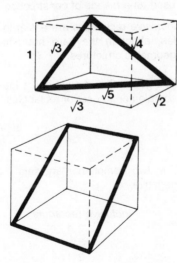

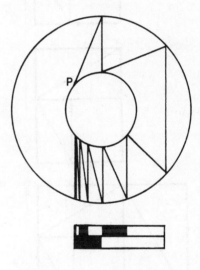

105

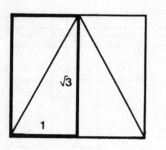

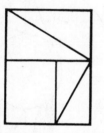

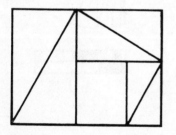

The *root three rectangle* has a diagonal length of 2 (units). Two $\sqrt{3}$ rectangles, juxtaposed, form a $\sqrt{3}:2$ rectangle, which embraces an equilateral triangle.

This is the spacious rectangle of the High Renaissance. It subdivides geometrically to provide right angles at key points in its area. It was later introduced into *modern art* by Le Corbusier and the Cubists about 1906.

The $\sqrt{3}$ rectangle *whirls* with the $\sqrt{3}:2$ rectangle as its complement to provide a centre of energy at one quarter of the sidelengths.

Whirling rectangles
A whirling rectangle grows by rotating through one right angle per generation. The rectangle grows such that the longer side becomes the shorter side of the next generation.

From an initial sidelength ratio of $1:b$, succeeding sidelengths will be $b^2\ b^3\ b^4\ b^5\ldots$

The new generation can include the existing rectangles or exclude them.

The diagonals of whirling rectangles turn at right angles, and can be used as a means of construction.

Inclusive rectangles are easier to construct than *exclusive* rectangles, although they are but different ways of looking at similar geometric structures.

The generation of a set of $b:1$ inclusive rectangles also generates a complementary set of rectangles.

$$\frac{b^2 - 1}{b}$$

The two complementary sets may be regarded as positive and negative.

inclusive rectangle	complementary
$\sqrt{2}:1$	$1:\sqrt{2}$
3:2	5:6
2:1	3:2
4:3	7:12
$\varphi:1$	1:1

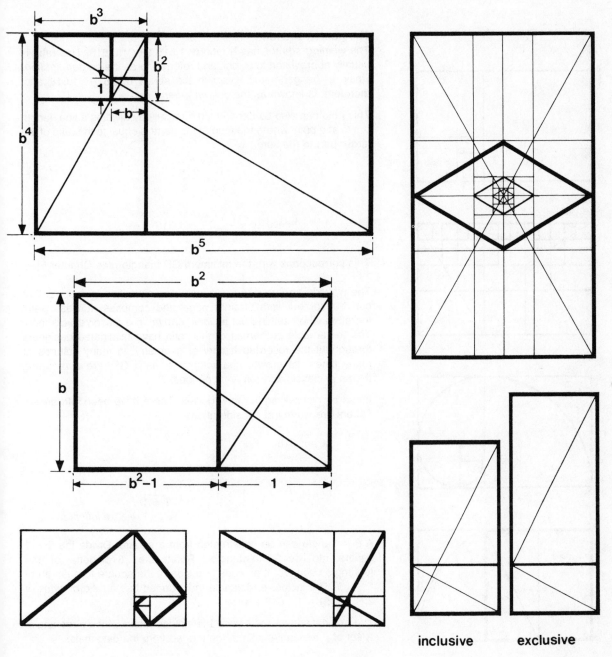

inclusive   exclusive

107

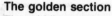

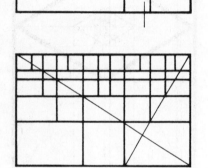

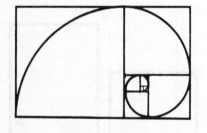

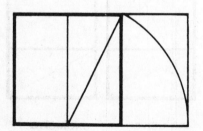

The golden section

The *whirling square* has a ratio of 1.618:1 or 1:0.618. This ratio is usually abbreviated to φ, phi, and referred to as the *golden section*. Unity is the geometric mean in the series 0.618, 1, 1.618 and, therefore, is known as the *golden mean*.

This ratio can also be derived algebraically by dividing a line, length $b + 1$, at a point where the ratio of the parts is equal to the ratio of the larger part to the sum.

$$\frac{b}{1} = \frac{b + 1}{b}$$

$$\text{hence } b = \frac{1 + \sqrt{5}}{2} = 1.618 = \varphi$$

This corresponds with the minimum GP triangle (see Chapter 5).

The *whirling square* offers a simple approximation to a spiral that can be set out with straight edge and compass. It was useful therefore when settting out an *ionic capital* in a mason's workshop. The remarkable properties of this ratio have fascinated designers throughout the recorded history of geometry, in many cultures at many times. Its growth characteristics, as a GP, are a recurring theme in classic and romantic periods.

It can be discovered in many guises. Three have been introduced. Others are worthy of consideration:

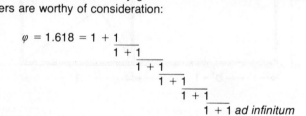

A φ rectangle can be constructed from a square. Divide the 2×2 square into two 2:1 rectangles. Rotate the $\sqrt{5}$ diagonal of one rectangle such that it extends one side of the square to a length of $1 + \sqrt{5}$. The inclusive rectangle thus formed has a ratio of sides of $2:(1 + \sqrt{5}) = 1:1.618$ approx.

The original square rests upon the 'golden mean' of the φ rectangle. A set of φ rectangles can be generated from the diagonals.

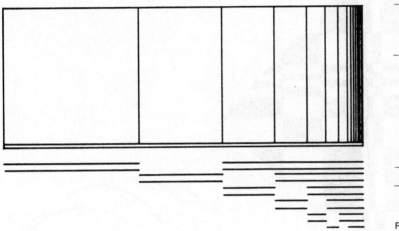

Ratios between sides of Rectangles	Percentages of preferences	
	Men	Women
1/1	2.74	3.36
6/5	0.22	0.27
5/4	3.07	0.00
4/3	1.97	3.36
29/20	5.85	11.35
3/2	22.33	17.22
34/21	34.50	35.83
23/13	21.64	16.99
2/1	6.25	9.94
5/2	1.43	1.68
Totals	100.00	100.00

Fechner's rectangles.

The φ rectangle was favoured by a variety of people when Fechner asked them to select the most pleasing *blank* rectangle from a selection put before them. It has been used as a canvas by many painters. Its ratio is highly dynamic with a dominant dimension that tends to restrict the internal space unless its structural squares are exploited. It is a constructivist tool, well suited to a Turner or a Barnett Newman, but likely to overpower an impressionist content.

The focus of a φ rectangle is at 0.724 approximately of the length.

The φ ratio can be derived from a series of integers named after Fibonacci (Leonardo of Pisa), an Italian mathematician of the thirteenth century.

Each successive term of the series is obtained by adding the preceding two: 0 1 1 2 3 5 8 13 21 34 55 89 144 233 . . .

The ratio of adjacent terms evolves from:

$$\frac{1}{1} \ \frac{2}{1} \ \frac{3}{2} \ \frac{5}{3} \ \frac{8}{5} \ \frac{13}{8} \ \frac{21}{13} \ \frac{34}{21} \ \ldots \ldots \text{to } \varphi$$

These ratios are members of a *family* and can be used as a means of progressive refinement, from 1:1, 1:2, 2:3 to φ.

When $r = 0.618$, S to infinity = 2.618. At any stage in the series it displays symmetry. The sum outstanding equals the preceding term.

109

The distribution of seeds on the head of a sunflower, some 15 cm in diameter, commonly has 34 logarithmic spirals unwinding in one direction and 55 in the other. Smaller heads can have ratios of 21:34 or 13:21.

A similar pattern can be observed in the heads of daisies and other flowers.

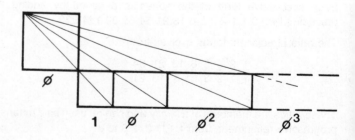

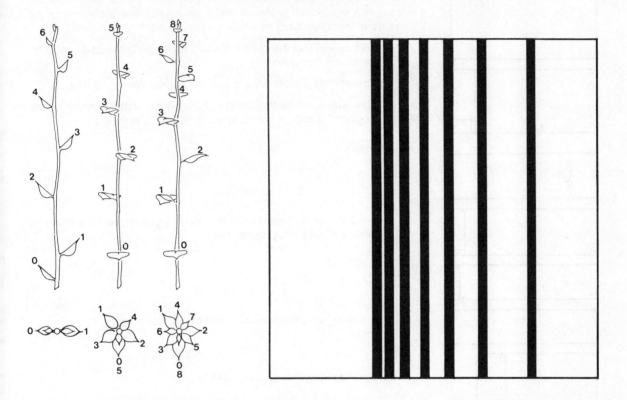

It cannot be mere coincidence that this family of ratios are to be observed in both nature and fine art.

Many books have paid credit to its usage in painting and architecture.

A common example in nature is the distribution of buds, branches or leaves upon the stalk of a plant. Their disposition is usually helical. Eugene P. Northrop refers to them as *m/n spirals*, where *m* is the number of revs and *n* is the number of branches. The illustrations show plan and elevation of typical cases. The φ ratio can also be evidenced in the intervals between branches.

Once one is conscious of the Fibonacci series, the frequency of their occurrence in nature becomes impressive.

The φ series of convergent intervals suggests depth. The constant width of the black bands is emphatically on the picture plane, setting up a tension between events and intervals.

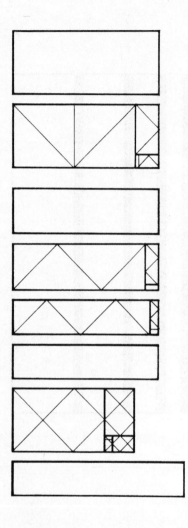

In the classic tradition another whirling rectangle has been regarded as a companion to the $\sqrt{2}$ and φ rectangles. The theta θ rectangle can be constructed by whirling a double square, exclusively.

This means that the complementary rectangle is the double square, hence, by formula $b = 1 + \sqrt{2}$.

The *whirling double square* has the overall ratio, $\theta = 2.414$

This was used by the great architect, Inigo Jones, known as the English Palladio, in his Banqueting Hall at Whitehall, London.

$$\theta = 2 + \cfrac{1}{2 + \cfrac{1}{2 + \cfrac{1}{2 + 1 \text{ ad infinitum}}}}$$

It is possible to generate *whirling treble squares*, with the inclusive ratio of 3.3028:1 approximately.

$$3.303 = 3 + \cfrac{1}{3 + \cfrac{1}{3 + 1 \text{ ad infinitum}}}$$

A *whirling quadruple square* has the inclusive ratio:

$$4.236 = 2 + \sqrt{5} = 1 + 2\varphi$$

This has intriguing design possibilities!

Other forms of Fibonacci series can be devised by adding, say, the preceding *three* terms in an integer series:

0 1 1 2 4 7 13 24 44 81 149 274 504 . . . ratio = 1.839:1

Adding the preceding *four* terms, the ratio becomes 1.928:1

In the limit, when each successive term equals the sum of *all* preceding terms, the population doubles at each generation and the common ratio is 2.

0 1 1 2 4 8 16 32 64 128 256 512 . . .

Again, the ratio 2:1 suggests a limit on normal growth rate. Beyond 2:1 the new generation overwhelms all that has gone before!

The monumental 2.414:1 scale of the θ rectangle can be humanised by introduction of its partner, the *inclusive* whirling double square (which is 3:2 exclusive); see numbers 1, 2 and 7 above.

The American Indian favoured the 5:1 rectangle. Eskimos are said to like the $\sqrt{10}$ rectangle.

The φ^2 series offers areas that have a common ratio based upon alternate terms of the Fibonacci series:

$$0\ 1\ 3\ 8\ 21\ 55\ 144\ \ldots$$
$$Or\ 1\ 2\ 5\ 13\ 34\ 89\ \ldots$$
$$\varphi^2 = 2.618 = 1 + \varphi$$

The φ^3 series offers *volumes* that have a common ratio based upon:

$$0\ 2\ \ 8\ 34\ 144\ \ldots$$
$$1\ 3\ 13\ 55\ 233\ \ldots$$
$$1\ 5\ 21\ 89\ 377\ \ldots$$

$$\varphi^3 = 4.236 = 1 + 2\varphi$$
$$\text{hence } \varphi^4 = 2 + 3\varphi$$
$$\varphi^5 = 3 + 5\varphi$$
$$\varphi^6 = 5 + 8\varphi$$

. . . the series is maintained in this dimension also.

Pell's series

Pell's series of numbers gives $r = 2.414$ by doubling the last number and adding its predecessor: 0 1 2 5 12 29 70 169 408. Another variation is to add the last two numbers and then double: 0 1 2 6 16 44 120 328 896 . . . $r = 2.732 = 1 + \sqrt{3}$.

Fechner's rectangles

Fechner (1801–1887), in his famous tests, found that people have preference for certain rectangles. The preferences were based upon judgements of single, blank rectangles, taken in isolation. They were not selected in terms of their capacity to contain or present any content, such as a drawing, but were rated solely for their entertainment value as pure shapes. In this context, it is not surprising that the common square got a low vote. The overwhelming preference for ratios between 3:2 and 7:4, in the region of the φ rectangle, is noteworthy. He also found that a majority of museum paintings were framed at 3:4 landscape format and 5:4 vertical.

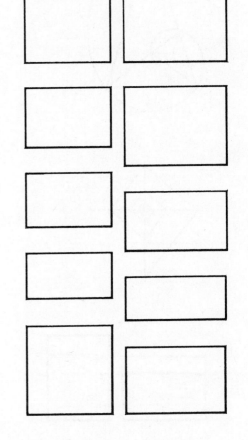

Check your preferences against Fechner's findings, given on page 109.

5:4	6:5
3:2	4:3
34:21	23:13
2:1	5:2
1:1	8:5

The square has become fashionable in recent years. Perhaps geometrical preferences are subject to cultural and social influences.

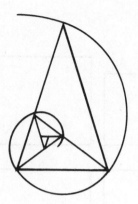

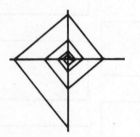

Whirling triangles

Whirling triangles help our understanding of spirals.

Considering *similar* triangles, programmed so that the longest side of one triangle becomes the shortest side of the next, they subtend similar angles at the *origin*, the centre of rotation.

The whirling equilateral triangle is the simplest, completing a regular hexagon in one revolution.

In any two similar triangles, the ratio of areas equals the square of the ratios of corresponding sides. Therefore, when whirling a 3, 4, 5 triangle, the corresponding sides of adjacent triangles are in ratio of 5:3. Their areas are in ratio of 25:9.

Whirling a right angled triangle so that the medium side of one becomes the shortest side of the next produces a spiral sitting neatly on the x and y axes.

114

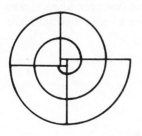 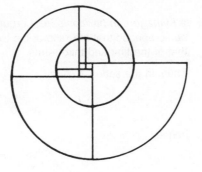

Spirals

It is possible to construct an approximation to a spiral using straight edge and compass. Whereas to construct a circle the compass has a fixed centre and radius, to form a spiral the centre and radius are programmed to vary in order.

For the radius to increase by r per rev, four centres are set in a square $r/4$ apart. From them the four quadrants can be described. Further revolutions can be drawn from these same four centres.

For the radius to double every rev, an enlarged control square will be needed for the second and subsequent revs.

If the radius is required to treble per rev, then the control square must be $r/2$.

For greater accuracy, eight centres can be used, in the form of a regular octagon.

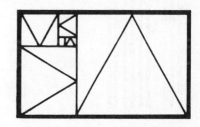

For a spiral of even greater accuracy a master circle would be ideal. Perhaps with a string wound about it?

For a GP spiral, the windlass would need to be conical!

The ascending chord 3, 4, 6 has a complementary descending chord 6, 5, 3 when the intervals are reversed.

Pythagorean harmonic ratios

Pythagoras was the most influential of early Greek mathematicians. He settled at Croton, a Greek city in Southern Italy, and founded a school that influenced both arts and sciences. The Greek musical scale, for example, used a linear harmonic system that came to be accepted in sculpture and architecture.

A *Pythagorean harmonic triad* requires that any three terms should be so spaced that the ratio of the two intervals should be similar to that of the first and third terms.

Thus, in the series, a, b, c

$$\frac{c}{a} = \frac{c - b}{b - a}$$

hence,

$$b = \frac{2ac}{a + c} \qquad c = \frac{ab}{2a - b}$$

For example, if $a = 3$ and $c = 6$

$$b = \frac{2 \times 3 \times 6}{3 + 6} = \frac{36}{9} = 4$$

The harmonic triad is: 3, 4, 6.

If $a = 4$ and $b = 6$, c is found to be 12. A series of harmonic triads emerges in this case: 3, 4, 6, 12, infinity.

Whenever a second term doubles the first, the third term becomes *infinity*; beyond human measure. Again it is found that the ratio 2:1 is particularly significant to mankind. Beyond it the Pythagorean harmonic joins the Gods.

Pythagorean harmonic triads are laborious to calculate and few develop into an integer series. Those commencing at small numbers are:

	1 2 inf	
2 3 6 inf	2 4 inf	
3 4 6 12 inf	3 6 inf	3 5 15
4 6 12 inf	4 8 inf	4 7 28
5 8 20	5 10 inf	5 9 45

and the longest available is: 12 15 20 30 60 infinity.

116

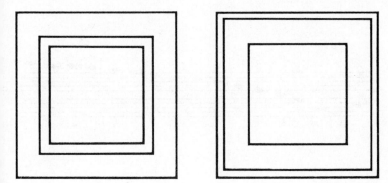

The Pythagoreans studied the mathematics of stringed instruments. For a given material, at constant temperature, tension, air pressure and humidity, a plucked string was found to vibrate such that:

$$\text{frequency} \times \text{wavelength} = f \times \lambda = \text{a constant.}$$

Nowadays wavelength is measured in metres and frequency in cycles per second, cps, or *Hertz*, Hz.

The Pythagoreans could not count the frequency, for their technology was not sufficiently advanced. However they could hear and recognise approximations to consonance that are pleasant sounding. They devised five and seven note scales based upon simple subdivisions of a string.

The Pythagoreans believed that numbers have a separate existence outside of our minds. Numbers are the elements of all things and the whole of heaven is a mathematical and musical scale.

They found that halving the length of a string causes it to double its frequency of vibration and sound an octave higher. This provides a perfect second harmonic or first overtone to the fundamental note of the full length string. This was used as datum so that a string of length $a + b$ has a half length of

$$\frac{a + b}{2}$$

The Pythagorean musical proportion was therefore:

$$\frac{a + b}{2} : b$$

HM GM AM

Harmonic squares by areas 2, 3, 6 and 6, 5, 2 offer reciprocal movement in and out.

The HM also forms a triad with the AM and GM of any two magnitudes—eg, given 3 and 27, the AM is 15, the GM is 9 and the HM is 5.4, forming a suitable series 3, 5.4, 9, 15, 27.

117

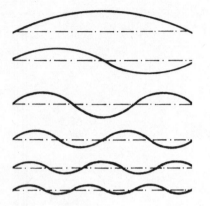

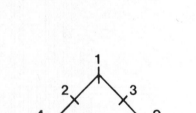

The Platonic Lambda guided simple subdivision of a string:
- 1:2 is an octave
- 2:3 is a fifth
- 3:4 is a fourth
- 8:9 is a tone

Some European musical scales

The European *diatonic* (eight note) and *chromatic* (12 note) scales have evolved via medieval forms, via Newton, Bach, Helmholtz and many others, from Pythagorean musical proportion.

When two strings are tuned to vibrate at the same frequency the plucking of one will cause the other to vibrate. This is *resonance*. The vibration is transferred from one to the other through the air.

The note of a plucked string is known as the *fundamental* note. But the quality, the timbre, of the note is described by the presence of overtones. The first three or four can be detected by a trained ear; they are the octave, the fifth, the next octave and the following third, ranging vertically in frequency above the fundamental note. The relative amplitude of overtones provides the character of a musical instrument and is fine evidence of the presence of harmony in nature.

The simultaneous plucking of strings tuned to a fundamental and its second harmonic, or octave, produces a pleasant and concordant sound. This is much enriched by adjusting the length of one string to two-thirds the length of the fundamental. This is known as a *major* fifth.

The Greeks discovered that pleasing harmonics could be produced by the Law of Small Whole Numbers. Ratios of string lengths of 1:2 and 2:3 are generally accepted and most people find 3:4 and 4:5 to be pleasant harmonies. But as the numbers increase dissonance becomes apparent.

It has not yet been possible to devise a precise series of notes within an octave such that each has another note providing its natural harmonic, a major fifth.

118

The familiar scales are approximations. The early European 12 semitone scale evolved to provide a series of good fifths with one *howler*, or *Wolf Interval* on a little used note. Transposition, changing the key of a piece of music by moving all notes up or down by a fixed amount, was not possible other than by retuning the instrument.

Johann Sebastian Bach wrote his *Well Tempered Clavier* to recommend an alternative method of tuning. All the C's were related as octaves, as before, but instead of having most of the fifths in perfect harmony with one Wolf Interval, all were tuned slightly flat so that the howl is spread in the ratio of 1.49831 instead of 1.5 for each major fifth.

Today we can consider the series of 12 semitones to be logarithmic, with $r = 1.0595$ approximately (the fifth becomes 1.4983) which again spreads the howl. This common ratio is found by taking $a = 1$ and $ar^{12} = 2$, giving a GP with 12 intervals between one and two.

The pitch to which instruments are tuned can vary. Standard orchestra pitch gives A = 440 Hz. Popular pitch, when C = 256 Hz, gives diatonic A = 427 Hz and logarithmic A = 430 Hz.

The ear can accommodate fine differences in frequency as Bach proved. Slight but alternating differences in frequency enrich the note, as in the vibrato of a good singer.

A *pentatonic musical scale* can be produced quite easily upon a piano by playing the five black keys only, commencing with F sharp. Running up the scale, play the three-group first. This is one of the oldest known scales, going back at least 4000 years. In *tonic sol-fa* this scale uses the notes: *doh*, *ray*, *me*, *soh*, *la*, *Doh*, thus providing the major harmonics of the tonic note, *doh*.

The pentatonic and later the diatonic scales were established by subdividing a vibrating string in the ratios:

doh	ray	me	fah	soh	la	te	Doh
1/	8/9	4/5	3/4	2/3	3/5	8/15	1/2

1:2 is an octave   doh to Doh
2:3 is a fifth   doh to soh
3:4 is a fourth   doh to fah
4:5 is a third   doh to me

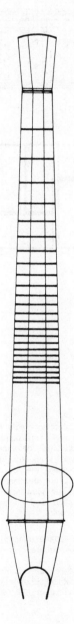

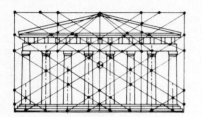

The *whole tone scale* is a scale consisting of whole tones only. This permits only six intervals within the octave, instead of the seven intervals of the conventional diatonic scale. Fundamentally there are only two whole tone scales. One commences at C and the other at C sharp. Whatever note is taken as starting point, any whole tone scale will correspond with one or other of these. The lack of a leading note (such as *te* in tonic sol-fa) and of semitones gives this scale a wandering, ephemeral quality that was well suited to Impressionism.

Resonance

Resonance can occur in any medium capable of vibration. As previously mentioned, if two strings are tuned to the same pitch, the vibration of one will radiate through the adjoining air molecules at the velocity of sound (about 720 mph at sea level) to impinge upon the second string. This will vibrate in unison with the surrounding air at its resonant frequency. The transmitted waveforms are essentially sinusoidal; the resultant form becoming an addition of the available harmonics.

Resonance can also be induced by using a natural harmonic, with a proportionate reduction in amplitude. For example, if one of the tuned strings is reduced to two-thirds of its length and then plucked, it will sound the major fifth *soh*, and cause the other string to vibrate at *doh*, with harmonics. But not as loudly as when the first string was plucked at full length at *doh*.

Top: Suggested schemata for the Parthenon, using φ. Note the number of columns and, thus, intervals. The outermost intervals were reduced while the columns were slightly thickened; thereby increasing the real and apparent sturdiness of the structure, making due allowance for variation of light penetration, and enhancing the welcome in the centre.

Above: The Japanese *tatami* mat is based upon a double square.

Right: A subtle dynamic symmetry is evident in this geometrical scheme for the Dome of the Rock, Jerusalem (688–692 AD).

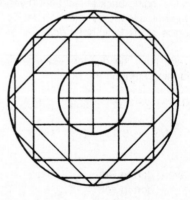

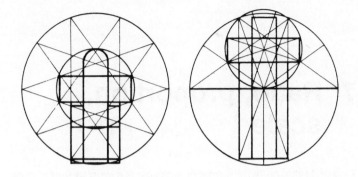

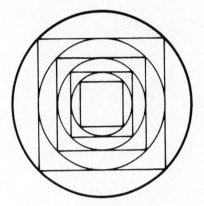

A famous example of resonance is Caruso's reputed feat of shattering a wineglass by singing a note at its resonant frequency.

Resonance also occurs in our nervous system. Colours appear to resonate. Painters like to use *echoes* and know that a large area of, say, greyed red can be caused to resonate by the addition of a touch of high chroma red, at the correct frequency.

Similarly shapes and textures, sounds, words and phrases resonate in the mind. The process of *trigger and response* that forms and informs our awareness is based on resonance. Words like compassion and empathy record the human capacity for resonance . . . *sharing the same wavelength*.

It is possible to conceive a myriad variations on a theme of AP's and GP's. They can be combined and permuted so that their common difference or ratio is no longer constant but is itself in AP or GP. Such disguises contained the magic of numbers in the middle ages and, even today, have their fascination: eg, in the series 4, 2, 1, 2, 7, what is the next term?

Top left and centre: Two Gothic standard church plans (Moessel).

Top right: The $\sqrt{2}$ series can be derived by 'squaring the circle'.

This, the $\sqrt{3}$, φ, θ series and their derivatives have fascinated artists, architects and scholars alike through the ages.

7 Ratio, proportion, scale

If we state that nothing is great or small by its own standard of great or small, then there is nothing in all creation which is not great, nothing which is not small.

Works, Chuang Tzu (Fourth/third century BC)
Translated by Lin Yu-tang

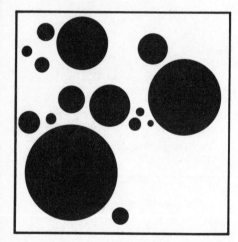

Solution to problem on page 121:

$4 \times 2 - 6 = 2$
$2 \times 2 - 3 = 1$
$1 \times 2 - 0 = 2$
$2 \times 2 + 3 = 7$
$7 \times 2 + 6 = 20$

Defining a scale

Ratio, the comparative magnitude of two events, is a basic measure of our lives.

Proportion is the repetition of a ratio: a is to b as c is to d. Thus we can judge similarities.

A scale is a series of magnitudes having a programmed rate of change, a common difference, a common ratio, a dynamic ratio, or perhaps some exotic mixture.

The decimal system is a mixed scale.
The series: 0 1 2 3 4 5 6 7 8 9 10 is an AP, with $d = 1$.
Millions, thousands, hundreds, tens, ones, tenths, hundredths etc, are in GP, with $r = 10$. They are then added, column by column.

The number 3597.6 is interpreted as:

$$(3 \times 10^3) + (5 \times 10^2) + (9 \times 10) + (7 \times 1) + (6 \times 1/10)$$

Scales in everyday usage are usually AP supplemented by GP.

Rhythmic patterns can be generated by superimposing two or more . . . but not too many . . . scales. But they need to be wedded; either by *keying* to produce a *consonant beat frequency* or by a transition from one scale to another (see 'Overtones', Chapter 6). In music this transition is known as *modulation*.

In architecture, a building complex may comprise differing functional volumes, demanding varied spacial grids.

Such a complex may be brought into unity by identification and emphasis of common characteristics. These may be shapes that change scale and texture, or scales that change shape. Colour and other stimuli can be used in the same way.

Shared services, materials and spaces offer regions of modulation between specialised functional zones.

Any journey through the complex should be rhythmic, involving *introduction*, *realisation* and *confirmation*. Echoes amid variety give unity and zest.

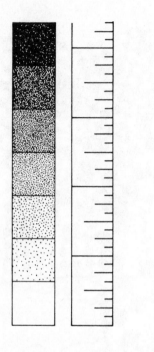

Intrinsic scale

Scales of qualities are comparable with scales of quantities.

A sensory scale may be conceived as a sensory structure. It provides an array of preferences; a series of *more than's* and *less than's*; a hierarchy that can release emotions without destroying the overall unity of the series.

A series of hues from red to yellow, of similar chromatic steps, is seen as a visual structure. The diatonic and chromatic scales in European music are aural structures.

All *things* that have *presence* have an *intrinsic scale*, a personal scale. All of the parts express their contribution to the whole. Both the sciences and the arts tend to confirm that intrinsic scale is an expression of functional efficiency.

Living creatures evidence countless variations upon a carbohydrate theme. Each mutation, by trial and error, uses procreation to find the highest survival rate in the prevailing circumstances. The creature becomes scaled into its environment and sacrifices some of its intrinsic scale.

It is well known that those species that are beautifully adapted to a particular environment are most likely to succumb to an adverse change of climate. They are unable to adjust to new conditions.

Adaptability requires an intrinsic scale that can be modulated or subordinated.

A work of art is a *thing* and has an intrinsic scale. Its internal space-time grid is essential to its existence within its own defined boundary. A small painting can suggest a vast landscape, using a scale that is unrelated to the room in which it hangs. A suitable frame can act as a modulator between the scale of the painting and that of the room. A mural commissioned by the architect would be designed into the architectural space, acting in most cases as a modulator between the human and architectural scales that it serves.

The scale of seven values forms a visual structure.

The inch scale is a familiar AP.

124

In a townscape, civic sculpture can modulate between the human scale and that of building and landscape. The dimensions of a plinth supporting the sculpture can be critical.

Objects tend to appear smaller and heavier as they are raised above eye level. This is often referred to as the *moon effect*. It is applicable in a variety of graphic forms and is much exploited by newspapers.

Monumental scale describes a set of dimensions that are more than human, in excess of 1:1, but not beyond human grasp. Most civic sculpture tends to be scaled up beyond life size, to compensate for its inanimacy.

If a real man is 6 foot of living, vibrant flesh and bone then, if it is to challenge him, his bronze replica must be over 7 feet tall. When it is raised on a plinth, then it needs to be larger still.

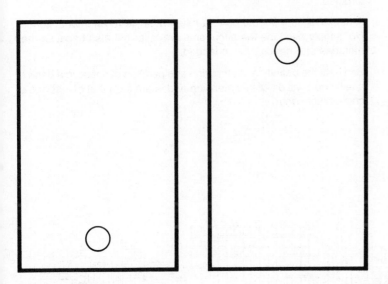

The *moon effect* is influenced by an adjacency factor, positive or negative, between the object and a frame of reference.

Architectural scale

Architectural scale should be intrinsic to the function and structure of a building. If it is to house ants, its scale and form, and therefore the materials suited to its construction, will differ from the dwellings of foxes, or hens, or humans.

The scale of a building should express the interaction between the activities that it embraces and the materials with which it is constructed.

A senior school should have a different scale to an infants school. Not simply because the occupants are taller but also because their attitudes and needs have changed.

Similarly the definition, distribution and partition of space in a bank or a law court will differ in dimension and intent from that of a sports or community centre.

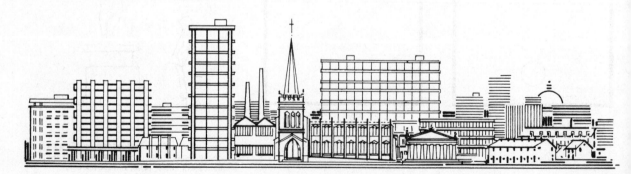

Human scale

Experience suggests that the scalar ratios that best serve our human needs lie between 1:1 and 2:1. The doubling process marks a limit beyond which ratios soar into monumental and overwhelming scales.

Human scale is, however, something more than a measure of physical dimensions. It embraces emotional and intellectual aptitudes and attitudes that influence and are influenced by our sensory responses. The act of sitting, for example, demands a peculiarly human posture that is revealed in both the emotional and physical characteristics of a chair. It is not enough to establish correct dimensions and ergonomics in terms of structural materials and production costs. The chair needs something more. A good chair will seem inviting:

'Please sit on me. I am strong and comfortable.'
'Sit upright and eat your dinner.'
'It is a privilege to sit on me.'
'It is sheer luxury to lounge with me.'
'I am just a perch for peeling the potatoes.'
'Let's relax together.'

And so it is with all those things that humans use: pots, pans, tools, toys and sailing boats.

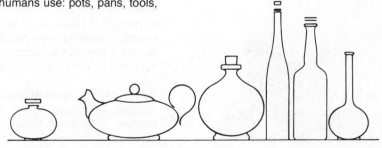

127

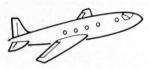

All tools, utensils and structures have an optimum size at which they serve mankind efficiently and it is with these that we express human scale.

The relative size of an object is important, therefore, in establishing both its human function and our attitude towards it.

The growth of a simple cube may serve as an example. When it is small and easy to cup in the hands, it is a tool, a utensil, a personal ornament, even a missile; but its scale is very much a human scale. Its geometry is subordinate to ours.

As its diagonal grows beyond 12 inches in length, the cube begins to command respect. Raised on to a suitably elegant stand it could be exhibited as an *objet d'art* . . . to be observed but not touched.

In this transition range its geometry is asserting an independence. It is interesting to contemplate the effect upon international soccer if we were either to halve or to double the diameter of a standard soccer ball.

As its diameter grows, the cube challenges man until it exceeds his height and begins to assert dominance, particularly if it is upended and balanced upon one corner.

At twice his height, the cube achieves dominance until at, say, a diameter of 15 feet it becomes a UPO, an unidentified poised object . . . perhaps from Jupiter?

Inscrutable, impassive, yet delicately poised, in the market square of a town such a UPO could frustrate and fascinate the populace. Its magic may be enhanced by strange hieroglyphs etched into its surfaces, and in a primitive society it could well be idolised, whilst wise men debate its significance.

At even greater size, the cube becomes immeasurable unless it can be brought to human scale by punctuation. The introduction of a few horizontal rows of openings, suggesting floors, with terracing and sloping ways, can suggest an architectural function and the cube becomes an extraordinary feat of human structural engineering.

Such human definition of detail is necessary in any large structure to establish its relative size. It is needed, for example, in a jetliner. Imagine a jumbojet without its rows of portholes and painted insignia.

We have seen large warplanes that lack these features and give virtually no clue to their dimensions except at the cockpit; and they are ominous, frightening beasts!

In our towns it is the street furniture, the steps, railings, doorways and people that set the human scale. Modulation through an intermediate stage is needed if they are to interrelate with multistorey buildings. The monumental scale of civic sculpture, its modern allies, streetlamps and, of course, trees and shrubs, can be *modulators*.

An architect introduces transition elements into his building. His *detailing* describes a physical and sensory scale of values.

Similar scaler principles apply at the factory bench, in the control cabin with its dozens of dials and switches, in a report to a board of directors or in a Van Gogh painting.

Modulation from one scale to another is achieved by the introduction of transition scales and although these are most easily illustrated in numerical form, they are valid in most applications of human relationships. On the industrial scene, transition scales between management and staff are provided by grades of middle management, personnel officers, social and works committees, suggestion schemes, and news sheets.

Plenty of dials demonstrate a need for grouping, hierarchy, scale.

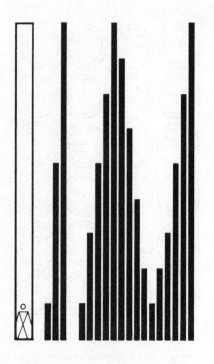

Modulation

An external view of a tower block from ground floor entrance level can be used to illustrate a linear form of modulation. For the sake of example, the tower is assumed to be nine units in height, where one unit is of average human height. The problem is to bring them into a comprehensive scalar relationship, using integer relationships only.

Using an AP, the difference can be halved, forming the triad 1, 5, 9. But this does not offer a rhythmic series, and the intervals of four units overpower the puny human at ground level. Of course, one might wish to do just that. If so, why halve it? Better to retain the stark impact of 9:1, which is *plenty*:1.

At the other extreme, a full integer series could be offered: 1 2 3 4 5 6 7 8 9! This too is into the world of plenty.

The AP 1 3 5 7 9 is rhythmic, but the initial ratio of 1:3 is very powerful. It might be appropriate to a status building? However a finer scale will be needed to detail between 1 and 3. Limited to an integer series, this can be achieved by a subordinate statement at 2: hence 1 2 3 5 7 9.

1 2 4 6 8 9 offers a false symmetry – false because an event on the ninth floor is smaller and heavier than a similar event at ground level. The *moon effect* prevents vertical symmetry above a ground level. Other possibilities are:

1 2 3 6 9
1 2 3 4 5 6 7 8 9

There is no right or wrong. Each sequence has a character. In practice, functional requirements will limit the available options. In each case the initial step of 1 to 2 is at the limit of human ratio and may seem stark, and even harsh, unless qualified by finer detailing.

It may be desired, for dramatic reasons, that the unit figure be brutally confronted by the towering 9. But if the full significance of *nineness* is to be experienced, an ultimate compatability must be offered by a scalar structure. One possibility might be the sequence:

9:1 9:1 6:1 9:1 6:1 3:1 3:1:2
9:1 9:1 6:1 9:1 6:1 3:1 3:2:1

Taking a lesson from Descartes (Chapter 2) flowpaths are offered to facilitate: 'running them over . . . so that I seemed to have the whole in intuition before me at the same time'.

The designer is creating a *melody*.

In his book *Introducing Music*, Otto Károlyi reminds us that a scale by itself is not a melody, but a skeleton. It is the quality of *inner tension* that makes a melody.

He distinguishes broadly between three kinds of melody:
(a) a step by step progression
(b) wider leaps, but *orderly*
(c) a combination of a and b.

He notes that 'melody is inseparable from rhythm. Melody without rhythm becomes shapeless and meaningless'.

In his book, *The Evolving House*, Albert Farwell Bemis proposed the standardisation of a 4 inch (10 cm) module to be used throughout the building and allied industries. The dominant motive was economic but, inevitably, this has great aesthetic potential.

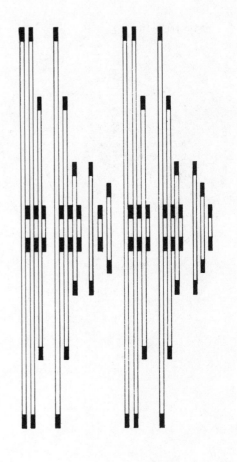

Melody from Beethoven's Ninth Symphony, fourth movement.

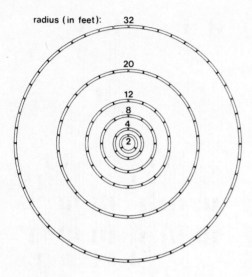

radius (in feet): 32

20

12

8

4

2

In Frank Lloyd Wright's project for a house for Ralph Tester, in Palos Verdes, dating from 1938, a series of cylindrical pavilions for the rooms are grouped about an open patio. The rectangular roof embraces them into a unity.

Two principal materials are used: concrete in the substructure of the curved terraces and the swimming pool, and plywood sheets for the circular rooms. The massive cylindrical columns, 4 feet in diameter, would have been built from Wright's poured masonry of large local stones set roughly in concrete.

The module for the plan is a standard 4 foot wide plywood sheet – the size that it comes from the manufacturers. Plywood bends readily in one direction, gaining rigidity.

In this concept, the plywood has a dual function. It is used as a structural and finishing material in the rooms. It is also used as cylindrical formwork for all concrete works. This 4 foot module gives the *measure* for the whole design.

The plan drawing shows how the circular rooms and columns are related on a 4 foot square grid. The centres of all circles lie on grid points.

Their diameters conform to a 4 foot module and also grow into a Fibonacci series:

radii in feet:	2 4 8 12 20 32
number of 4 foot panels in circumference:	3 6 12 18 30 48

By taking $\pi = 3$, the error of 0.142 provides intervals, or tolerances, to receive jointing, door frames and mullions.

The modular areas 4 and 9 can form combinations by addition and subtraction:
4589101213 . . . ; 12 is critical.

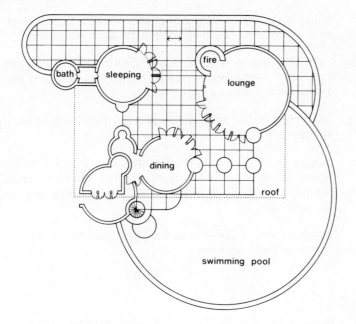

Combinations and permutations

Combinations of two modules by simple addition brings variety and rhythm into scale.

Our sensitivity to addition is such that given any two magnitudes in a collection or set, their sum is also of that collection.

Using rods of length 2 and 3 units the available series becomes: 2 3 4 5 6 7 8 9 . . . critical integer is 2.

Using rods of lengths 3 and 4 units:

3 4 6 7 8 9 . . . the critical integer is 6, meaning that all succeeding integers can be built.

Using rods of lengths 4 and 5, the critical integer is 12.

Using rods of lengths 3 and 7:

3 6 7 9 10 12 13 14 15 . . . the critical integer is 9.

Note: In a combination, the order of sequence of the modules is not important.

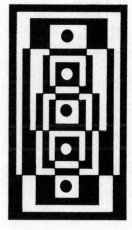

133

AbCd ACbd AdbC
AbdC ACdb AdCb

bACd bCAd bdAC
bAdC bCdA bdCA

CAbd CbAd CdAb
CAdb CbdA CdbA

dAbC dbAC dCAb
dACb dbCA dCbA

Ab AC Ad AE
bA CA dA EA

bC bd bE
Cb db Eb

Cd CE
dC EC

dE
Ed

Permutations are an extension of combinations requiring that the order or sequence of differing objects be taken into account.

If we have n objects in given places and we interchange the places of some or all of them, we are said to permute the objects and any one arrangement is called a permutation.

Given the series of differing objects A B C D, to permute four from four see illustration.

Twenty-four variations are possible. This represents $n! = 4!$ permutations. Similarly, permuting 5 from 5 gives $5! = 120$ permutations, but permuting any 2 objects from 5 gives 20 permutations as shown in the illustration.

Where there are r places to be filled by objects from a set of n, the number of permutations is:

$$_nP_r = \frac{n!}{(n-r)!}$$

Note: When $r = n$, take $(n - r) = 1$. Thus permuting 3 from 4 gives the same number of permutations as 4 from 4.

The number of permutations of n objects taken all together when there are p like objects of one kind, q like objects of a second kind and r of a third kind, is:

$$_nP_{pqr} = \frac{n!}{p!\,q!\,r!}$$

A *combination* is a set of objects chosen from a given group, when no significance is attached to the order of the objects within the set:

$$_nC_r = \frac{n!}{r!(n-r)!}$$

Note: When $r = n$, the number of combinations $= 1$.
Combining any 2 from 5 gives 10 combinations (see above).

Also, factorial numbers are products of integer series:
e.g, factorial $5 = 5! = 1 \times 2 \times 3 \times 4 \times 5 = 120$
Similarly $3! = 1 \times 2 \times 3 = 6$ and $7! = 5040$

134

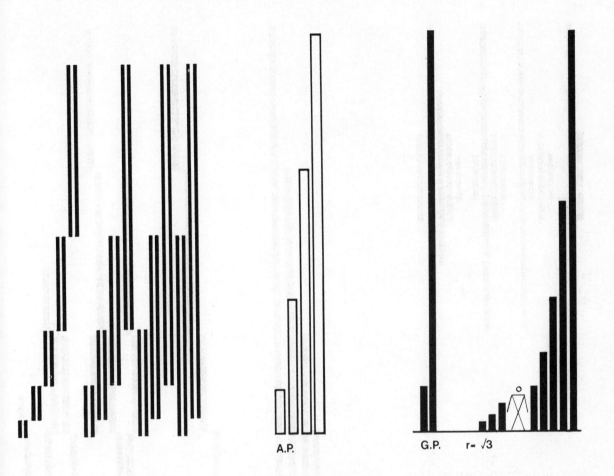

A.P.

G.P.   r= √3

GP scales

A suitable scale to solve the 9:1 problem can be in GP. The $r = \sqrt{3}$ series is an obvious choice; r falls between 1:1 and 2:1 and offers four intervals between 1 and 9. It might well be linked with the AP, 1 3 6 9, to give it stability.

GP's have a tendency to soar out of human range unless they are gripped by an AP.

A GP can also provide a convergent series less than one. This means that the common ratio can be applied to furniture and furnishings down to the smallest detailing.

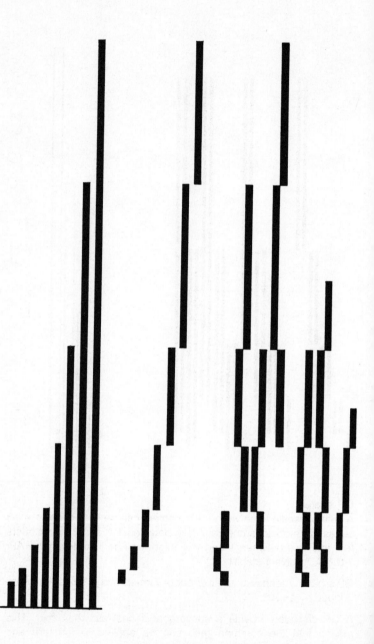

Above: Comprehension of the ratio 2:7 can be aided by reference to a base, forming groups such as 1217 and 1271. An AP scale in the series 1247 emerges to produce intervals of 1, 2, 3.

Right: Variations in a truncated φ series. The basic structure is converted into intervals and then regrouped schematically *so that the mind can run over them freely* (ref: Descartes).

Once a structure has been established by the senses the inflection and transposition of its constituent terms can cause it to appear rhythmic and alive.

136

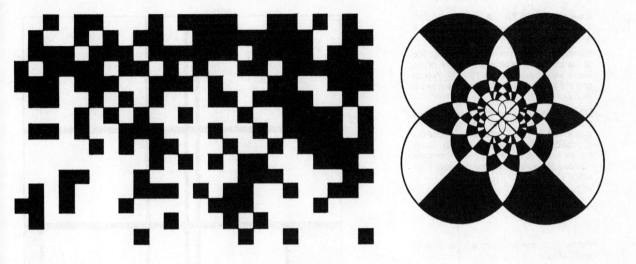

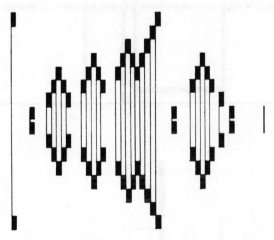

Above left: An arithmetic distribution of squares. Each particular site is random, but the distribution is graduated.

Above: GP series of circles with r = √2. The dominance of the outer leaves is established by eliminating the penultimate group in the series. This pause emphasises the conclusion, and illustrates a useful dramatic tool.

Left: Graphic interpretation of a melody, made famous by Astaire and Rogers.

Drawing derived from a painting by Piet Mondrian. A 5:4 canvas is energised by a finely judged hierarchy of rectangles.

Mondrian's work extended the deductive philosophy of *Neoplasticism*. Many of his works were based upon a 16 × 16 interval grid (16 subdivides neatly and also offers φ ratios of 1:2:3:5:8.

Mondrian required art to *attain an exact equilibrium* through the creation of pure plastic means composed on two absolute oppositions (vertical and horizontal). *Using the rectangular relationship—the constant relationship—establishes the universal individual duality:unity.*

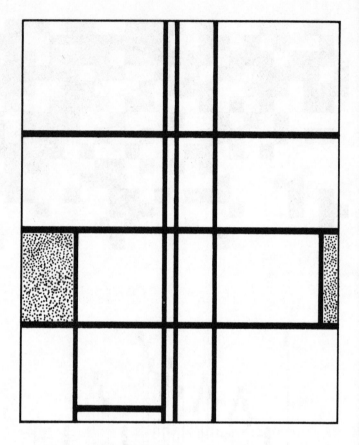

Human scale can be zoned in terms of walls and ceilings.

The toe wall marks a boundary.

The sit-upon is a civilised barrier, but can be dangerous in the dark.

Waist height is companionable but shoulder height is for viewing only; requiring a clear decision before clambering over. Above head height, exclusion is asserted; only a determined effort will surmount it. Up to about twice human height is still within man's grasp (with the help of a companion).

Internally, a low ceiling, just clearing the head, can be cosy in small spaces. A touch height ceiling is practical, domestic, but can be oppressive over large areas. A high ceiling, up to twice human height, is spacious. Higher than this is monumental.

138

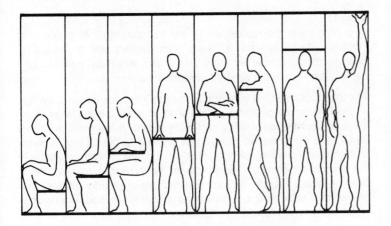

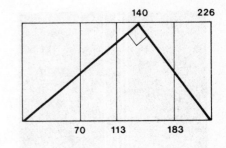

Corb's modulor

Le Corbusier's 'modulor', finalised in 1948, was based upon a φ GP. This he linked, with some artistry, to a right angle set into a double square.

Having recognised the exciting scalar possibilities of a φ series, Corb selected a classic eye level at 6 feet (183 cms) from ground level. He then projected both convergent and divergent series from this datum.

The resultant Fibonacci series is:

1 2 4 6 10 16 27 43 70 113 183 296 479 . . . the *red* series.

He found that the rate of change accelerated too rapidly and developed a second series to double the first:

2 4 8 13 20 33 53 86 140 226 366 592 . . . the *blue* series.

The resultant mixture feels like a duple space . . . reminiscent of *duple time* in music.

But perhaps the most important property of Corb's modulor lies in its recognition of the need for a scale . . . and having the courage to use it!

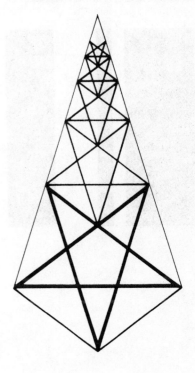

A φ series can be generated from a regular pentagon.

139

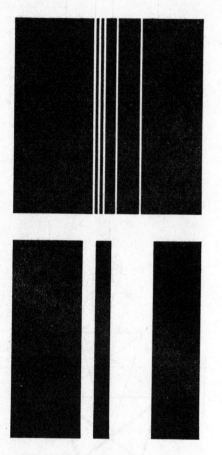

Modules

Two properties are necessary to the establishment of a scale: a *module*, which provides a basic, standardised unit or repetitive building block, and a *grouping procedure* which by permutation, combination or simple similarity orders the scale.

The intrinsic properties of a module directly influence and restrain the scales that can be constructed from it. If the module is too large, then it will restrict the availability of combinations. If the module is too small then the grouping procedures needed to bind it into a comprehensible scale may be too complex and difficult to manipulate. If the module is coarse then it cannot be expected to produce a delicate scale, though an experimental designer may attempt the challenge. Certainly, if a module does not have a human dimension it is not likely to produce a human scale.

This has become one of the major challenges of twentieth century design, well illustrated by its architecture. Advances in engineering now offer massive structural members scaled to the processes that gave them birth. The rolling mill, prefabrication yard, mechanical handling plant, bulldozer, crane and concrete mixer require a module that is intrinsic to the scale of their activities. At the same time, the human being who uses the machines and who will use the buildings has a different scale of values, based upon a different module. It is the architect's problem to integrate the two scales: a problem that has preoccupied modern architects from Mackintosh to Lasdun.

It can be argued that every dimension of contemporary society is facing a similar problem.

Linear dramatisations of the φ series.

Orders of scale

Ratio scales are the most advanced available to us and very often are in excess of needs. It is sound practice to select a scale of the lowest order that will do the job. The ideal design has tolerances for *the loosest possible fit that will not rattle.*

Nominal scale has no sequence, but merely recognises membership of a group . . . like soccer shirts.

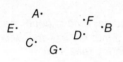

Ordinal scale is an order of preferences that is not quantified.

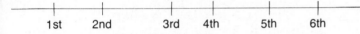

| 1st | 2nd | 3rd | 4th | 5th | 6th |

Interval scale has an arbitrary origin, the unit is assumed to be constant only under linear transformations, by addition or subtraction.

0 1 2 3 4 5 6 7 8

Ratio scale has a non-arbitrary zero, a constant unit and is invariant under similarity transformation, by multiplication or division.

0 1 2 3 4 5 6 7 8 9 10

Hence GP's, Pythagorean harmonic series and the chromatic musical scale are all ratio scales.
AP's and the whole note and pentatonic musical scales are interval scales.
Any suggestion of a hierarchy is an ordinal scale.
A grouping procedure introduces a nominal scale.

8 Simple oscillatory structures

I still reserve the right at any time to doubt the solutions furnished by the modulor, keeping intact my freedom which must depend upon my feelings rather than my reason.

Le Corbusier

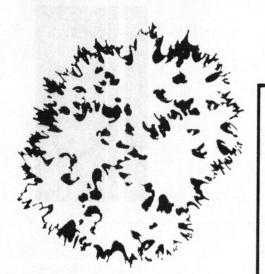

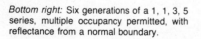
Bottom right: Six generations of a 1, 1, 3, 5 series, multiple occupancy permitted, with reflectance from a normal boundary.

In this programme, the first generation has three items, of magnitudes 1, 2 and 3, turning through 180°. The second generation is a repeat of the first. If adjacency and multi-occupancy are forbidden, growth ceases after two generations. If they are permitted, four generations complete the introvert figure, left.

The need for pulsation

Walt Disney once revealed that his key discovery, making it possible to animate his Mickey Mouse and other cinematograph drawings, was not the technique of hinging and synchronising the limbs to move at 24 frames per second. It was the introduction of *pulsation* into their forms so that they appeared to swell and contract rhythmically. It is this quality that gives them the semblance of life!

In his description of *melody*, Otto Károlyi states that analysis of large numbers of melodies shows that an ascending melodic line is sooner or later balanced by a descending one, and vice versa.

Oscillation seems to be a property of all forms of energy. Certainly it is a property of life and a need for a balance of reciprocating flows is observable throughout the arts and sciences. It applies to any structure, physical and sensual. A structure exists by a set of laws, principles, perhaps even *axioms* that appear to bind the parts into a unity. Each structure has a *programme*.

A study of simple programmes that encourage oscillation between growth and decline can be both instructive and a spur to the imagination. This chapter examines a selection, using graphics as a medium.

143

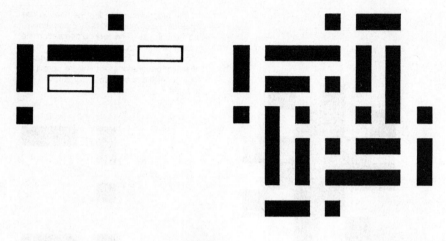

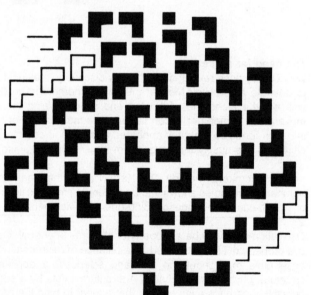

In the introvert, clockwise 1, 3, 5 series each generative five unit has two offspring, 1 and 1. When adjacency and multiple occupation are permitted, the figure becomes extrovert, expansionist. When denied, as illustrated, the figure is introvert.

In the anticlockwise, extrovert evolution of L's, each unit has two offspring, adjacency forbidden.

Designing into a boundless, regular, squared grid, let black represent the occupation of any square.

Let *adjacent* mean adjoining and parallel with the sides.

Therefore squares diagonally adjoining are not adjacent.

Above left: A 1, 1, 3, 5 series, multiple occupancy permitted, reflecting diagonally on the boundary of a square within an AP tartan grid.

Above: A marching, extrovert programme.

This 1 2 4 series will repeat, generation after generation, into eternity. It can be read in either direction, but with a difference of inflection. The 1 2 4 2 series is better balanced. It oscillates.

The 1 2 1 4 series is more jagged.

145

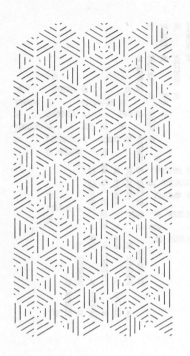

Programmes into a triangular grid.

Planar growth and decline

Unless stated to the contrary, all rotary generations in these examples are clockwise on a rectilinear grid.

Introvert series occur when a programme inhibits itself and can grow no further.

Extrovert series are apparently limitless in growth. To comprehend them we must examine a part as being typical of all other parts . . . as in Leibnitz's infinite universe! The part is at once somewhere and anywhere. To fix it locally, the part is finely focused and the peripheral area diffused, greyed and lost. Attention can be concentrated also by a symmetrical change of scale from the centre of interest, by AP or GP.

The growth of an extrovert series can be restrained by generation within a boundary that is absolute and does not permit flow across it. This is not to be confused with the *framing* of part of a limitless series, a microcosmic view of the macrocosm.

The boundary can be used as a reflecting surface so that the angle of incidence equals the angle of reflection.

The generations could be colour coded to reveal the evolutionary process.

In the ultimate, within a reflecting boundary, all squares will be occupied. Whether adjacency be permitted or not, the evolution of the series will be halted, or swamped in a black mass, unless earlier generations decline and make room for their successors.

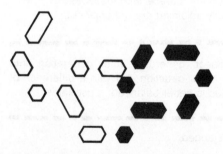

Top left: A series can be colour coded to represent an ageing process, thus revealing multiple occupancy.

Top right: A 2, 3, 1, 1 reflective series on a diamond square grid.

A unit can be rotated and counterchanged within the grid.

147

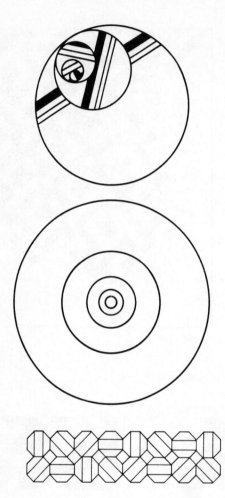

Rotary generations take many forms, however they are all based upon rhythmic rotation through an angle and could be expressed graphically as a waveform along a
time axis.

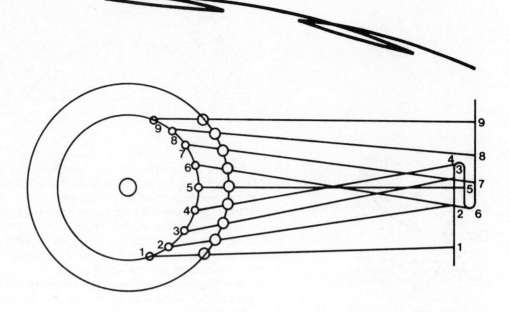

Our solar system

After the conquest of North Africa by Alexander the Great during the fourth century BC, the city of Alexandria was founded as a seat of learning.

In its massive library both Babylonian and Greek records of the heavenly bodies, going back hundreds of years, were housed, studied and debated.

The records showed that the heavenly bodies subdivided into two groups: the Sun, the Moon and the containing sphere of the background stars orbited the earth in near circular paths. The abundance of records enabled Hipparchus to use the properties of *similar triangles and sine tables* to calculate the diameter of the Earth and the distance of the Moon with amazing accuracy, to within a few miles of today's agreed figures.

But the five known planets, Saturn, Jupiter, Mars, Venus and Mercury, were a different problem. Their paths about Earth were variously epicyclic and prompted a study of a geometry of curves for some 2000 years. The mathematician Aristarchus suggested that the problem could be simplified if all the planets, including Earth, were to orbit the Sun but, after much controversy, his argument was lost. During the second century AD the astronomer Ptolemy summarised all the geographical knowledge amassed in his *Geographia*. The Ptolemaic theory, putting the Earth at the centre of the universe, went unchallenged, except by mystical nonsense, for over a thousand years.

A model of successive views of an outer planet as seen from an inner planet as they revolve in concentric orbits about a sun.

Planets of our solar system known today are:

Planet	Diameter (miles)	Solar distance (millions of miles)	Sidereal period (Earth days)
Mercury	3 100	36	88
Venus	7 700	67	225
Earth	7 900	93	365
Mars	4 200	142	687
asteroids		c 300	years
Jupiter	88 000	483	11.9
Saturn	75 100	886	29.5
Uranus	28 300	1783	84.0
Neptune	31 000	2793	164.8
Pluto	4 000(?)	3666	248.4

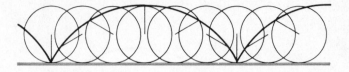

By the time of Copernicus, in the fifteenth century, the interaction of 77 mathematical circles, forming cycloids and ellipses as necessary, was required to account for the apparent motion of the Sun, Moon and five planets about the Earth. His calculations, putting the Sun at the centre of a solar system in which the Earth was one of six planets, reduced the number of circles required to 31. Within a hundred years, Kepler resolved these by translating the planetary orbits into ellipses with the sun at a focus of each ellipse. Today we observe the planetary orbits to be near ellipses as the solar system revolves about its common centre of gravity, to which the Sun is the major contributor.

The cycloid

The *cycloid* is the locus of a point on the circumference of a circle rolling on a straight line.

Therefore, the length of the base line from cusp to cusp is $2\pi a$, where a is the radius of the circle.

The length of a complete arc of a cycloid is $8a$.

The area between one arch and the base is $3\pi a^2$, which is three times the area of the generating circle.

The arc of a cycloid offers the path of *quickest descent* between two points. In the example, if the two balls are released from *A* together, the ball on the cycloidal path will arrive first at *B*.

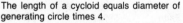

The length of a cycloid equals diameter of generating circle times 4.

If the two rollers are released simultaneously from *A*, that on the cycloidal path will reach *B* first.

Two epicycloids and a hypocycloid, each with five cusps.

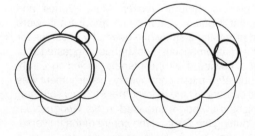

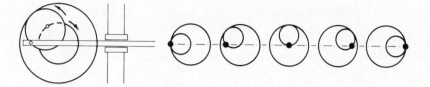

A *curtate cycloid* is generated when the point P is inside the generating circle; OP is less than a.

A *prolate cycloid* is generated when the point P is outside the generating circle; OP is more than a.

A *hypocycloid* is formed when the rolling circle is inside a master circle.

An *epicycloid* is formed when the rolling circle is outside a master circle.

The properties of the cycloid, can be adapted to the hypocycloid and epicycloid.

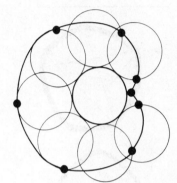

If the rolling circle in a hypocycloid has a radius half the length of the fixed circle, point P simply moves to and fro along a diameter.

C, the centre of the rolling circle, can be attached to a revolving circle that is concentric with the fixed outer circle. As the central circle rotates, it causes the rolling circle to give point P a reciprocating action. This mechanism was much used as an ancilliary pump in nineteenth century steam engines.

When a disc is rolled about a disc of equal diameter, the roller makes two revolutions about its own centre. This principle is used in differential gears.

If a particle moves under gravity along a smooth curve in the form of a cycloid with its cusps pointing vertically upward, the time of descent to the lowest point is independent of the starting position.

The *Geneva stop* is an intriguing device for translating continuous rotary motion into intermittent rotary and stopped motion. It is, therefore, an elementary timing device.

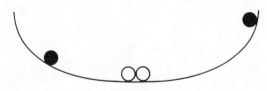

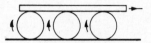

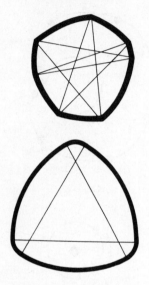

Rollers

It is reasonable to suppose that man discovered the roller before developing the wheel. Their difference is important. The roller is independent of the vehicle that it transports so that, if the rollers have a circumference of three feet (or, say, one metre) then the slab will move forward six feet (say, two metres) per rev. This is known as the *roller and slab* theorem.

Rollers do not need to be circular in order to offer constant breadth. *Curves of constant breadth* can be irregular; however the simplest are based upon the equilateral triangle, the regular pentagon and septagon.

The introduction of short radius curves can soften the corners. Such curves develop an *organic flavour* that is particularly useful to designers.

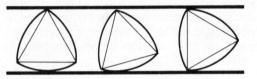

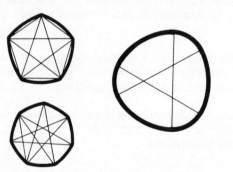

A curve of constant breadth must remain in contact with two parallel lines as it is rotated. Any of these could be used as rollers but only the circle has a constant centre, permitting a hub.

152

Transition curves

Rounding off is a familiar device for softening harsh corners. It can serve both utilitarian and aesthetic purposes; however its effect can be crude when a simple radius curve joins two straights.

When travelling along an edge or a line, the senses, the fingers, the eyes are subject to the same physical laws as other moving bodies. They have inertia, mass and momentum and obey centrifugal force. If a railway engine travelling along a straight length of track is suddenly introduced to a radius curve, it will jump the rails. The railway engineer, therefore, provides a *transition curve* to ease the engine from one radius to another while adjusting the *superelevation*, or cant, to counter the centrifugal force. The length of the transition curve depends upon the total change of radius, the velocity of the engine and the permitted superelevation, bearing in mind that the cant must not be so great that if an engine is halted it will topple over.

The desirable rate of change of curvature will vary with a design specification. Railway transition curves are usually related to the velocity cubed – a cubic curve is comparatively easy to set out with a theodolite. An exponential curve might be more accurate. In general design where practical considerations are paramount, a series of short circular arcs with radii in AP or GP will offer sensory continuity of the transition.

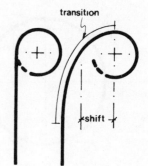

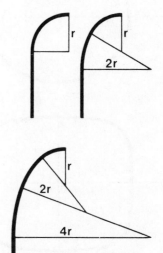

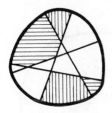

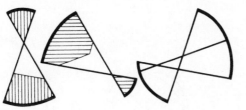

Bottom left: Non-circular rollers can be constructed by assembling vertically opposite pairs of acute angled isosceles triangles.

Above: The introduction of a transition curve requires a lateral shift of the line.

Movement along a curved path is an acceleration. The length of a transition curve reveals the rate of change of acceleration.

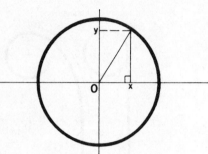

The superellipse

An ellipse, and the other conic sections, the parabola and the hyperbola, as discussed in Chapter 11, offer beautiful transition curves. The circle is a special case of the ellipse in which the two axes are equal in length.

The *Theorem of Pythagoras* can be applied to the rotating vector of unit length to reveal, as it describes a circle centred on the origin *O* that:

$$x^2 + y^2 = 1^2 = 1$$

It can also be shown that a general equation for an ellipse is of the form:

$$\left(\frac{x}{a}\right)^2 + \left(\frac{y}{b}\right)^2 = 1$$

where *a* and *b* are the maximum and minimum radii.

If the *indices* are raised, say, from 2 to 5/2, then the closed curve produced has more *character* than a simple rectangle or a simple ellipse . . . it becomes a *superellipse*.

An approximation to such forms, which will be discussed as an aesthetic later in the book can be achieved by the projection illustrated.

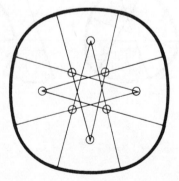

The superellipse is, in effect, a continuous oscillatory transition curve, having four fold symmetry. The ever changing acceleration charges it with energy; a semblance of life that is discussed in Chapter 14.

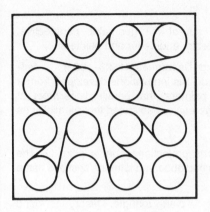

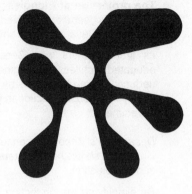

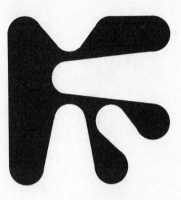

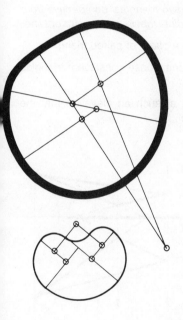

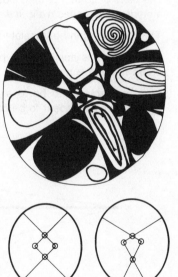

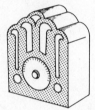

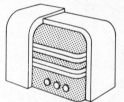

The drawing technique of shared radii can be used to construct a variety of curvilinear shapes.

Transition curves were temporarily eliminated from the *pure* geometric shapes of the twentieth century: in part, as a reaction to Art Nouveau but also as a means of getting a *firm grip* upon design.

The peg and string method of devising near biomorphic forms has been used by Naum Gabo and Armin Hofmann. The absence of transition curves is disguised by the pulsation of positive and negative, convex and concave curvature.

The projection of triangles

Projective geometry evolved out of the geometric perspective, beloved of Renaissance architects, engineers and painters.

Its first exponent was Gérard Desargues (†593–1662), a self-educated architect and engineer. His innovations developed from a deduction, long accepted by painters, that parallel lines *meet* at infinity. Previously, Euclidean geometry had stated that parallel lines *never* meet.

Desargues's Theorem concerns projections from a point *O*. The illustration shows how painters had observed differing sections of the same projection.

By simplifying the projection to a plane triangle, Desargues found that:

The pairs of corresponding sides of two triangles' perspective from a point meet, respectively, in three points that lie on one straight line.

This property can be translated into a *chain* of paired triangles.

The theorem is applicable to polygons whose constituent triangles share the above properties.

The perspective can be to a point at such an elevation that the projection lines appear to be parallel.

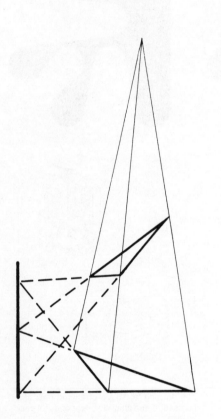

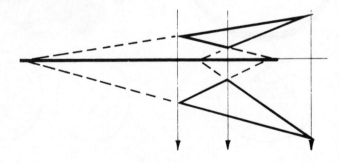

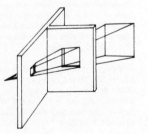

156

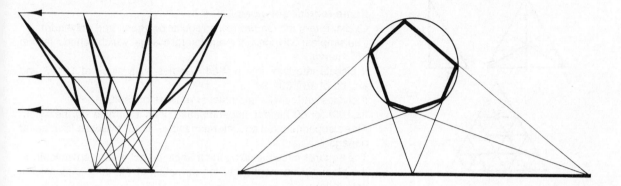

Blaise Pascal, of *Pascal's triangle*, extended the theorem to:

If a hexagon is inscribed in a circle, the pairs of opposite sides intersect, respectively, in three points which lie on a straight line.

Brianchon's Theorem (circa 1820) states:

If a hexagon is circumscribed about a circle the lines joining opposite vertices meet in one point.

In Chapter 6, a *dynamic* series was developed between parallel lines using a control point on one of the parallels and a GP was projected between parallel lines using a control square.

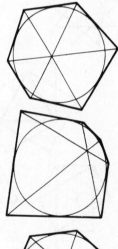

It is possible to programme variations on these by using both divergent and parallel curved and straight lines. Their important quality is that they present a rate of change that is clearly and definitely structured.

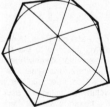

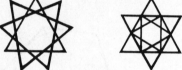

Some regular polygons

Cyclic, rotary motion produces regular polygons and polyhedra.

The simplest polygon is the equilateral triangle which echoes itself at 60° intervals.

It bisects into two right angled triangles, with sides of $1:2:\sqrt{3}$ and angles of 30°, 60°, 90°.

It divides and stacks into smaller replicas of itself.

Its 180° (or 60°) image superimposed upon it forms a *star hexagon*.
Three superimposed equilateral triangles at 40° intervals form a star nonagon.

The squares circumscribing the triangle do not mesh conveniently in the plane, but are critical to the formation of the three dimensional octahedron.

The regular *hexagon* comprises six radial equilateral triangles. It is an isometric view of a cube.

Three superimposed $\sqrt{3}:1$ rectangles at 60° intervals give a continuous planar structure. The node heights are: 0.866 and 1.732.

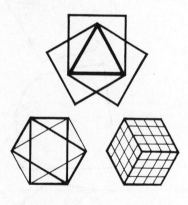

The water molecule, H_2O, has two hydrogen atoms attached to the big oxygen atom at angles that discourage the formation of equilateral triangles. As a snow crystal grows in free fall, the angular deviation within the molecules sets up stresses and the hexagon will not close completely. The resultant strain tends towards symmetry as the crystal grows, so that although snow crystals exhibit great variety of detail, little difficulty arises in their recognition.

In this respect they share a property of living organisms.

158

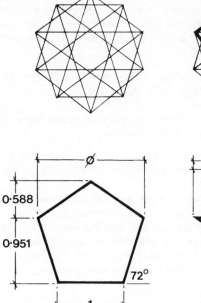

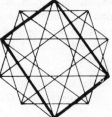

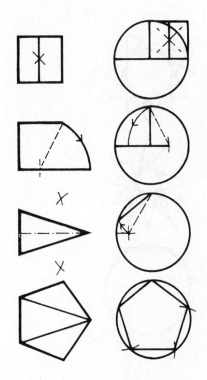

The regular *pentagon*, in association with the hexagon, has been credited with magical powers throughout recorded history. Looking hard at one's hands, and at life generally, it is not surprising!

Two complementary regular pentagons can be superimposed to form a decagon. This reveals much of the interstructure of the pentagon which conforms to a Fibonacci series. The node heights are: 0.951 and 1.539.

The regular *decagon* can be formed by rotating a φ:1 rectangle at 36° intervals.

It came as no surprise to mystics that DNA is found to function like a right handed helix in which each tread is of the same size and turns at the same rate of 36° per tread.

On each tread the *chemical lattice* is coded in hexagons and pentagons!

Two methods for construction of the regular pentagon.
The pentagram:

$$\frac{x}{y} = \frac{y}{z} = \varphi$$

159

The regular septagon is the most inaccessible of the primary polygons . . . probably because it cannot be constructed accurately with only ruler and compass. The three node heights, compared with unit base, are: 0.782, 1.757 and 2.190. Its external angle is 51° 26′ approximately.

The regular octagon is a rotating θ:1 rectangle (see Chapter 6). Its three node heights are: 0.707, 1.707 and 2.414.

The regular duodecagon is formed by the superimposition of four equilateral triangles per rev, at 90° intervals.

Alternatively, it records the rotation of a $2 + \sqrt{3}$:1 rectangle at 30° intervals. The node heights are: 0.5, 1.366, 2.366, 3.232, 3.732.

Polygons with more than seven sides are into the range of *plenty*. However we are sensitive to parallels and symmetry so that polygons with an even number of sides can *fold* into the elementary range. Polygons with eight, ten and 12 sides are instantly recognisable, whereas nine, 11 and 13 sided polygons are not. The nonagon is easier to comprehend if its three fold symmetry is revealed.

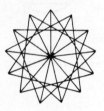

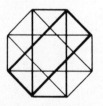

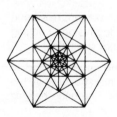

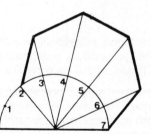

A useful ruler and compass construction for a regular polygon of n number sides upon a known sidelength is:

(1) Using the base of the polygon as radius, draw a semicircle.
(2) Mark off n number equal intervals on the arc.
(3) From the centre of the circle produce straight lines through points 2, 3, 4, 5 . . . to n.
(4) From point 2 cut off side lengths to form polygon.

Labyrinths and mazes

Reciprocal movement can be suggested by constructions that offer alternative paths. In past centuries these led to considerable artistry in the devising of labyrinths and mazes.

The maze in Chartres Cathedral (thirteenth century).

The 'Little world of me'.

161

Top: On a square grid selected diagonals are switched through 90°.

Bottom left: Diagram of the maze at Hampton Court.

Right: Variation on a maze by Greg Bright.

162

Reciprocity in vegetation

Rooted vegetation radiates in two directions. The root hairs absorb water and simple inorganic compounds of nitrogen, phosphorus, calcium, potassium, magnesium, sulphur and iron. These, with certain trace elements, are taken up the woody fibres and much of the water evaporates at the leaf surfaces, while photosynthesis takes place.

Light energy from the sun is absorbed by the chlorophyll in the leaves and the water molecules are split. The hydrogen in the water combines with carbon dioxide in the atmosphere to form organic compounds while oxygen from the water is released into the atmosphere.

Rooted vegetation takes water upwards and sunlight downwards. It takes carbon dioxide and gives oxygen. It is, therefore, the complementary life form to the animals of Earth.

Many artists and ecological scientists hold the view that both practical and aesthetic fulfilment are conditional upon an interaction of animal, vegetable and mineral properties.

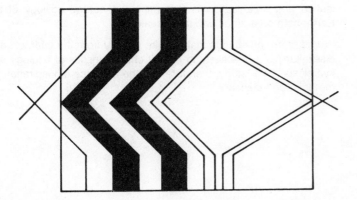

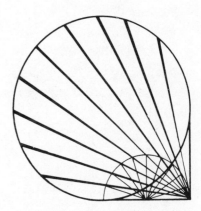

The projection from a semi-circle is reminiscent of certain forms of seashells.

163

Symbiosis

Nature, as we observe it, is built upon reciprocal relationships of dissimilar organisms, bacterial, vegetable and animal. Such dependence is referred to as symbiotic, under three broad headings:

(1) *Commensalism*, in which food or space is shared, without harm to either organism and with possible benefit to one.
(2) *Mutualism*, in which both partners benefit.
(3) *Parasitism*, in which the host is subject to varying degrees of injury while the parasite benefits, albeit temporaily.

Typical examples of mutualism, which is the aspect most commonly referred to as symbiotic, are:

(a) The bacteria that decompose compost heaps of organic waste to form humus that in turn feeds new vegetation.
(b) Pilot fish of the pompano family (*Carangidae*) who keep the company of sharks.
(c) Starling-like oxpeckers who live on the backs of large animals such as elephant, rhinoceros and cattle, in equatorial Africa. These birds clamber all over and under their hosts, devouring whatever bloodsucking ticks and flies they find. The large animals not only tolerate and, by their presence, protect the birds; they also use them as lookouts for predators.

Contemporary science is revealing complex symbiotic relationships that contribute to a shared environment to establish a balanced ecology. It is a matter of concern that much of mankind's industrialisation and urbanisation is disrupting the natural ecology of the Earth, both on a small and large scale.

Works of art, any things that acquire identity from the interaction of dissimilar parts, are likely to exhibit characteristics of ecology and symbiosis. Their study, therefore, can be a source of inspiration for the artist and designer.

9 The moving point

The Moving Finger writes; and, having writ,
Moves on; Nor all your Piety nor Wit
Shall lure it back to cancel half a line,
Nor all your tears wash out a Word of it.

from *The Rubaiyat of Omar Khayyam*
English version by Edward Fitzgerald

Note: Omar Khayyam (1050–1132 AD) was a Persian mathematician.

The Theorum of Pappus

It was Pappus, one of the great mathematicians of Alexandria in the fourth century AD, who recognised that space could be filled by a moving point.

A point moving in one dimension produces a straight line.
This line, moving in a dimension at right angles to the first, defines a rectangle.

The rectangle, moving in a dimension at right angles to the previous two, defines a rectanglar prism.

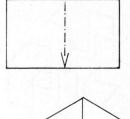

This concept can be used when the point moves along curved paths to describe more complex areas and volumes. It has made possible the massive evolution of mechanics in modern times and has inspired *Constructivist* art forms that regard space as a continuum. Open planning and inside-outside sculptural and architectural forms of the Modern Movement are expressions of the *moving point*; works which use string, wire, glass, perspex, standard steel sections, footpaths and textures to define movement through space . . . concepts evolving out of the work of many brave pioneers, such as van de Velde, Mackintosh, Wright, Braque, Picasso, Balla, Klee, Arp, Gabo, Van Doesburg and Mondrian, are all expressions of the moving point.

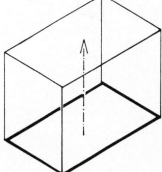

The *Theorem of Pappus* is basic, therefore, to all scanning mechanisms; however, recent developments in mathematics, particularly the work of Mandelbrot on *Fractals*, permit a three dimensional symmetry of movement. The path is a continuum, of infinite length, defining a finite space.

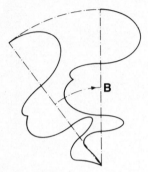

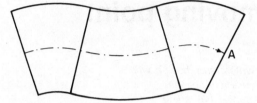

If *A* is the centre of a straight line travelling along a curved path, the area traversed can be calculated by multiplying the length of the line by the length of *A*'s path. No matter how the path of *A* wriggles on the plane, this calculation will be applicable provided that:
(a) The line is always at right angles to the path.
(b) Deductions are made for areas swept more than once.

The area swept by a curved line is described by the *effective length*, perpendicular to the path of *B*. *B* is the centre of the effective length, the centroid of the line.

The area swept by the curved line, in the plane, compensates at each end of the quadrilateral so that the area is: length of *B*'s path times the effective perpendicular length of line.

A line can be programmed to vary in effective length.

These principles can be projected into a third dimension to describe complex volumes; and then into a time dimension, as in the cinema and television.

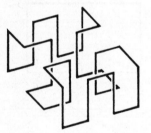

Lines of infinite length
It is possible for a moving point to describe a path of infinite length that yet encloses a finite area.

A star hexagon can be produced by superimposing two equilateral triangles in opposition. The perimeter of this figure is 4:3 longer than the original triangle.

The perimeter can be increased further by superimposing equilateral triangles on the prongs of the star.

The process can be repeated indefinitely. At each stage the perimeter lengthens by 4:3.

166

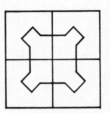
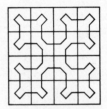
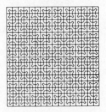
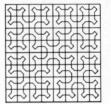

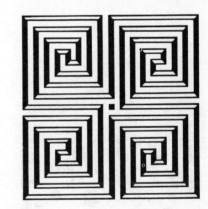

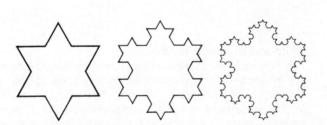

A Greek spiral was a means of using a line to describe an area.

In the year 1912 the Polish mathematician, W. Sierpinski, constructed a limiting curve that can completely fill a square. The principle can be extended to fill both space and time.

167

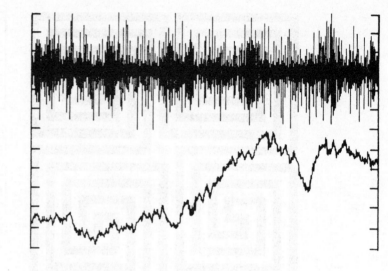

white

brownian

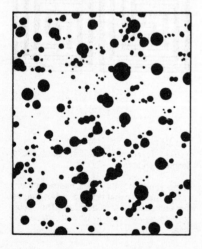

White and Brownian Motion

This method of lengthening a perimeter indefinitely can be applied to any polygon or shape and can be extended to the complete occupation of an area or volume. The study of such curves, originating perhaps in the Ancient Greek spiral, can be traced in modern times from the work of Giuseppe Peano in 1890 and Helge von Koch in 1904 to Mandelbrot's book, *Fractals: Form, Chance and Dimension* (1977).

This concept of a line of infinite length has a remarkable property in that its detail is unaffected by a change of scale. A magnification or a diminution reveals the same pattern. Mandelbrot compares it with the phenomenon of *scaling noises*. Normally when a tape of a sound is played faster or slower, its pitch and character are changed. But scaling noise behaves quite differently. If the sound is played at a different speed, only adjustment of the volume control is necessary to make it sound as it did before.

168

White motion gives the simplest form of scaling noise. It is a completely random distribution, within limits, about a mean which sounds and looks like the snow-like flurries on television screens when there is no input.

White melodies can be produced by using random spinners that are weighted about a datum to produce a sequence of notes. A simple spinner using a pentatonic scale might be subdivided into five symmetrically weighted sectors. Each note could then be generated by random use of the spinner.

Brownian motion is a form of scaling motion characteristic of the random movements of particles and molecules suspended in a liquid. Each molecule moves, step by step, along a random path through the liquid. But although each step is random, the path has sequence and location; yet it does not have a datum. A spinner for the production of *Brownian noise* would require simple numerical instructions such as: −2, −1, 0, +1, +2.

Use of these instructions on a spinner to produce a random walk on the notes of a piano must end, after perhaps much meandering, by wandering off the keyboard.

The initial generations of a line of infinite length as discussed in *Fractals, Form and Chance* by B. B. Mandelbrot.

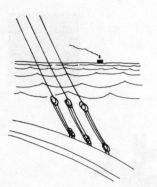

The location of a point

The following experiments cannot be entirely satisfactory on the page of a book for they are influenced by other illustrations, the rectilinearity of the page, the text and the general environment.

However, using graphics as a research medium, suppose that a dot is dimensionless and floating in a void. Can it be lost? No; for it belongs anywhere and nowhere. It can have location, and thus suffer loss of location, only by relationship with another event. At minimal level, this would be a second dot. Of course, the second dot could be *me*, permitting a dialogue between *subject* and *object*.

This experience can happen when at sea. In a vast ocean, empty of all else but one's own boat and a tiny speck on the horizon, attention is drawn to the other boat. Vision moves to and fro between the vessels, setting up a visual and, if one has been long at sea, an emotional tension between them.

Science finds that a surface tension on the water can draw the boats together, like toy boats in a bathtub. But also there is a magnetism, a gravitational force or curvature of space, call it what they will, an *attraction* between them.

If we attempt the role of bystander, then two dots are observed in reciprocal tension. The force between them has some correspondence with Newton's finding that *the gravitational force is inversely proportional to the square of the distance between them*.

Perception of the two dots swings along the easiest path. The vision can wander about the void but one part of a void is like another and there can be no consciousness of movement until two locations have been defined, either by two dots or by the displacement of one dot, which requires memory of its path.

The dots mark the extremities of countless possible paths which, if they were recorded, would become lines.

The distance between two points

In normal circumstances, certainly on this printed page, the shortest unhindered distance between two points is a straight line. Drawing such a line, between the dots but not touching them, provides a path to guide the eye and ease its journey. The stress between the dots is increased or *charged*, and becomes a useful method of bringing attention to a *pair*.

When the straight line touches and incorporates the dots, the force field is *discharged*. The eyes can travel freely along the series of dots comprising the line. All are equal; but as in Newton's universe, the terminal dots have emphasis . . . they have neighbours on one side only. This too is a useful design tool: a dazzling, disquieting pair, or *duality*, can be resolved by discharging them into a line. If their terminal positions still retain too much emphasis, then the line can be continued beyond them.

Paul Klee found that if any path other than a straight line is offered between two nodes, the stress can be increased. Derivatives of this concept have become a major symbol in modern art. They can be seen very clearly in the work of Juan Miró.

An embracing two dimensional path connecting powerfully juxta-posed terminals is a means of securing space. It is an emphatic *enclosure*: the more so because it permits movement, through its mouth, between outside and inside.

Countless examples can be studied in living creatures, seaboard harbours, great castles and manor houses, pots, bottles, soccer goalposts and pinball machines.

It is a favourite military tactic . . . the pincer movement!

In a suitably designed circuit the terminals will have a forcefield between them, similar to the potential difference on the plates of an electrical condensor.

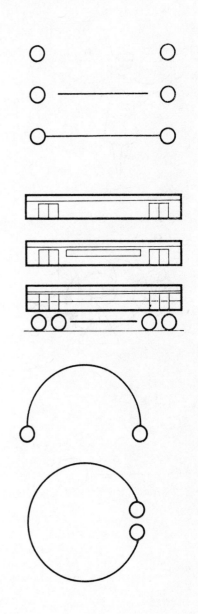

171

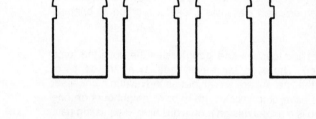

Any dissimilarity between the dots suggests weighting and they will cease to be dimensionless. However small they may be, the introduction of a hierarchy makes them again more important than the interval between them.

A study of three dots
Study of three dots, charged, discharged and variously weighted reveals that:
(1) Symmetry, as presented in a void by the equilateral trio, is static.
(2) Conversely, asymmetry suggests movement and the movement is *towards the greater concentration of energy.*
   Note: Asymmetry is not necessarily chaos or limbo. The word is used to define an order or programme that is not constructed symmetrically.
(3) Asymmetry suggests hierarchy.

When a trio of dots are in GP by both size and interval, the group is most stable when the largest is on the shortest arms and the smallest is on the longer arms. The forcefield is maximised and the dots appear to behave like a solar system, orbiting about their common centre of gravity.

Variations upon the embrace – welcome!

A few of the symbols of Juan Miró.

172

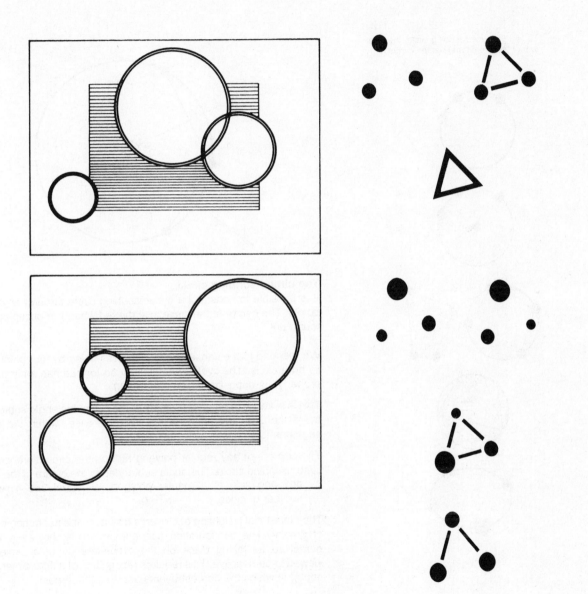

To find the circumscribing circle, the bisectors of the chords meet at the centre, O.

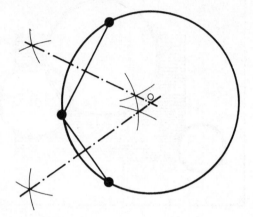

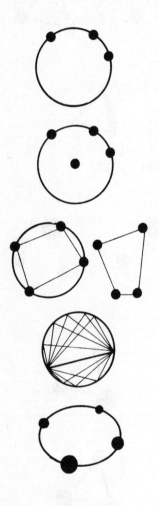

The circumscribing circle

It is possible to construct a circumscribing circle through any three points. The centre of the circle is stabilised when it is occupied by a fourth dot.

We respond to the sense of completeness given by four points that lie on a circle. The *cyclic quadrilateral* so formed has an important property; its opposite angles add to 180°.

This is linked with another property of the circle: the angle subtended by a chord at any point on the circumference, within the same segment, is a constant.

The corners of any regular polygon rest on the circumference of a circumscribing circle. The angle subtended at the centre of the circle by any one side of a regular polygon will equal 360°/n, where n = number of sides.

The differential weighting of n events displaces their common centre of gravity. The configuration can appear stable, however, when perceived as taking place on the circumference of a circle and viewed in perspective. This requires recognition of a third dimension, depth, in which the nearest events are also the largest.

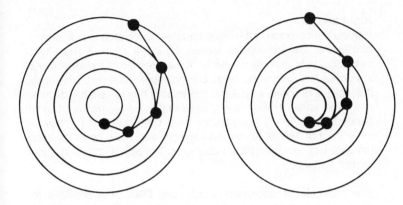

The spiral

The alternative distribution programme on a plane, the spiral, requires a minimum of five events for its spiral form to become evident.

Three examples are:
(1) AP by distance from centre and preceding dot
(2) GP by distance from centre and preceding dot
(3) AP by distance from centre, at fixed angular intervals.

An arrangement of more than four similar events into a circular orbit emphasises the centre, which may be occupied or not. Consequently, when interest is to be directed upon the *series* of events, a *spiral* is needed.

Experiments with seven and more dots remind us, almost uncannily, of the growth and decline of living creatures. The two spirals illustrated have vitality as extrovert and introvert gestures.

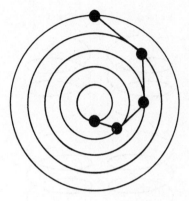

The spiral and its three dimensional expression, the helix, have a *handedness* that is intrinsic. A clockwise spiral remains clockwise whatever its orientation in the plane. To change from clockwise to anticlockwise it must go through a third dimension to become a *mirror image.*

Similarly, no matter how it is turned about, a right handed helix remains a right handed helix. To change to a left handed helix it must pass through a fourth dimension. This too could be a mirror image.

The two dimensional spiral and the three dimensional helix are *asymmetric.*

175

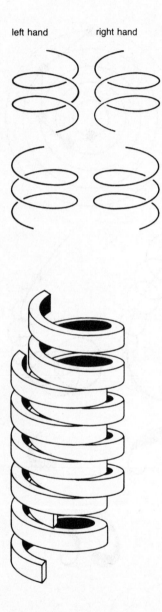

left hand   right hand

Only helices of the same hand entwine together.

Right and left

Helices are common in the plant world: in stalks, stems, and tendrils, and in the arrangement of leaves around a stalk. A majority of climbing plants coil right handedly, in the direction of a woodscrew as it is driven into the timber. There are, however, thousands of varieties that coil the opposite way. A species usually has its own handedness that never varies. Honeysuckle, for example, always twines into a left handed helix. A very few species have both right and left handed varieties. For helices to entwine together they must be of the same handedness, like the strands of a rope. Helices of opposing hands cannot embrace.

The molecule of deoxyribonucleic acid, DNA, that provides the programme for living creatures, is formed by a pair of right handed helices in parallel. Science is still puzzling on the handedness of all sub-units of protein and nucleic acid in earthborn living cells. It is a mathematical possibility that our mirror images exist on another planet. Perhaps, in the primordial soup, left and right handedness were in free competition until some small chance advantage became overwhelming through the evolutionary progress. But it is more likely that a physical restraint influenced the swirling liquids – just as bad weather cyclones and hurricanes are anticlockwise in the northern hemisphere and clockwise south of the equator of spinning planet Earth.

Neither does science know why a majority of humans prefer using their right hands to their left hands. But perhaps more important, why a minority of persons are left handed. Certainly left handed people are ill-served in western society. They become so accustomed to handling scissors, screwdrivers, drawing boards, drills and similar mechanisms in what is, for them, the more difficult posture, that they do not demand proper service from manufacturers. I write on paper turned clockwise through 70°, with an understanding born of experience.

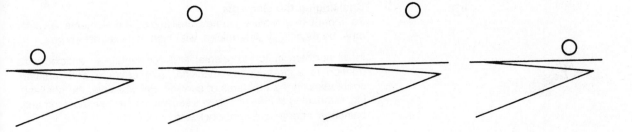

Clockwise

The Earth's land masses are largely in the northern hemisphere. Consequently the most influential civilizations originated north of the equator and share a common view of movements in the heavens.

The Sun, the Moon, the planets and stars seem to move *clockwise* across the northern sky.

Pictorially this visual time sequence can be used to suggest morning, high noon, afternoon and evening. The clockwise journey can suggest the rotation of the seasons and the rise and fall of life's cycles.

All motion is relative. One object moves relative to another. The *railway train effect* gives a good example of visual counterpoint, when two trains are halted on opposing lines in a station. As one train starts to move, a passenger gazing through his carriage window, observes movement but is unsure whether it is his own train that is moving or the train on the opposite line. To form a judgement he seeks further information. Is his carriage vibrating? Is the platform moving with respect to himself? This means that to all change there must be counterchange. If something is getting bigger then its measure is getting smaller. As an object approaches and enlarges, the surrounding background recedes . . . so it is with the intellect, the emotions, loves and hates.

To the northerner, the apparently clockwise movement of the Sun and the stars results from an anticlockwise rotation of the earth. To a southerner, in Australia for example, the movements are reversed.

Mathematicians have chosen the anticlockwise rotation of a vector to be positive. The events that it scans during its journey are conceived as the experiences of a positive vector. It is moving against the sun.

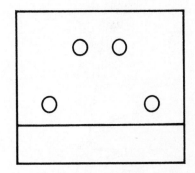

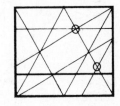

In the rectangular canvas, the four suns are located by an equilateral triangle. To find the time of day, use a slip of white paper to blank out three of the discs.

177

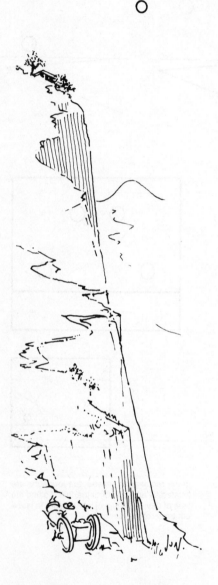

It's a long way to Tipperary, Mandalay and Bedford Square. What is the time of day?

Challenging the elements

To undertake a positive journey, challenging the elements, a vector must be thrustingly determined, with high motivational energy.

In all northern cultures, oriental and occidental, an anticlockwise rotation is aggressive as mankind, with courage and fortitude, contends with the problems of survival. For example, the challenging, rampaging storms of Turner's seascapes are, like most romantic paintings, energetically anticlockwise.

A good theatrical director knows that aggression comes from the right wing of a stage. When filming a combat he pans round two adversaries so that, as each in turn assumes the aggressive role, he is observed moving in from the right. Attack from the left is retaliatory.

In battle scenes the villainous attackers move in from the right and the valiant defenders, usually the good guys obstinately rejecting defeat, are on the left.

In another mood, secure and easy movement, optimistic and pleasantly anticipatory, goes with the sun and the moon; westwards . . . the migratory direction of the human race in modern times. At the end of the film, the *successful* hero moves left to right out of the frame, to follow the setting sun.

178

Experiments with a mirror confirm that the meaning of many famous paintings can be inverted or negated by reversing the picture. The demeanour of a virgin can be converted into that of a coquette. And so it can be for a building or a workbench. There is a right and there is a left way in which to rob a bank. The handedness of a sequence of activities affects their human significance, materially, emotionally and intellectually.

Movement in depth

Movement in depth has emotional effects, probably inherited from primordial survival patterns. An object advancing directly towards its target, unflinching and undeviating, is threatening unless the approach is relieved by a *smile* or some gesture that establishes friendly intent.

To suggest a casual relationship, the approach needs to deviate, hesitate and show a certain sensitivity by inflection to minor incidents along the way and a disinterest in the awaiting subject. Its behaviour thus offers the subject ample opportunity to assess and accept the amiability of the approach.

Of course, the subject could be deceived and get a nasty shock. But that is in the nature of art and artfulness: the establishment of laws so that we can break them.

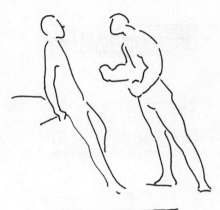

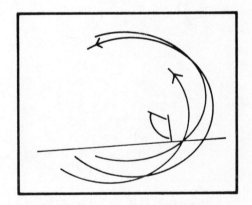

179

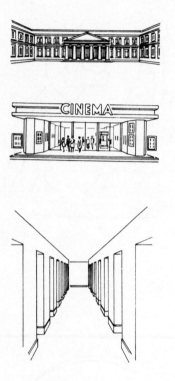

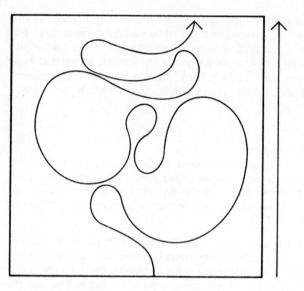

The embrace can be used as an architectural welcome.

A long repetitive corridor or tunnel produces an *Alcatraz* syndrome.

Top right: Two very different paths. We enjoy winding paths packed with friendly variety and affording appetising glimpses of future delights with their assurance of survival into the middle and far distance.

The emotional overtones of movement away from the subject are entirely dependent upon the manner of the retreat. The artistic variations are inexhaustable but can be summarised under three headings:

(1) The retreat backwards: the object has his attention and face directed towards the subject . . . in love or fear . . . as he moves pace by backward pace into the middle distance; then turns and hastens away.
(2) Withdrawal at a gentle gait, slowly accelerating, with frequent turning salutes to the subject . . . epicycles?
(3) The determined stride into the distance without a backwards glance.

These descriptions are theatrical but are applicable in many contexts. They can describe a street, a landscape, a hotel or a prison corridor, an industrial complex, a workbench, a symphony or a painting.

Movement in depth cannot be rhythmic unless it reveals at least three stages: foreground, middleground and background. Motions occurring in one ground may acquire differing emotional and physical attributes in another ground. A man brandishing a sword 100 feet away, preferably on the far side of a river, is a very different experience to the same man brandishing the same sword just 10 feet away.

Similar principles apply to the gestures of friendship and sexuality!

In *horse opera*, the aggressor in the black hat moves in from the right . . . .

181

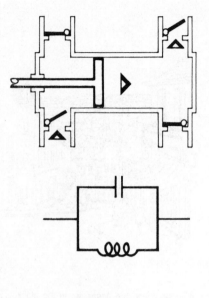

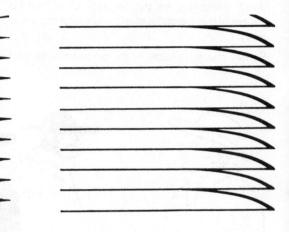

The valves of a reciprocating pump are designed to enable one side of the moving piston to suck fluid whilst the other expels fluid.

In electronics, an oscillatory circuit is based on the reciprocal charging and discharging of a condenser through an inductance.

It can be argued that Monsieur Guillotin was the true founder of democracy by eliminating class distinction in public executions.

Reciprocal motion

Reciprocal motion, positive and negative at constant mean velocity, is unnerving, mechanistic and inhuman. It can be an hypnotic. Certain frequencies, such as seven cycles per second, are of ill-repute.

When aimed directly towards the subject, reciprocal motion is fearsome. Children are taught, for sound historical reasons, that to point is rude. In the past, and even today with gun in hand, it is threatening. Without the gun but armed with suitable words, symbols or grimaces, a pointing gesture can be intimidating to the recipient.

The reciprocal motion of pointing is asymmetric. The thrust forward has more concentrated power than the withdrawal. It can be compared with a civil engineer's piling hammer, when the great weight is hauled to the design height and released by a slip catch. At the moment of impact the kinetic energy possessed by the hammer is proportional to its mass times the square of its velocity.

Asymmetric reciprocal motion is common in electronics: rapid charge and slow discharge of a condensor is fundamental to oscillatory circuits. In another context it becomes syncopation and *swing*.

182

Electromotion

Confirmation of the three dimensionality of localised space can be found in electromotion. When a length of wire is suspended in a magnetic field, the wire will move at right angles to the magnetic flux whenever an electric current is passed along it. A mnemonic for this phenomenon is to set the first and second fingers and thumb of the left hand at right angles to one another. If the first finger points from magnetic north to south and the second finger points in the direction of the electron flow, from negative to positive, then the thumb is the direction of the electromotive force.

It is this force that translates electricity into rotation in an electric motor. It is also this force that converts the motion of a turbine into the electrical output of a generator.

The left hand can also be used to demonstrate the magnetic flux surrounding a wire carrying a current. When the fingers are curled round the wire and the thumb points in the direction of the electron flow, the fingers will point in the direction of the current's magnetic field.

The flow of a magnetic field is taken from magnetic north pole to magnetic south pole. This means that the giant magnet that serves our earthly navigation has its south pole in the northern hemisphere and its north pole in the southern hemisphere. The Earth's magnetic flux is, therefore, from Antartica to the Arctic and a compass needle aligns itself with this.

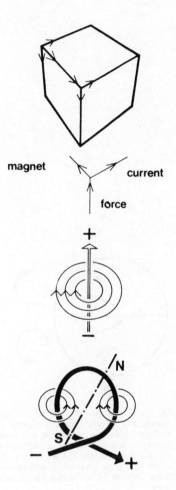

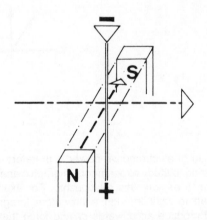

Coiling the wire into a loop permits directional flow of the magnetic flux through the loop. When the suitably insulated conductor is wound round a rod of soft iron it forms a bar magnet.

183

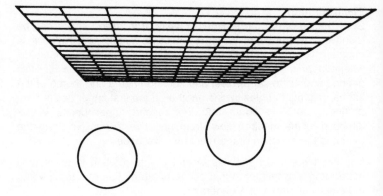

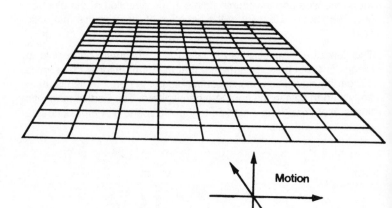

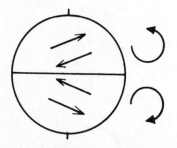

On Earth, the westerly winds that blow against the sun are aggressive, whilst the easterly trade winds are warmer and kinder. In the northern hemisphere, a bad weather cyclone has a centre of low pressure that sucks air at ground level in an anticlockwise spiral, to form its *eye* into a right handed helix.

These patterns are associated with the Coriolis force that expresses the Earth's rotation. A maximum velocity at the equator reduces to a theoretical nil at the poles.

An average hurricane disperses the energy equivalent of about 10 000 atom bombs.

The aggressive anticlockwise spiral is a common phenomenon in the northern hemisphere. It can be used to encourage competition on a racecourse and, by inversion, to reduce aggression in public places.

The triad of electromotive power is therefore asymmetric. It will be interesting to study experiments in graphic and theatrical design that attempt to explore this relationship. For example, an energy flow from left to right through a flow from foreground to background should produce an upwards driving force that becomes diagonally anticlockwise.

184

Emotional spirals

The emotional content of a spiral is expressed through a combination of at least two properties: is it opening or closing, slowly or rapidly?

A spiral opening clockwise is happy and optimistic.
A spiral opening anticlockwise is aggressive.
A spiral closing clockwise is going to sleep.
A spiral closing anticlockwise is in pain.

Similar principles apply to helices:
A right handed helix, moving forward, is anticlockwise and aggressive.
A right handed helix, moving away, is the departure of a friend.
A left handed helix, moving forward, can be a jolly challenge to a dance.
A left handed helix, moving away, is a vanquished enemy.

In all cases the movements are assumed to be continuous. The introduction of *epicyclic* forms can augment or suppress the emotive content.

A useful mnemonic reminds us that movement with the heavens is passive; movement against the sun and the moon and the stars is aggressive and/or courageous!

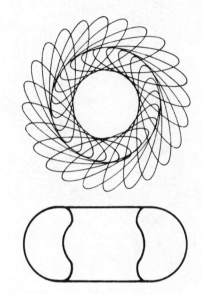

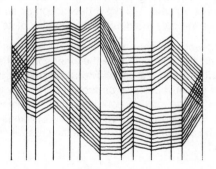

The ends of a helix can be joined to form a continuous ring or torus. If each revolution of the helix slips inside its neighbour a beautiful form emerges, common in nature, with a section approximating to the above drawing. Mechanically, it has great flexibility, malleability and elasticity.

Bottom left: The continuous linking of parallels can be used to suggest a third dimension.

185

10 On lines and edges

Hamlet: Do you see nothing there?
Queen: Nothing at all; yet all that is I see.

from *Hamlet, Prince of Denmark*, William Shakespeare

A line is a line in many ways.

It can be the mind's abstraction for an edge, a crack, a fissure or a chain of *dimensionless* points, linking their extremities.

How long is a piece of string?
As long as it takes to get from one end to the other!

A line can be the contour, the silhouette, of a series of magnitudes such that the mind may run over them, as Descartes required, until they are entirely memorable. The line then becomes the envelope of a series of events.

It is the trace of a moving point; a record of its passing, to guide and ease subsequent trips and become firmly established with use.

But, although in its twisting and turning a line may circumscribe an area and even a volume, it is not a description or an experience of them. It can define only the quantity and quality of its journey.

A means of describing area and volume by line was mentioned in Chapter 9. The struggle to explore the inner space of their materials has driven sculptors to dig deep. The ageing Rodin hacked with a scalpel at the sensitive, sinewy perfection of his clay figures. Gabo, Moore and Hepworth took sections and punched holes to get at the space within. Architects have reduced their buildings to glass clad skeletons in the search for space . . . but the creative challenge is far from resolved.

The location of the perimeter of a square can be described by continuous lines.

186

A line is a path that can offer an interesting and varied journey; rhythmic and with occasional, pleasurable surprises. Thus is one tempted to take the journey again. This is as true for a line of music by Mozart or Gershwin as for the skyline of Salisbury Cathedral or the Taj Mahal. It is absolutely vital to the sales of a popular car, a hi-fi radio, a camera or an evening dress. From the hand of a Toulouse-Lautrec, a Michelangelo or a Picasso, a line becomes a poem of infinite sensitivity with a bitter-sweet irony inflected by compassion and love.

The human eye, which is but an extention of the fingertips, enjoys travelling not only along a line but also between two that provide an open roadway. In its journeying the eye needs guidance and will reject ambiguity as a form of dazzle. Therefore, the line seeks direction and magnitude at each brief episode of the journey. If it is to take the eye with it, the line becomes a series of vectors. They can vary in length, weight and continuity, but their direction should never be in doubt, if they are to maintain a co-ordinated space and time.

The artist goes first. Before him lies a dark, trackless, formless, chaotic field, which he probes with the antennae of his techniques and ideas, seeking by his action to transform it into pure presence.

Designs based upon *interpenetration studies* by Paul Klee.

187

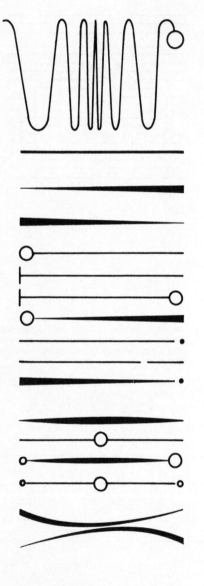

The charging of lines

A uniform straight line is ambiguous. The eye can move in either direction and seeks a greater concentration of energy at one end of the line. The eye moves towards the thicker, heavier end of a graduated line.

If the line wriggles or curves then the movement is towards the tighter curves. The line can be *charged* by setting one form of energy against another: one end against the other, one length against another.

Stress in the centre of a line fixes the eye and is an irritant. This can be countered by applying energy nodes to the ends of the line, forming a triad that will then require a hierarchy.

A discontinuity in the line, involving a jump, attracts the eye and has energy. This can be used as a *full stop* . . . charging both the line and the dot.

Lines can acquire emotional attitudes such as elegance, determination, anger, fatigue, tension, kindness.

Harmonic lines

Simple harmony occurs when an event is supported, strengthened or echoed by others. Harmonic lines are most commonly in two forms:

(1) *Parallels* that may be straight, or curves of similar radius, concentric curves or mixtures of these.
(2) Straight or curved lines that *radiate* from a common centre, but do not necessarily pass through it.

And combinations of these.

One opposing or discordant curve in a set can deter rotation and suggest a clasping, a containment of area that contradicts the radiation.

To be harmonic, simple radiating curves should be of the same hand. Complex curves need to share parallelism or radiation through part of their length. Some traditional theses require that they be tangential (in fact or promise).

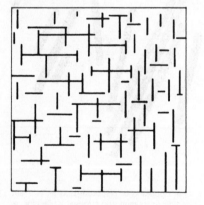

A transition in hierarchy of opposing vertical and horizontal lines developed by Mondrian, in about 1915 (detail of major composition).

Linear discord

Maximum linear discord is achieved when lines cross at right angles. The eye is held and the point is static. The resulting cross is an hypnotic. In its upright form it represents the vertical thrust of life across sedimentary layers of earthly matter. Mondrian and his colleagues in de Stijl considered this discord to be the ultimate concord and spacial equilibrium.

Opposing lines – the cross

A vertical line is highly energetic in its defiance of gravity. Its physical attributes are shared visually. More energy is needed to move the eye vertically than horizontally. It is more difficult for man to look up than to look down. He respects, *looks up to*, objects placed on a pedestal . . . but only within limits! A line stretching beyond the range of his vision, above or below him, becomes a fearsome thing – at its worst when curving over and behind him.

A horizontal line is calm and secure. We are accustomed to the infinite length of the horizon all about us. Even when it is hidden from view, we *know* it is there, securing the plane on which we act our lives.

It is the withdrawal of this assurance that contributes to the widespread dissatisfaction with home life in a tower block. If the blocks were truly large, as Corb originally envisaged them, then they could become honeycombed hills. Their vast horizontal planes of activity could then provide a substitute horizon.

190

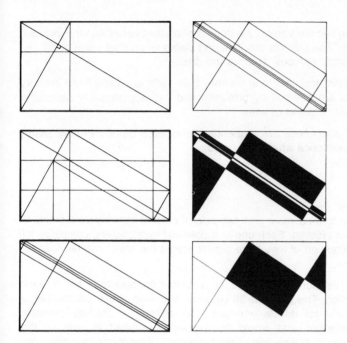

When the right angular cross is in the *diagonal* position, with two lines in conflicting 45° slopes, it becomes the most combative linear symbol available to us . . . like crossed bayonets. It is the grid for a scene of battle, whether it be the *Rout of San Romano* by Uccello or *Guernica* by Picasso.

Whereas both vertical and horizontal lines have stability, sloping lines are in a state of change from one condition to the other. They are dynamic and stressful, needing props or ties to gain a semblance of equilibrium. Lines can thus represent the cycle of growth, fulfilment, decay, death, rebirth . . .

In summary: horizontal lines represent repose, calm, eternity, security, the material of earth.
Vertical lines represent presence, life, man, God, potential and (sometimes) kinetic energy, dreams and aspirations.
Sloping lines suggest movement, change, kinetic energy.

Rectangles whirling on a master diagonal.

A vigour of random needles.

191

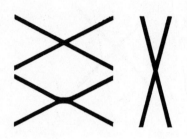

When two lines cross, the degree of discord varies with the included angle. The clash is absolute and stable when they cross at 90°. As the angle reduces, so does the discord.

As lines approach one another their form is inflected. All sensory forms are affected by proximity and this is particularly noticeable amidst networks of lines.

Only when lines are perpendicular to each other can they assert independence when they cross.

Grids

When formed into a grid, two sets of parallel lines create a series of similar crosses. Each one is a potential hypnotic and competes for the attention. If they have similar voices the effect can be dazzling unless:

(a) The number of lines is restricted to about seven in each direction. This provides 36 squares, and even at this low number, a potential for dazzle emerges. The 16 central squares compete for attention and would be happier if reduced to nine by the elimination of one line in each direction. This tends to confirm the findings of psychologists who report an optimum memory faculty for five items in any one dimension.

Painters have been consistent throughout the ages by dividing their canvases into nine areas. Three by three is the minimum rhythmic

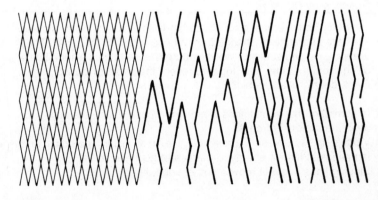

192

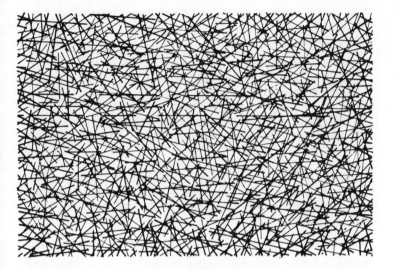

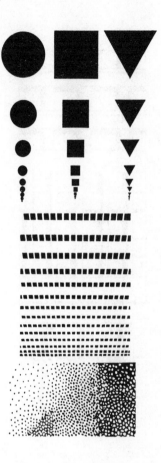

The essential character of a grid is retained to fine focal limits.

subdivision of an area. It is also the most versatile structure on which to build complex graphic detailing.

(b) If the number of lines per set becomes *plenty*, dazzle will certainly arise unless a method of grouping or pattern is introduced into the grid. This requires the introduction of patterning into the grid (see Chapter 2).

(c) If the grid is taken just beyond *plenty* into *multitude* a network establishes a positive, negotiable *space*. It becomes a special measure. Therein lies the popularity of tiled and wood block floors, the patterns of architectural fabrics and fenestrations.

(d) Deeper into multitude the grid becomes *texture*. But textures vary in quality, from deeply to finely etched, rounded to jagged, course to smooth, and seek to be brought into rhythmic, scalar relationship with larger, sculptural elements.

The concrete finishes of buildings, for example exposed aggregates or fluting, can affect the apparent scale at short distances, beyond which the texture is lost into the surface *colour*. These distances vary with lighting and climate, the character (sharp or smooth edges) of the aggregate, its colour and the degree of weathering.

Size of exposed aggregate		Distance from viewer	
50–35 mm	2–1½ inch	40 metres	125 feet
35–25	1½–1	30	100
25–20	1–¾	25	75
20–12	¾–½	15	50
12– 6	½–¼	10	30

193

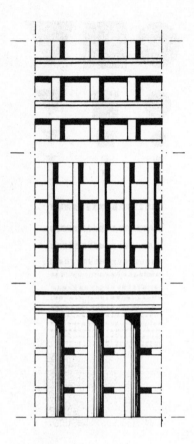

The dazzle effect of grids can be subdued by establishing a hierarchy of one set of parallels over another. This can be achieved in many ways:

(1) by differing frequencies and wavelengths in the two sets
(2) by differing rhythmic groupings so that one set of parallels is more energetic than the other
(3) by *flexing* one set of parallels more than the other. Architecturally this can be achieved by chamfering, softening or rounding one set of edges. Graduated chamfers can convert a set of lines into vectors.

Hierarchy in a grid is most readily achieved by superimposing one set of parallels over the other. This suggests the third dimension, depth. The lines now represent the leading edges of receding planes that can cast shadows.

Normally the leading set will be in harder focus than the rear set.

A reversal of focus can be exciting. The leading set can be rounded into a near cylindrical section while the rear set retains hard edges. When used as a counterchange this is the columnated classical tradition.

Recently, photographers have discovered, via the zoom lens, the aesthetic possibilities of putting a distant object into hard focus while the foreground is fuzzy. Memorable examples can be found in films such as *Butch Cassidy and the Sundance Kid* and *Lawrence of Arabia*. The latter film also exploited the effects of atmosphere on visual distance.

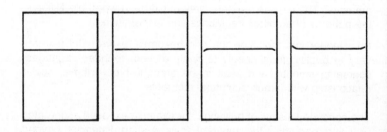

The dazzle of a grid can be alleviated by weaving, permitting parallels to alternate in domination. Tartan patterns and plaids are applications of this theme.

When lines cross, focus upon the near line throws the far line out of focus in the immediate vicinity of the cross. This has led to the legitimate graphic device of *breaking* the further line as it passes behind the near line.

A simple proof is to cross the first fingers of your two hands, one at 30 inch range, the other at 15 inches. It is not possible to focus upon both simultaneously. This observation leads to a common visual problem arising in painting when a line in the background is brought hard up to the edge of a foreground object. The works of the masters have usually lost background lines, most times by diffusion, as they pass behind foreground incidents.

A crossing of curved lines softens the hypnotic. The four quadrants are no longer symmetrical.

Eliminating one limb of a cross, the remaining effect is of one line butting against another. If the junction is right angular, movement is arrested; the point is static unless other stresses are introduced. The need for a hierarchy is essential, particularly if such junctions occur near the edge of a design. In a good painting, an horizon line butting the vertical edges of a canvas would be lost into the atmosphere and probably turned slightly downwards at the ends. Apart from losing the hypnotics, the end curvature (what a transport engineer might call a *filter road*) can suggest the positive robustness of the earth swelling *beyond* the frame.

Upwards curvature at the ends is reminiscent of liquid in a glass.

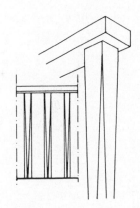

A graduated chamfer can convert a linear element into a vector, having magnitude and direction.

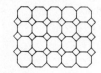 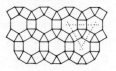

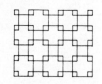 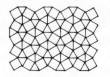 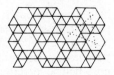

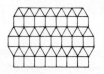

 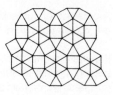

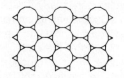 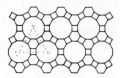

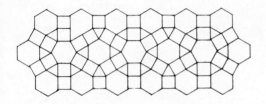

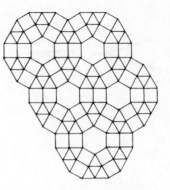

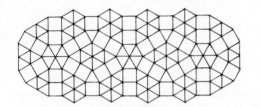

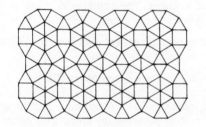

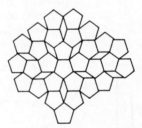

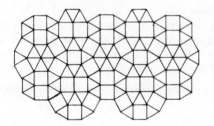

The triangle, rectangle and hexagon form the only regular tessellations suitable for development into space grids of uniform thickness, as discussed in Chapter 13.

Of these, the planar hexagonal grid cannot fold.

Many semi-regular grids have been discovered, a few of which are shown.

Areas of shapes, based on unit side length are:

Square: 1.00000 triangle: 0.43301
hexagon: 2.59808 octagon: 4.8284
duodecagon: 11.19615

The square based grid at bottom left uses pentominoes: simply connected sets of five squares.

The pentagonal grid, bottom right, is attributed to Dürer.

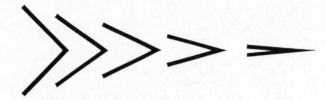

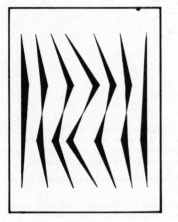

Arrows

Half of a right angular cross is a corner, an arrow. Attention is drawn along both lines to the point of juncture with sufficient energy for the eye to jump an interval to a target. The optimum distance of the target depends upon the energy of the arrow.

The velocity induced by arrows is dependent mainly on the angle of juncture; there are fast arrows and slow arrows.

Arrows have a sensory effect only when a target is offered.

The conventional arrow symbol signifies the existence of a target. It is disappointing, therefore, to experience an arrow that points at nothing and nowhere.

A series of arrows becoming progressively tighter increases the velocity. A series that becomes looser slows the movement. Arrows provide a second linear means of expressing movement, and therefore the passage of time upon a canvas.

The properties of an arrow can be enhanced or reduced by ancilliary lines or dots.

Arrows can point up to heaven or down into hell.

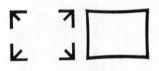

Arrows occur at the corners of polygons and tend to make the sides seem concave. It is a problem that applies throughout viseo-tactile design and is discussed in Chapter 14.

The arrow and its target should differ, with a clearly established hierarchy of sensory weight.

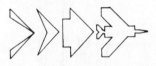

Graduated lines can strengthen or weaken an arrow. Closure of the arrow to form a triangle transforms it into a symbol. A symbolic arrow can function only if it has a target, explicit or implicit.

At what stage does a graduated line become an elongated triangle? When the overall dimensions have a ratio exceeding 7:1. The critical ratio varies with local conditions.

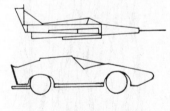

The arrow, expressed as a *wedge* form, can minimise turbulence and drag in supersonic flight and in automobiles travelling beyond about 75 mph (120 km per hour). The wedge also happens to be erotically fashionable at this time.

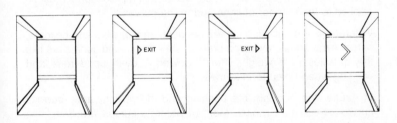

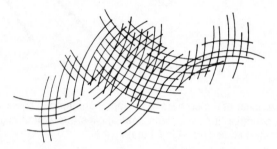

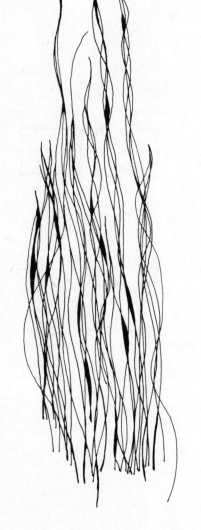

Emotive curves

A straight line can be defined as a curve of *infinite* or very large radius. Mathematicians find it useful to assume that a tiny part of the circumference of a large circle can be regarded as straight. Perhaps this is why straight lines do not suggest movement along their length as effectively as slightly curved lines.

When the complete line has only one curve in it, it is a *simply curved* line. If it curves in positive and negative directions it is a *compound curve*.

Fast compound curves are most effective when hierarchic and interweaving, apparently at random but with avoidance of competing energy centres. In other words, careful grouping procedures must be applied to the number of lines and to the curves.

Whereas fast compound curves suggest smoke, silks and delicate, tenuous traceries drawn by a breeze, slow compound curves are like the muscles of a weight lifter – powerful, even ponderous and writhing when taken to extremes.

In nature, the packing, the pushing and the pulling rarely permits curves of constant radius. Most of nature's curves are *bent*, like bending a length of brass rod for use as a ruler. The curves approximate to hyperbolae and incorporate the principles of *transition curves* discussed in Chapter 8.

200

A group of too many curved lines, without the structural rigidity of straights, tends to become sweet and sentimental. Many aesthetes have insisted that the essence of drawing lies in the relationship between compound curves and straights. It was an awareness of this contrast that led to the Cubists' interest in the violin and the guitar as plastic forms around 1910.

Hogarth devised a *line of beauty* that has an uncanny similarity to a woman's back! Delacroix based his combative, romantic works on the compound curve. He recognised the vigour that these imparted to the works of Rubens and Veronese. John Ruskin, writer and art critic, champion of Turner and the Pre-Raphaelites, also favoured the reverse curve.

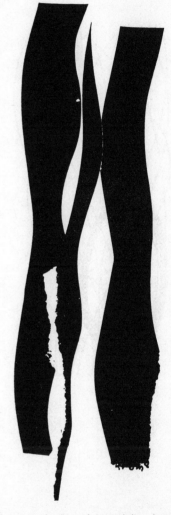

The romantic 'line of beauty' has been associated with curvature of a woman's back and is an asymmetric reverse curve.

The guitar outline evolved into the classic profile of Picasso's middle and late periods.

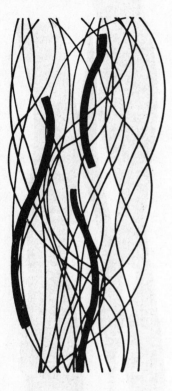

Art Nouveau offered an ambiguous space invaded by interactive, complex, flame-like curves.

Art Nouveau

Such flourishes evolved into Art Nouveau in the 1890s, which, in its search for new sensory experience, contributed to the emergence of the art forms of the twentieth century. In Art Nouveau the movement, the flow, the rhythm of a design became pre-eminent. The sinuous yet elegant complex curve was decorative yet was charged with tension and emotion: to such extent that at its best Art Nouveau assumed an organic quality. Henri van de Velde, the movement's leading theorist, believed that ornamentation and functional forms should appear *so intimate that the ornament seems to have determined the form*.

A prime mover of Art Nouveau was A. H. Mackmurdo, but so were many famous artists – from Aubrey Beardsley, book illustrator, to Henri Guimard, designer of Paris Métro stations; from the glassware of Louis Conford Tiffany to the architecture of Antoni Gaudi and early Frank Lloyd Wright – that any list of them is likely to be incomplete.

202

Du Cubisme

Du Cubisme, by Gleizes and Metzinger, was published in 1912. This manifesto proclaimed:

What the straight line is to the curve the warm tone is to the cold in the domain of colour.

It was with such proclamations that the Cubists confirmed our lurch into the twentieth century and confronted us with the sometimes harsh realities that are alternative to the Renaissance view of mankind and certainly far removed from the *elegances* of Art Nouveau, Tiffany's, the Moulin Rouge and the Paris Métro. Even so, they are not unrelated . . .

Above left: Curvilinear structure of *Zombor* (1949–53) by Victor Vasareley. Note the meticulous asymmetry of bent curves.

Top: A linear analysis of *Still life* (1920) by Juan Gris.

Above: Expanding perspective in a Mogul picture *c* 1585 (after Thouless).

The first phase of Cubism, about 1906, had rejected the traditional single point view of objects in order to explore their structure, both internal and external. Influenced by Cézanne, early Cubists such as Picasso and Braque recognised a continuity of space and found that initially this required a rejection of the continuity of line associated with Art Nouveau. The penetration of total space required fragmentation of the object and its environment and the adoption of superimposed multiviews, translucency and transparency.

High or analytical Cubism, the second stage, lasted from 1909 to 1912. To permit absolute fidelity to the fragmentisation process, texture and surface colour were largely excluded from the paintings.

Late or synthetic Cubism (1912–1914) continues with variations today. Tactile qualities, colour and personal *handling* were reintroduced, incorporating collage and the bringing together of disparate materials for emotionally provocative purposes, and encouraging the innovation of individual forms of symbolism.

Orphic Cubism originated in 1912 to exploit the emotional, musical qualities of colour. Cubism was used as a vehicle for the laws of simultaneous contrast of colour, derived from Chevreul via Gauguin, Van Gogh, the Symbolists and the *Fauves*, by Robert and Sonia Delaunay. At an early stage the Delaunays recognised the importance of juxtaposing curved and straight lines of colour, a quality taken to maturity by Matisse.

Purism

Après le Cubisme, published by Le Corbusier and Ozenfant in 1918, accused the Cubists of turning to mere decoration. Purism was to be unsullied by ornament, fantasy or individuality and was to be inspired by the machine. Its severity was echoed by parallel opinion in the Netherlands (de Stijl) and Germany (the Bauhaus) and its most famous painter in France was Fernand Léger. Its widespread influence in architecture has linked it with a joyless form of economic and technological *functionalism* that was not the intent of its originators. The works of Léger and Corb have, on occasion, a great deal of fun in them.

At their most severe, Purism and its allies virtually eliminated modulation and transition curves from their works. Linear elements were largely restricted to the straight edges and radius curves that symbolised machines.

Schemata of *Violin and Pitcher* (1910) by Georges Braque.

204

The quality of a line

An important property of line is its texture and resolution. It can be consistently hard like the cutting edge of hardened steel, or it can offer the irridescence of tulle draped into a soft light.

Firm and decisive edges belong to rocks, crystals and the mechanisms of man. Intermittent, soft, broken, variable and dotted lines suggest the cylindrical, conical and ellipsoidal forms of living organisms.

If a cube is sidelit and viewed against a neutral background, its vertical edges can be seen in sharp relief. A cylinder viewed under similar circumstances will reveal edges that are *soft* as they turn away from the observer. The quality of edges, and therefore the lines that express them, is conditioned by the manner in which a surface retreats from the observer.

An edge expresses a change of spacial quality from one density to another. The change need not be abrupt. In fact, most living creatures prefer a transition zone of bark, moss, hair, fur or clothes. Many examples of ornamentation in the arts are functional in this way. The elaborate carving and tiling that *clothes* most traditional architectural forms; the row of badges and lamps that decorate the grille of an enthusiast's motorcar; the roses and shrubs in front of a suburban house; all act as buffer zones between differing activity spaces.

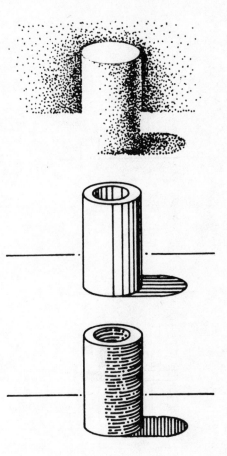

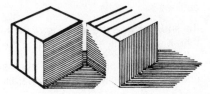

When parallel lines are closely hatched the eye prefers to assume that light flows along them. Therefore a form is softened by hatching, fluting or texture that wraps round it and is hardened by lines that run lengthwise.

The interrelationship of planes is affected by the direction of the hatching. The eye can read the lower cylinder as standing in a pool of water!

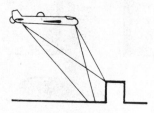

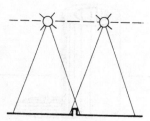

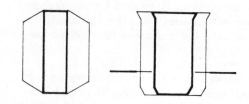

Use of parallax in synchronised photographs and radar to reveal the height of objects on the ground was developed during World War II.

The principle is currently used by one camera taking timed exposures from an orbiting space satellite.

The view of a matchbox held close to the viewer's nose gave a clue to the multiple vision of Cubism and Futurism.

Allowing for parallax, the weaving pattern above needs wider gaps either side of the verticals.

Parallax

Our attitude towards edges is affected by our binary form. We have two hands, two ears, two eyes, two nostrils. To fully comprehend space we need stereoscopic touch, hearing and vision. Nowadays we are all conversant with the effects of multispeaker audio transmissions. The principles of parallax apply in all senses. When examining a sculptural form, a symmetrical examination of opposite sides by left and right hands simultaneously is more informative than a single handed action. The embracing stereoscopic action gives a truer measure of volume, mass and space.

The translation of bifocal vision to design upon a canvas was a major concern of Cézanne. He realised that we can see more than half way round a small cylinder and that three views are available: that of the right eye, that of the left eye and the total sensation, giving three outlines.

If a line, perhaps the far edge of the table, passes behind a beaker, then it will be only semi-evident in the proximity of the beaker.

Since most people have their eyes set side by side, only vertical edges are normally affected by parallax.

Parallax, both visual and tactile, reinforces the feeling that verticality is more vibrant, more assertive, more claspable than horizontality.

This probably explains why little children favour *tall* animals, that they have never seen in reality, to animals that slither and scuffle across the ground. Giraffes and upstanding bears are more popular than snakes, rats and spiders.

Linear analysis of *Navigable Space* (1954) by Singier.

A teenager. Note the slender hips and plump legs.

11 A geometry of curves

Past, considered as receding back
established in the view point present
from mutually conceptual planes projects
an undreamed future that awaits ahead.
As pale projections on retinal film
spring new found reason from forgotten form
so seen are things beyond us to construe
the very fabric of a higher skill
perceiving through reflecting all as will.

from 'Kaleidoscope', Christopher Ryan

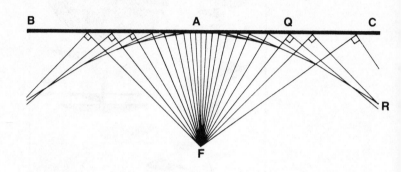

A geometry of curves has evolved from attempts to solve the spacial problems of engineers, architects and astronomers in terms of the physical, sensory and emotional properties of lines. Historically it has been convenient to explore them as an evolution from the works of Euclid.

In Chapter 5 the equation for a straight line was given as: $y = mx + c$ where m is the slope and c is the point where the line cuts the y axis

The parabola

The Cartesian equation for a horizontal parabola is usually given as $y^2 = 4ax$, where the vertex of the parabola passes through the origin and the curve has *one-fold symmetry* about the positive x axis. Distance a locates the focus of the parabola on the x axis.

The parabola has the important property of reflecting to its focus all lines parallel to the x axis. A paraboloid can be used therefore as a mirror in telescopes to focus a maximum of light from a distant star or galaxy at a viewing point that can be some ten metres or more above the mirror.

Conversely a parabolic mirror can be used behind a spotlight to project a parallel beam from a point source of energy.

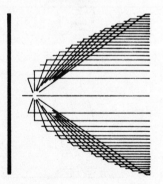

208

To draw a parabola

Draw a straight line *BAC* and mark focus *F* a right angular distance from *A*.

Place a set square *PQR* such that right angle *Q* rests on *AB* and side *PQ* passes through *F*.

Draw line *QR*. Repeat the exercise with *Q* in many positions on *AB*. The overlap of the series of lines *QR* forms the *envelope* of the parabola. *A* is the vertex and *F* is the focus.

To draw a parabola with an included angle exceeding 140°, draw two straight lines and mark on each a series of equal intervals. The second series need not be equal to the first. Number them in sequence 1, 2, 3 etc, left to right on each line. Join corresponding numbers to form an *envelope*.

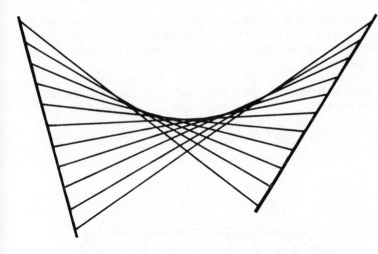

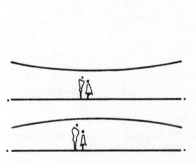

A parabola is the locus of a point that moves such that it is equidistant from a fixed point, the focus, and a straight line, the directrix.

At any location of the parabola *PM* = *PF*.

209

U.D.L.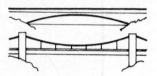

B.M. Dia

Properties of a parabola

All parabolas are similar. Focal length a determines the *magnitude*.
The simplest Cartesian equation is $y^2 = 4\,ax$.
The polar equation is $2a = r(1 - \cos\theta)$.
The area bounded by a parabola is two-thirds of the rectangle having the same base and height.
It is the form assumed by a hanging chain under a uniformly distributed load, UDL. Compare with the catenary.

The cable of a suspension bridge can be considered as parabolic when the horizontally distributed applied load greatly exceeds the self-weight per unit length of cable. It is the bending moment diagram for a simply supported beam under UDL. Thus:

$$M \text{ at any point} = \frac{wx}{2}(l - x) \text{ and}$$

$$\text{maximum } M \text{ at mid span} = \frac{wl^2}{8}$$

Inverting the situation, a shell can be paraboloid when the applied (live) load greatly exceeds the self weight and is distributed *horizontally*.

The parabola is the section of a right circular cone on a plane parallel to the slope of the cone. The name *parabola*, meaning equal, derives from the work of Appollonius (circa 250 BC). Translated into Cartesian terms:

the parabola is $\qquad y^2 = 4\,ax \qquad\qquad$ (equal)
the hyperbola is $\qquad y^2 = 4\,ax + px^2 \qquad$ (throwing beyond)
the ellipse is $\qquad\ \ y^2 = 4\,ax - px^2 \qquad$ (falling short)

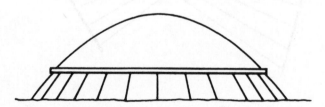

The curvature of a ceiling can render a space introvert or extrovert.

UDL on a simply supported beam gives a parabolic bending moment diagram.

Conic sections: circle
ellipses
parabola
hyperbola

The quadratic equation, $y = ax^2$, can be plotted to form a parabola symmetrical about the y axis. The vertex passes through O and the focus is on the y axis at $a/4$.

If the equation is completed to $y = ax^2 + bx + c$ the function $(bx + c)$ moves the parabola about the grid. Similarly a family of vertical parabolas is of the form $y = ax^n$, where n is an even number.

Algebraically, quadratic equations can be solved by the formula:

$$\text{Let } y = ax^2 + bx + c = O \quad \text{then}$$

$$x = \frac{-b \pm \sqrt{(b^2 - 4ac)}}{2a}$$

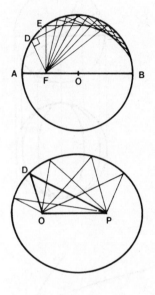

To draw an ellipse

Draw a circle, centre O and a diameter AOB. Let F be any point on AO.
To any point D on the circumference of the circle draw FD.
Using a set square, project the right angle FDG such that DG is a chord of the circle. Repeat for different positions of D.
The envelope of DG will be an ellipse.

AOB is the major axis of the ellipse. The minor axis passes through O at right angles to AOB.
The nearer F is to A, the narrower the ellipse.

The ratio of OF to OA is known as the *eccentricity*. Conventional symbols are used such that $OA = a$ and $OF = ae$.
The point F is one of two foci possessed by the ellipse.
For a circle eccentricity $e = O$.

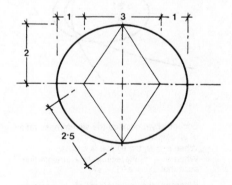

To draw an ellipse using a length of string, tie the string, length $= 2a(1 + e)$, into a continuous loop.

Fix pins at distance $2ae$ apart; these become the foci. Drop the loop of string over the pins, draw it taut to form a triangle with a pencil point. Keeping the string tight, draw the pencil around the foci.

If the two foci of an ellipse are points O and P, and D is any point on the circumference, then $OD + PD$ is a constant for that ellipse.

The circle is a special case of the ellipse, when the two foci are coincident.

The 53° 9′ ellipse is of special interest, related to the φ series. It exhibits the dimensions shown:
the axes have the ratio 5:4;
the eccentricity is 3:5;
$OD + PD = m + n = 5$.

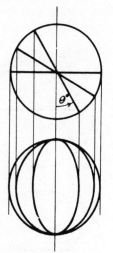

A circle may be considered as an ellipse that is seen *full frontal*, at right angles to the central visual ray of the eye, the *CVR*. As the circle is turned from the frontal plane 75°, 60°, 45° etc to the *CVR* so its minor axis becomes shorter.

Ellipses can thus be referenced in terms of their angle $\theta°$ of tilt to the *CVR*. At 0° the circle is seen edge on, as a straight line; at 90° it registers as a circle.

If the major axis is 2a, then the minor axis = 2a sin θ.

Properties of an ellipse
The Cartesian equation, origin at centre, is

$$\left(\frac{x}{a}\right)^2 + \left(\frac{y}{b}\right)^2 = 1$$

The polar equation is

$$\frac{l}{r} = 1 + e \cos \theta, \text{ where } l = a(1 - e^2)$$

The eccentricity e is less than 1.
The area $= \pi ab$, where a and b are the semi-axes.

The ellipse is a section of a right circular cone by a plane cutting at a slope less than the slope of the cone.

It is the orthogonal projection of a circle onto a plane inclined to its own plane. From a point outside the ellipse two tangents can be drawn, and they subtend equal angles at a focus.

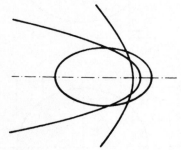

Eccentricity e decides the slenderness ratio of an ellipse.
When $e = 0$, the ellipse is circular.
When $e = 1$, the ellipse is a straight line, such that: $b^2 = a^2(1 - e^2)$.

Whereas the extremities of a parabola become parallel to its major axis, the asymptotes of a hyperbola cross one another. The axes of an ellipse are at right angles.

Desargues's Theorem for the projection of a triangle can be extended to the circumscribing ellipse.

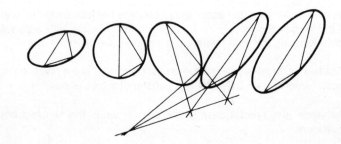

The five centred arch

The five centred arch can approximate to an ellipse. Given the major axis *AB* and the minor semi-axis *CD*, complete the rectangle *ACDE* and draw its diagonal *AD*.

EO is at right angles to *AD*, locating *O* on the vertical axis *DC* extended.

EO cuts *AC* at *X*.

Y is any point within triangle *XCO* such that *XY* = *YO*.

X, *Y* and *O* are centres of three circles.

Repeat for the other side of the arch.

Kepler published his discovery of the elliptical orbits of planets in 1609. The eccentricities of planetary orbits are small: the Earth about 1/60; Mercury about 1/5; Mars about 1/11; and Pluto about 1/4. Halley's comet has an eccentricity of about 0.9675 permitting it to visit us every 76 years. A majority of comets have either parabolic or hyperbolic orbits.

The Earth is an ellipsoid, probably due to its rotation. The equatorial diameter exceeds the polar diameter by 26 miles. This gives an eccentricity of 1/12 approximately.

Kepler found that the velocity of a planet varies such that the area swept by its arc in a given time is a constant.

Members of the solar system revolve about their common centre of gravity. This is dominated by the enormous mass of its central star, the Sun, as compared with its planets. Even so, their various masses, velocities and distances cause minor fluctuations in their paths.

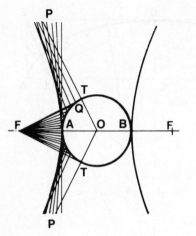

To draw a hyperbola

Draw a circle with diameter *AOB*. Mark any point *F* on *BOA* produced.

Using a set square, select any point on the circle *Q* and draw the right angle *FQP*, external to the circle.

Repeat for many positions of *Q*.

The envelope of lines *QP* will be a hyperbola. *AOB* is called the transverse axis and the complete hyperbola is symmetrical, with two foci, equidistant from *O*.

The distance of a focus from *O* compared with the radius of the circle is called the eccentricity *e*; *e* for a hyperbola exceeds 1.

If *OA* = *a*, then *OF* = *ae*.

The above drawing will reveal a limiting position for *Q*, at *T*. *FT* is tangential to the circle and *PT* extended passes through *O*. *PTO* extended is an asymptote of both halves of the hyperbola.

The slope of the asymptote to the transverse axis is such that:

$$\sec FOT = e.$$

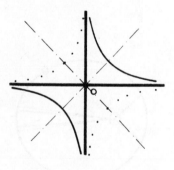

The rectangular hyperbola

If $e = \sqrt{2}$ the asymptotes are at right angles and the curve is called a rectangular hyperbola. The Cartesian equation is:

$$x^2 - y^2 = a^2$$

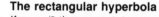

With the asymptotes as axes, the Cartesian equation becomes:

$$2xy = a^2 \quad \text{or} \quad y = \frac{a^2}{2x}$$

occupying the first and third quadrants.

A series of rectangles of equal area based on the origin *O* of a Cartesian grid have a hyperbola as their envelope. In each case, area *A* = *xy* hence

$$y = \frac{A}{x}$$

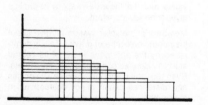

214

The difference of the focal distances is a constant. Whereas in an ellipse $m + n$ = constant, in a hyperbola $m - n$ = constant.

The growth relationships of m and n are in AP. As one grows the other grows in direct proportion. This property can be employed as a method of drawing a hyperbola.

A hyperbolic mirror will reflect light from a point source at focus F so that it is dispersed from focus F_1.

Alternatively a hyperbolic mirror can gather data from a distribution focused at F_1 and reflect them to F.

This property has given the hyperbola an important role in radar and radio communications generally.

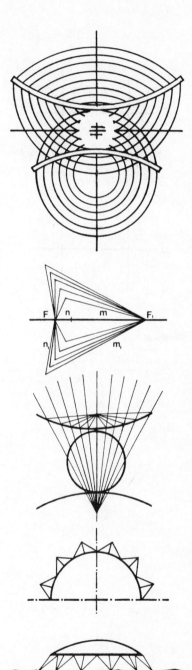

Properties of a hyperbola

The Cartesian equation is

$$\left(\frac{x}{2}\right)^2 - \left(\frac{y}{b}\right)^2 = 1$$

Using x and y axes as asymptotes, the Cartesian equation is $2xy = a^2$.

The polar equation, pole at focus, is

$$\frac{l}{r} = 1 + e \cos \theta$$

where $l = a(e^2 - 1)$

The hyperbola is a section of a right circular, double cone having a steeper slope than the cone.

It is the envelope of a series of parallelograms of equal area and sharing two sides.

Energy radiating from one focus is reflected by a hyperbola as if to radiate from the other focus.

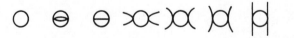

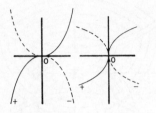

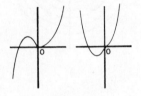

Graphs of
$y = ax^3$ $y^3 = ax$
$y = ax^3 + bx^2$ $y = ax^4 + bx^3$

The cubic curve

A cubic curve is a compound curve passing through O. Its Cartesian equation is $y = ax^3$ or $y = ax^5$ or $y = ax^m$ where m is an odd number.

Similarly vertical parabolas are of the form $y = ax^n$ where n is an even number.

At the point of contraflexion, at O, the cubic curve is horizontal. Its two halves are asymmetric and cannot be folded to be superimposed without first turning one of them over.

The negative curve $y = -ax^3$ has the opposing slope. Reversing the axes reverses the curvature:

$$y^3 = ax$$

The addition of parabolic and cubic curves

When a cubic curve is added to a parabola the resultant curve will depend upon which *order* is higher, odd or even.

The curve of $y = ax^3 + bx^2$ will give a cubic curve with a pronounced s form near the origin.

The curve of $y = ax^4 + bx^3 + cx^2$ will give an essentially parabolic form with a *ripple* appearing near the vertex.

In all cases the addition of a straight line component $(px + q)$ would serve to move the curve about the grid.

Roulettes

Of the many curves that have been explored by mathematicians, the roulettes are formed by a curve rolling along another, fixed curve and are fundamental to mechanics. The *cycloids* have been mentioned.

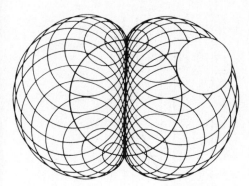

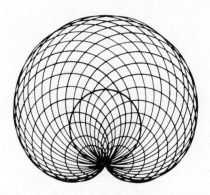

The conchoid

A curve of great interest to Ancient Greeks, and used to provide entasis in their columns was the conchoid.

To draw a *conchoid of a straight line*:
Select a point A that is not on the straight line.
Select a straight edge BCD that is bisected at C.
Place BCD so that it passes through A and cuts the fixed straight line at C.
Slide BCD along to trace relative movements of B and D, while the straight edge always passes through A and cuts the fixed straight line at C.

Three cases of the conchoid arise: with the fixed distance less than, equal to or greater than the distance of A from the fixed line.

Other forms of the conchoid are based upon fixed curves that are not straight. The *limacon* is a conchoid of a circle. If the fixed distance equals the radius of the circle, it becomes a *cardioid*.

It is possible to draw conchoids of the ellipse, hyperbola, parabola and other curves.

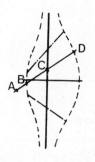

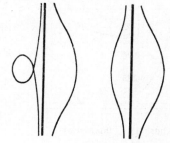

The nephroid; the cardioid; the conchoid

217

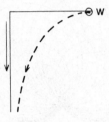

If a string is attached to load W which is free to slide without interference, then movement of the string in the direction of the arrow will cause W to describe a tractrix.

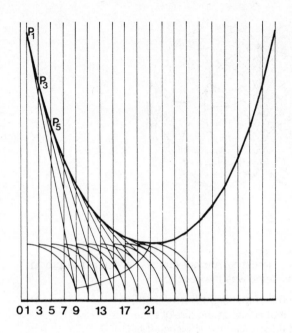

0 1 3 5 7 9   13   17   21

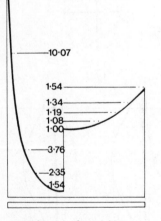

y = cosh x ,   from tables

A catenary can be constructed from table of $y = \cosh x$.

To draw a catenary and tractrix

Mark equal intervals upon a baseline and number them 0, 1, 2, etc.
Erect verticals upon the odd numbers, 1, 3, 5, 7, etc.
With points 0, 2, 4 etc, as centres draw quadrants of circles with radius = 9.
Let P_1 be the top of the catenary, on vertical line number 1.
From P_1 draw a tangent to circle centre 2, at T_2.
Where this tangent P_1T_2 cuts vertical number 3, mark P_3.
From P_3 draw a tangent to circle centre 4, at T_4.
The points P_1, P_3, P_5, etc, will lie approximately on a catenary.

The catenary is the evolute of the *tractrix*.
To draw the tractrix, draw the tangent to circle centre O, from P_1 to find T_0.
Join T_0, T_2, T_4, etc, to obtain an approximate tractrix.

Continue to find points T_6, P_7, T_8, P_9, etc until the tractrix and catenary meet. This locates the vertex of both tractrix and catenary and their vertical axis of symmetry can be erected.

The right hand half of each curve can be drawn as a mirror image.

218

Properties of a catenary

Length of arc of a catenary: let the length of arc from P_1 to the vertex $= s$, then

$$s = \sqrt{(y^2 - c^2)}$$

where c is height of the vertex above the baseline.

The Cartesian equation is $y = c \cosh(x/c)$. This means that a catenary can be obtained by plotting the values of hyperbolic cosines obtained from tables.

$$s = c \sinh(x/c) \qquad y^2 = s^2 + c^2$$

A catenary is the locus of the focus of a parabola as it rolls on a straight line.
It is the evolute of a tractrix.
It is the form of a uniform chain hanging under its self-weight.

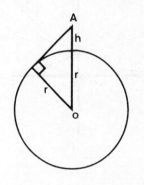

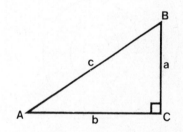

Trigonometrical ratios

The trigonometrical ratios sine, cosine and tangent were used by Hipparchus during the second century BC to calculate the diameter of the Earth and the distance of the Moon with amazing accuracy: 7900 and 238 000 miles respectively.

There is evidence that the Babylonians were using sine tables, recorded in cuneiform symbols on clay tablets, long before Hipparchus.

In any triangle ABC, right angled at C

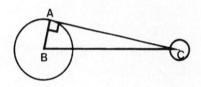

$$\text{Sine } A = \frac{BC}{AB} = \frac{a}{c} = \frac{\text{side opposite angle } A}{\text{hypotenuse}} = \frac{1}{\text{cosec } A}$$

$$\text{Cosine } A = \frac{AC}{AB} = \frac{b}{c} = \frac{\text{side adjacent to angle } A}{\text{hypotenuse}} = \frac{1}{\text{sec } A}$$

$$\text{Tangent } A = \frac{BC}{AC} = \frac{a}{b} = \frac{\text{side opposite angle } A}{\text{side adjacent angle } A} = \frac{1}{\text{cot } A}$$

These can be plotted as Cartesian graphs as described in Chapter 4.

In angular measure 1 rev $= 2\pi$ radians $= 360° = 400$ gradians.

The principles used by Hipparchus were:

To climb a mountain of known height and measure the angle between the horizon and the vertical.

Then $\sin A = r/(r + h)$, giving the Earth's radius r.

He established a system for locating points on the Earth's surface similar to our latitude and longitude.

To find the distance BC between the centres of the Earth and Moon, $\cos B = AB/BC$ where B is the latitude.

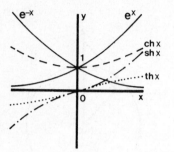

Hyberbolic trigonometrical ratios

Whereas $\sin \theta$, $\cos \theta$ and $\tan \theta$ are projected from a circle, $\sinh \theta$, $\cosh \theta$ and $\tanh \theta$ are based upon a hyperbola.

$$\cosh x = \text{ch } x \text{ (abbreviation)} = \frac{e^x + e^{-x}}{2}$$

$$\sinh x = \text{sh } x = \text{shine } x = \frac{e^x - e^{-x}}{2}$$

$$\tanh x = \text{th } x = \text{than } x = \frac{\text{sh } x}{\text{ch } x} = \frac{e^x - e^{-x}}{e^x + e^{-x}}$$

$$= \frac{1 - e^{-2x}}{1 + e^{-2x}}$$

Hyperbolic functions are commonly used in *kinetics* :eg, the speed of waves in water over a shallow bottom is given by:

$$V^2 = 1.8 L \, th \left(\frac{6.3d}{L} \right)$$

where V is velocity in knots and L is the wavelength in feet.

The equiangular spiral can be related to the tractrix. If four dogs are stationed at the four corners of a square and released such that A chases B, while B chases C, C pursues D and D follows A, the path of each dog will describe an equiangular spiral. In these curves the tangent at any point makes a constant angle with the radius drawn to that point from a fixed point.

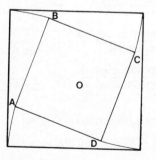

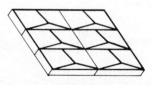

The equiangular spiral can be related to the tractrix.

220

The hyperbolic paraboloid

The *hyperbolic paraboloid* can be formed from an array of parallel rods, resting equidistant on a horizontal plane to form a square. Their midpoints should be fixed and hinged along their central axis so that they can be rotated at equal intervals into the form of a helix. Thus, on a square plan *ABCD, corners B* and *D* rise above corners *A* and *C* and the plan view becomes rhombic. Positive curvature of edges can be trimmed away, if necessary, to give straight edges in plan.

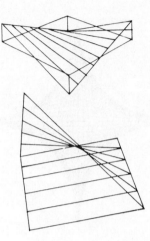

The surface curves in two directions to form the hyperbolic paraboloid, with a positive parabolic section in one diagonal of the rhombus and a negative parabola in the other. A horizontal slice through the shell will reveal a hyperbola.

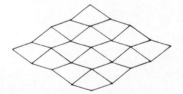

It will be found that a second set of parallel rods, at right angles to the first group, can overlay them. However the second helix will have the opposing hand to the first helix. Thus a construction can be in laminated form, helix upon helix, to produce a very rigid, lightweight, integral shell of invaluable use to architects.

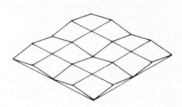

Hyperbolic paraboloids can be grouped to form undulating shells that present a continuous waveform.

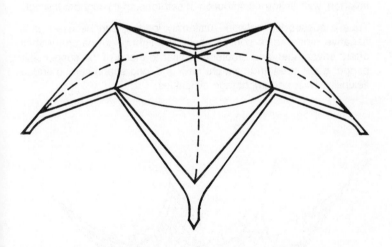

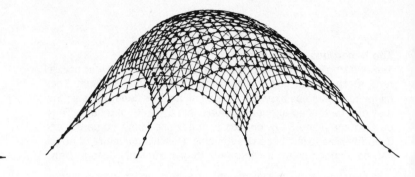

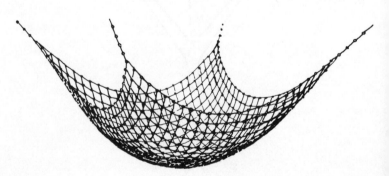

The astroid can be a graphic representation of interrelated hyperbolic paraboloids.

Shells

Shell structures can be formed from *catenaries*.

A condition of the catenary is that the force in the hanging chain be a constant when the uniformly distributed load is per unit length of the chain. The distribution of loading can continue to obey these conditions when chains are suitably linked to form a hanging network in three dimensions. These may be simple or complex, forming *saddles* when intermediate chains are shortened.

If the chains are converted to rods, theoretically the system can be inverted, with uniform distribution of self-loading throughout the net.

Thus a suspended network, uniformly loaded, can be used as a negative model for a convex shell. The lightweight catenary shell offers advantages and problems similar to those of the suspension bridge: good strength to weight ratio and long spans versus undue flexibility, twist and anchorage difficulties.

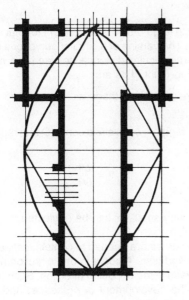

The Vesica piscis

On the diameter of a circle an equilateral triangle is described centrally such that its apex just touches the circumference. The height of the triangle therefore equals the radius of the circle and its sidelength is 1.155 r. Using this as radius, circular arcs are drawn from the apex through the other corners of the triangle to produce the form of a *fish*. This was a mystical word in Ancient Greece under which Christ was later denominated. The *Vesica piscis* became an important emotional symbol and also a practical geometrician's tool throughout Gothic architecture, sculpture and painting.

The intersection of two similar circles about an equilateral triangle became the Greek symbol for justice. This, in turn became a basic geometry for the pointed gothic arch.

By approximating $\sqrt{3}$ to 1.75, the magic number 7 could be invoked. The equilateral triangle already proclaimed the magic of 3.

Placing a square or a cross upon the circle increased the geometric possibilities. These are under renewed scrutiny, in our own day, by Vasareley.

Geodesic shells are discussed in Chapter 12.

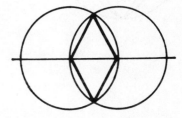

Above left: Schematic plan of New College Chapel, Oxford.

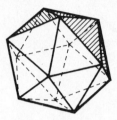

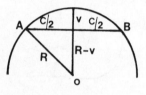

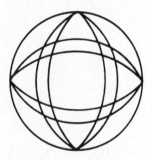

The versine

When dealing with large radii it is convenient to refer to them in terms of their versines. The versine of a circular curve for a known length of chord is the perpendicular distance between the mid-point of the chord and the mid-point of its arc.

These can be related by Pythagoras' Theorem for a right angled triangle.

Given chord AB, length $=c$, on circle centre O and radius R, to find the versine, v:

$$v = \frac{c^2}{8R}$$

Note: when v is very small, v^2 can be neglected.

Complementary curves are needed to contain, define and stabilise a particular space and time. A curve in one direction needs balancing by a curve or curves in the opposing direction. Such an equilibrium is a first stage in the development of *presence*, and can be readily observed in living organisms.

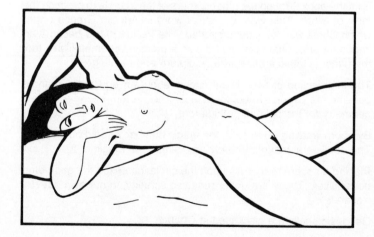

Right: Linear structure of a painting by Modigliani, 1917.

224

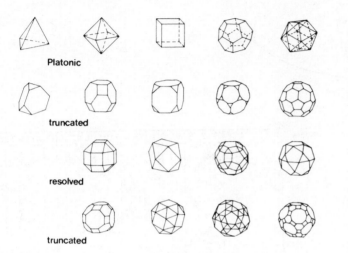

Platonic

truncated

resolved

truncated

12 A geometry of solids

Nature, that framed us of four elements,
Warring within our breasts for regiment,
Doth teach us all to have aspiring minds.
Our souls, whose faculties can comprehend
The wondrous architecture of the world,
And measure every wandering planet's course,
Still climbing after knowledge infinite,
And always moving as the restless spheres,
Will us to wear ourselves and never rest,
Until we reach the ripest fruit of all

      Tamburlaine the Great (Part One), Christopher Marlowe

The five Platonic and 13 Archimedean solids.

Early models of the cosmos were based on concentric spheres (they still are in most minds). Platonic cosmology contained elements: Tetrahedron – fire; Octahedron – air; Icosahedron – water; Cube – Earth; Dodecahedron – ether.

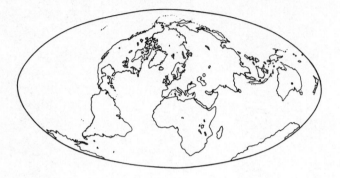

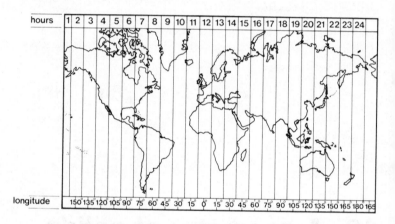

Top: Bartholomew's 'Nordic' projection gives the Antipodes half the scale of the North Polar Basin. If the scales were equal the projection would be Cartesian.

Above right: The international time zones, reviewed in June 1962 for the *Times Atlas of the World*, uses a Mercator projection.

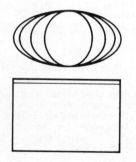

Stereographic drawings

Some of geometry's greatest advances have followed attempts to solve the problems of navigators.

Stereographic drawings translate the surfaces of solids onto a two dimensional plane, some form of charting. Two projections are well known.

The *Cartesian projection*, narrowing towards the poles, is practical for detailing and is used in most coastal and ordnance surveys.

The *Mercator projection* gives a popular, rectilinear picture of the Earth's surface but grossly exaggerates dimensions near the poles. Canada looks as big or bigger than Africa, which is not correct. On a Mercator projection, Great Circle routes appear as curves.

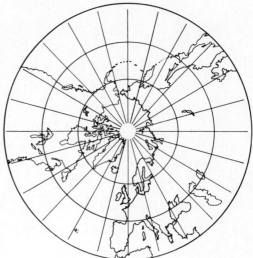

More recently, in an age of man-made satellites, the *polar stereographic projection* and the *equatorial stereographic projection* have become important. By comparing photographs obtained on slightly different orbits or times, the topography of the body is revealed.

As mentioned in Chapter 10 under 'Parallax', the techniques perfected during the 1939–45 War for taking synchronous photographs are now performed automatically by satellites.

Futurism

Effects of parallax have influenced the work of many twentieth century artists.

Between 1909 and 1915, the Futurists, an Italian group who exhibited in Paris, were inspired by moving pictures. They recognised the staccato slicing of time, at so many frames per second, as an aggressive *march of mechanisation*.

In 1909, Marinetti, the writer, announced 'a new beauty, a roaring motor car, which runs like a machine gun'.

In 1910 they issued two manifestos: 'We wish to represent machines or figures actually in motion ... movement or light destroy the substance of objects.'

The best Futurist works went deeper into the human paradox than these early statements imply. By 1911, Umberto Boccioni who was dead by 1916, was grappling with the emotions of modern life; the impact and anxieties of living in the stroboscopic uncertainties of a mechanised urban environment.

Although Futurism succumbed to the ravages of the First World War and its surviving adherents were later to be put to flight by Mussolini, many of its observations and its leading artists, such as Severini, Picabia, Boccioni and Balla continue to inspire the main stream of modern art.

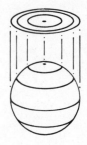

Gnomonic projection (limited polar stereographic) of the North Polar Basin.

Equatorial and polar projections.

227

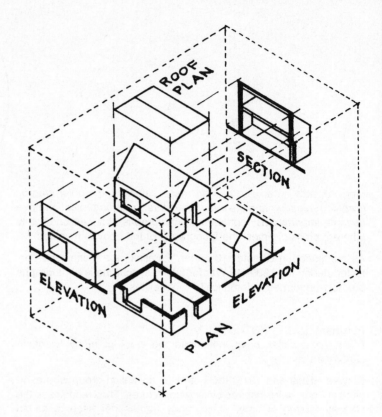

Orthographic projections

Orthographic projections are right angled views ideally suited to the study of everyday objects.

The object can be sited within an imaginary transparent cube, offering six possible views on the axes of three dimensional space. The views are taken from *infinity* and translated onto each intervening face of the cube.

In architecture, the *worm's eye view* is rarely required. The master drawing is usually the ground floor plan, taken as a *section* at one metre height. It is the roof plan that would form the conventional orthographic projection onto the top of the transparent cube.

Elevations and vertical sections are treated similarly. The observer's line of sight is perpendicular to the plane of the cube and, therefore, all planes parallel to the drawing surface are represented without foreshortening or distortion. They are two dimensionally true to scale.

228

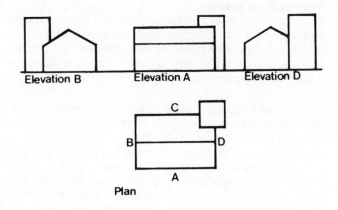

Elevation B **Elevation A** **Elevation D**

C

B D

A

Plan

Paraline drawings

Paraline drawings are useful because most people find them easy to understand, while their axonometric lines (lines parallel to the x, y and z axes) are *true to scale*.

Their construction suggests a three dimensional *depth*. But this does not diminish with distance and can be optically disconcerting if long lines are involved. Non-axonometric lines may not be true to scale. This varies from one method to another.

The *isometric* projection gives equal emphasis to all three dimensions, which are orientated at 120° intervals. Non-axonometric lines are *not* true to scale. *No* areas or shapes are true to scale.

Plan oblique projections provide a *plan true to scale*, with plan axes at 90°. Verticals are erected from the plan to provide vertical surfaces that are not true to scale.

A *45° plan oblique* projection is sometimes referred to as an *axonometric projection*.

Although a plan oblique projection can be set at any angle to the horizontal, the other common form is 60°, 30°.

Elevation oblique projection is uncommon. A vertical plane remains parallel to the drawing surface and is true to scale. The third dimension is taken at a paraline angle to the horizontal. It usually needs scaling down visually.

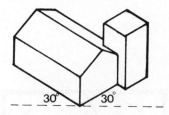

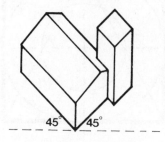

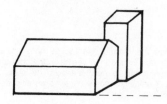

229

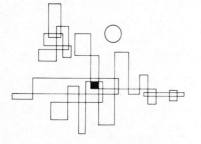

Geometric perspective

Perspective, the visual effect of distance, was first expressed in cave drawings. Early man observed that things appear to get smaller and to climb up the picture plane. As civilisation evolved painters noted that near objects can overlap distant objects. Overlapping remains a major tool of the designer as a means of establishing hierarchy.

There is evidence to suggest that by the time of Euclid these observations were occurring in a *cone of vision*. Certainly recent excavations at Pompeii reveal that the Romans made use of vanishing points. The earliest recorded study of modern optics was produced by Alhazen, an Islamic geometer of circa 1000 AD. A translation of his book appears in the Vatican library, annotated by Lorenzo Ghiberti. The development of geometric perspective during the Renaissance in fifteenth century Italy is credited to the architect Brunelleschi. Further contributions by Alberti, Masaccio, Uccello, Piero della Francesca and Dürer developed it into an instrument capable, in the visual arts, of freezing time. A specific point of view of a space, in a fleeting moment of time, could be held in utter stillness.

The subsequent evolution of geometric perspective in Europe has been devoted to means by which this property could be used and adapted to suggest movement and change: by the introduction of multiple points of view and interlocking spaces; by the concentration and diffusion of light and light sources; by the Impressionist fragmentisation of surfaces.

The basic assumption of *geometric perspective* is that although parallel lines never meet, they appear to do so at a *vanishing point*, on a distant backcloth.

The vanishing points for horizontal lines are located upon the horizon.

Until Cézanne decided to *realise his sensations*, geometric perspective sometimes presented a one-eyed view of the world, for the basic theory requires that the observer closes one eye.

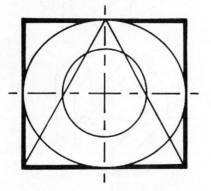

Since the human eye moves horizontally with less fatigue than vertically, the cone of vision tends to be flattened. The classic $\sqrt{3}:2$ rectangle nicely contains an elliptical backcloth.

230

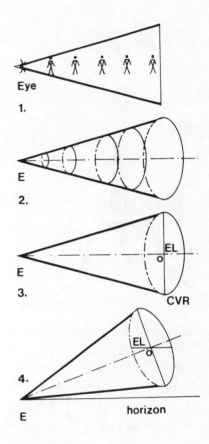

Eye

1.

E

2.

E

3.

EL
o

CVR

EL
o

4.

E

horizon

The cone of vision

The cone of vision is assumed to be right regular. Its major axis is the central visual ray, CVR, the centre line along which the eye is focused. The cone can be sliced lengthwise by two planes at right angles, offering a vertical-horizontal cross like a gunsight to the eye. The horizontal plane is *eye level*. The vertical plane is referred to, incorrectly, as the CVR: it should be the *central vertical plane*. These correspond visually with *x* and *y* axes in general geometry.

If the gaze is directed upwards or downwards, eye level will not coincide with the horizon.

The assumption that straight lines remain straight is not seriously incorrect if the internal angle of the cone is restricted to 30°. In practice it is enlarged to 60° and obvious distortions around the fringes of the work are *adjusted* by eye.

Parallels to the CVR meet at origin *O* in the familiar railway line effect. A depth scale can be devised by directing diagonals of a receding series of squares to VPd (vanishing point for diagonals). The squares are seen to diminish in GP.

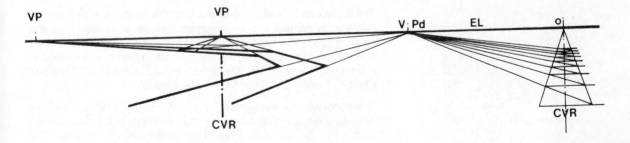

VP

VP

V Pd   EL   O

CVR

CVR

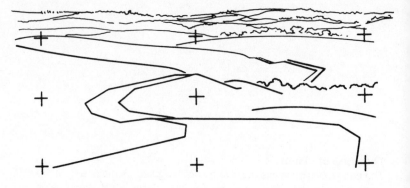

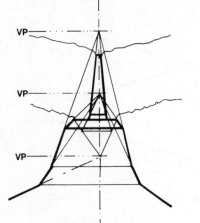

VP

VP

VP

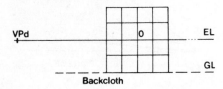

VPd | O | EL
| | GL

Backcloth

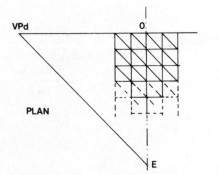

VPd

O

PLAN

E

Gradients in perspective

The railway slopes uphill when its VP or vanishing point is moved above eye level; for a downhill slope the VP falls below eye level, EL. For left and right movements the VP must move to left and right of the CVR.

A set of nine VP's can suffice to permit the representation of a winding, even helical path.

The short lengths of straight lines thus produced are vectors. These can be brought into continuous curves by freehand softening of the joints. This should not be overdone: *bent* lines emphasise the direction and structure of planes.

The geometric perspective box

The geometric perspective box created the stage upon which the great dramas of European painting, theatre, internal and external architecture and materialist thinking generally have evolved since the Renaissance.

The scale can be vast, embracing a mighty landscape, or it can be intimate, to contain a bowl of apples. Whatever its size, it is this *trapped* space that has fascinated both artists and scientists. It offers a stable, secure and finite universe to be explored by painters as emotionally diverse as Masaccio, Bellini, Hobbema, Vermeer, Claude, Turner, Cézanne, Monet and Picasso.

One observation is essential to the construction of a GP box and that is the location of the vanishing point for diagonals of the squared plan grid, VPd, on the eye level. This is conveniently simple. The observer's eye *E* on the CVR, and VPd, on the backcloth, are equidistant from origin *O*.

232

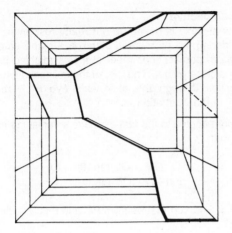

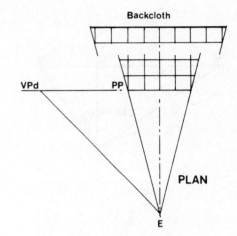

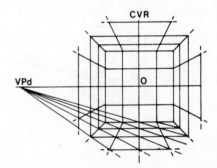

The method of projecting a geometric box forward from a backcloth is ideally suited to the exploration of *interiors*.

The great paintings of Europe since the Renaissance, even the major landscapes, have been conceived within a finite box. They are interiors, constrained by a rigid three dimensional matrix within which movement is permitted. Men of genius – Dante, Leonardo, Milton, Blake, Turner, Wagner, for example – have attempted to punch holes in the box or to replace it by a stack of boxes. However it is not until this twentieth century that variable space has become a conceptual reality (see Chapters 5 and 14).

Within the box it is possible to describe slopes and turns as numerical ratios, as tangents. The illustration shows a right handed square helix. A slope of one in two, with landings, is taken round the box.

An orthographic projection can be converted into a geometric perspective by inscribing the ground and roof plans on the bottom and top of the box respectively; and the left, right, fore and aft elevations on the vertical sides of the box.

Cross referencing within the box will circumscribe the geometric perspective view.

233

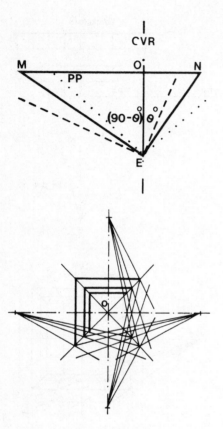

Two point perspective

Two point perspective is based on our ready response to the right angle. Considering the problem in plan (on a plane parallel to eye level) a series of parallel lines meet at their vanishing point on the backcloth (or picture plane). The VP_1 of these lines is located by the line that passes through the observer's eye E. It reaches the backcloth PP in the illustration at M.

Parallels at right angles to the first set have a vanishing point VP_2 at N. It follows that:

$$OM = OE \tan (90 - \theta)$$
$$\text{and } ON = OE \tan (\theta)$$

For example, if E is 100 metres from PP and θ is 33°, then:

$$OM = 100 \tan 57° = 154 \text{ m}$$
$$ON = 100 \tan 33° = 65 \text{ m}$$

Of course VP's can be found by projective geometry without calculations. Given the plan of a house, its VP's can be found simply by drawing parallels to its walls from E to the PP.

Vertical VP's can be found by similar calculations and projections.

The picture plane

Geometric perspective is based on similar triangles. Therefore the geometry is not affected if the picture plane (which receives the projection) is behind, intermediate to, or in front of the subject. Its position relative to E affects only the size of the projection.

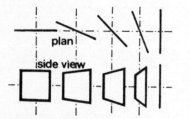

234

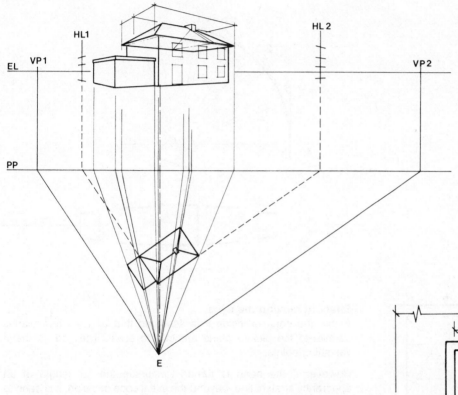

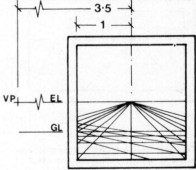

A single point view, without moving eye or head, restricts the vanishing point of diagonals of the square grid to a maximum range of 3.5:1.

Therefore a backcloth is restricted by the viewing frame.

Height lines

Height lines are a quick way of establishing a vertical scale. In plan, extend any vertical plane until it cuts the picture plane, PP. At that point, and that point only the vertical plane will be true to scale in the perspective drawing. A vertical scale, erected at that point, can be projected through the drawing by using the *VP* for the vertical plane. Such heights can then be *taken round* the drawing. Most drawings require only two height lines. One for working, the other as a check.

The finest check of all is: *Does it look convincing?*
Geometric perspective is an *approximation*, after all!

235

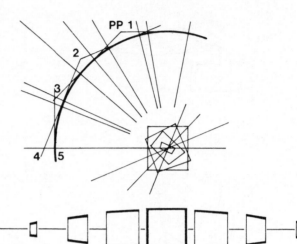

Top right: Restraints on the single point view show in plan and elevation the effect of rotating the head at 22½° intervals, horizontally.

Top: Effect of moving the head vertically.

Above: Introduction of two perspective boxes into the viewing frame suggests a panorama. This principle can be extended creatively (ref: Leonardo da Vinci, Turner, Cézanne, Cubism, late Monet).

Effect of moving the eyes

Within the cone of vision it is assumed that all lines and planes parallel to the picture plane are true to scale. They do not have vanishing points.

However if the head is turned to pursue the full length of an apparently straight line, beyond the initial cone of vision, it is seen to approximate to an ellipse, with a VP at each end.

Observation of this property led the masters of geometric perspective, such as Canaletto, Turner and Van Gogh, to use *positive curvature* to emphasise the spaciousness of their works.

A turn of the head or eyes turns the CVR. Rival visual boxes in a painting, building or landscape can thus be used to suggest spaciousness.

Vertical movement of the head reveals that a third VP, for parallel verticals within the cone of vision, is beneath one's feet. This series of squares is disquieting as it heads for the horizon unless it allows for the curvature of the Earth.

236

Three point perspective

If a cube is orientated so that three of its sides are viewed symmetrically, then three VP's will be equidistant. The diagram shows the limiting size of a cube to be viewed through a 60° cone. Gross distortion is present and, unless a *fish eye* view is required, the three point perspective should be restricted to a 30° cone.

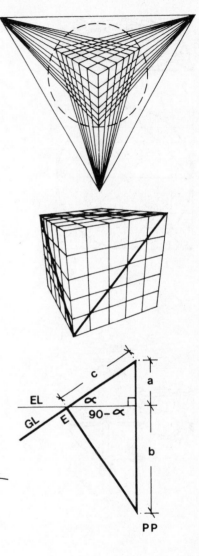

If one were gazing at the vertex of a tetrahedron, would the view be different?

Turning the eye reveals a different view through the cubic grid; the three point geometry is based upon a pyramid sliced from the corner of a cube.

A longitudinal section shows that the vertical distance between an horizon containing two of the VP's and eye level can be compared with the distance of the third VP below eye level.

If the angle between ground or datum level GL, and eye level EL is a, then

$$\frac{a}{b} = \frac{\tan a}{\tan (90 - a)}$$

therefore $c^2 = a(a + b)$

Three point geometric perspective can be constructed without resort to calculations. Several methods are available and can be found in any good book on perspective drawing. They must transfer a horizontal plan and height line to the sloping ground level, through the angle a.

237

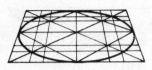

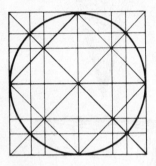

Curves in perspective

Geometric perspective is a vectorial process. Therefore all curves must be developed from a continuum of short straight lines, related to VP's by rectilinear grids.

Reflection as symmetry

Symmetry never ceases to fascinate the human being. A visual axis of symmetry is offered by a plane mirror; because light is reflected such that *the angle of incidence equals the angle of reflection*.

If an observer's eye is on the plane of reflection, perfect symmetry can be obtained. But that is theory! In practice the eye must be at least very slightly above the mirror plane to obtain a reflection. The resultant observation is asymmetric, but can be interpreted by association as symmetry in perspective.

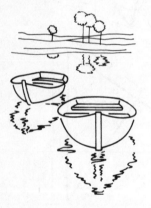

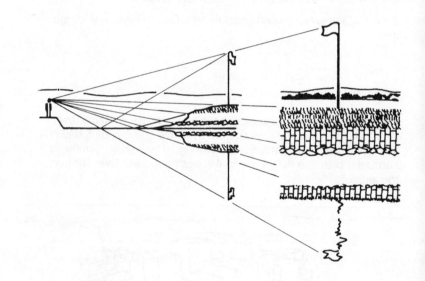

238

Sciagraphy

The art of shadow projection has evolved because our eyes work by recognising differences of lighting levels. We see, essentially, by comparing adjacent visual areas of value, or tone, reflectance, luminosity – quantities of energy per unit area: lux. Our basic vision is on the black-white scale through a series of greys.

Hues of the spectrum – red, orange, yellow, green, blue and purple – can be regarded as qualitative refinements to the quantitative black-grey-white scale. This is why a black and white television screen is satisfactory as a means of communication.

Sciagraphy has grown as a convention used by architects and engineers because it can be used to reveal detail in forms that might otherwise be lost in orthographic linear projections. Convention has it that the source of parallel rays of light is behind the observer's left shoulder at 45° to the x, y and z axes.

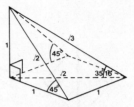

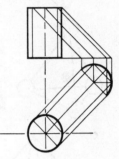

The Platonic solids

The Platonic solids, the tetrahedron, cube, octahedron, dodecahedron and icosahedron, were thought by Plato, the Athenian philosopher, to have universal significance.

They are completely regular solids: each has all of its faces repeating a regular polygon, triangle, square or pentagon.

They can be found by the close packing of similar spheres and are in two categories:

(1) The tetrahedron, cube and octahedron grow in succession, cycle after cycle, by each encasing its predecessor. The grid, made up of similar spheres, is a constant, no matter what the size of the solid. The packing is in AP.

(2) The dodecahedron and icosahedron alternate, one encasing the other, but the spheres must grow in size if they are to close pack. The initial icosahedron requires a void, representing the first term of a GP, at its centre. The packing is in GP.

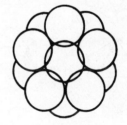

Top: Diagram of the resultant shadow projection at 45° to all three axes.

Centre: An orthographic projection of a vertical cylinder and its shadow.

Above: Initial packing of similar spheres to form Platonic solids.

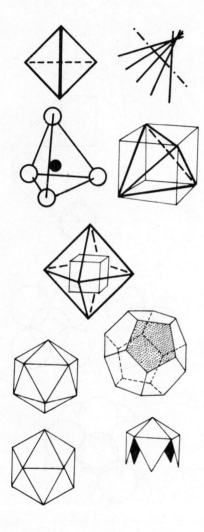

The *tetrahedron* has four faces, each an equilateral triangle. Resting on one face, an edge slopes at 54° 44′; a face slopes at 70° 32′.

Its full spacial beauty becomes evident when the leading edge is vertical and the remote edge is horizontal. The space between them is the third dimension.

If this third dimension is represented by a spine, a series of rods can rotate upon it, step by step, from the vertical to the horizontal. They form a helix. If it is not to be a positively charged convex curve, the intermediate rods need to be trimmed to form a straight edge.

The *cube*, clearly defining a three dimensional space, is the most readily comprehended of the Platonic solids. The tetrahedron is contained within the diagonals of its six faces. The vertexes of an octahedron are at midpoints of the faces of the cube.

The corners of an *octahedron* can be located by erecting a perpendicular, height equal to half the side length, on the midpoint of each face of a cube. The cross-section of an octahedron is a square, producing eight triangular faces.

The *dodecahedron* has 12 regular pentagonal faces. All the magic of the pentagon is transferred to this solid.

A group of six pentagons folds naturally to form a serrated hemisphere.

Each vertex can be regarded as a triangular pyramid with a base to edge ratio of φ. The angle subtended by a side at the centre of the circumscribing sphere is 41° 52′.

An *icosahedron* has 20 faces, each an equilateral triangle. It can be formed from the face-centres of the dodecahedron.

Both the dodecahedron and the icosahedron can be structured by rotating a φ rectangle about the centre.

A majority of materials in the Earth's crust are silicates with molecules comprising four oxygen atoms linked to one atom of silicon.

The pentagonal base of a pyramid formed by five equilateral triangles can be set upon each face of a dodecahedron to form a polyhedron of 60 faces. By further subdivision semi-regular solids of increasing variety can be devised. Alternatively, truncating the vertexes will produce the Archimedean solids.

The Archimedean solids

These 13 solids are formed by truncating, cutting off the vertexes, of the Platonic solids. The process can be repeated to produce complex patterns which introduce the regular hexagon and octagon to the faces. By Euler's Law for semi-regular solids: let V = number of vertexes; F = number of faces; and E = number of edges; then:

$$V + F = E + 2$$

Geodesic structures

The surfaces of regular and semi-regular solids lend themselves to *geodesic shells* in which all the vertexes touch the surface of a circumscribing sphere. A geodesic distance is the shortest between two points on the surface of a sphere. It is, therefore, the arc of a great circle, the plane of which passes through the centre of the sphere.

Geodesic shells have a repetivity of edges that is suitable for industrialisation or prefabrication of parts to form a lattice that is rigid and lightweight while offering equitable distribution of loading. It can be used at both small and large scale, in the construction of aircraft and in the architecture of their vast shelters, hangars, stadia and the like. The principles can be applied to ellipsoids, *sausage* forms, barrel vaults and rings such as the torus.

Buckminster Fuller has made a life-time study of geodesic domes. His books and publications are authoritative.

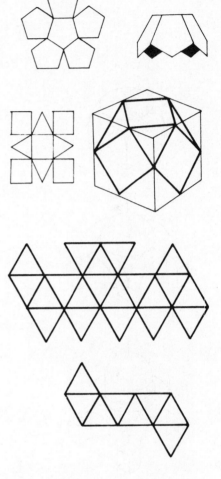

The cubeoctahedron, dodecahedron, icosahedron and various other semi and demi-regular solids have been used as models for geodesic domes.

Particular favourites are the truncated octahedron (dymaxion) using squares and hexagons, and the truncated icosahedron, using pentagons and hexagons (the international soccer ball).

Below: Surfaces of the icosahedron and the octahedron.

241

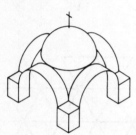

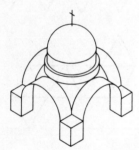

Pendentives

The problem of securing a round dome to a square plan was solved in Mesopotomia some 4000 years ago, using the spherical pendentive.

Geometrically, it is a segment of a sphere with radius equal to one half the diagonal of the square bay to be covered by the dome.

Later designs introduced *lanterns* under the dome and used ellipsoids, paraboloids and more complex curves.

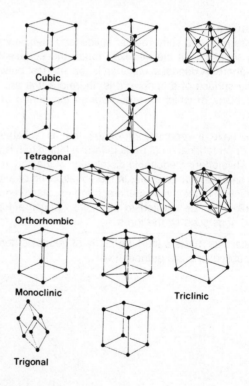

Bravais lattices.

242

Bravais lattices

Only 14 kinds of unit cell can form an extended regular lattice. In crystallography, each lattice point can accommodate more than a single atom. Despite the restraints of symmetry in the growth of crystals, a great variety of materials, using different groups of atoms and molecules, become possible. But all will conform to one of the 14 *master* lattices.

Crystal structures can be dislocated by sheer, fault or *edge dislocation* which involves the sliding of crystals along a sheer plane. They are also subject to *screw dislocation* and a mixture of the two, *mixed dislocation*.

Our observation of these, as recordings of the frozen energy of nature, can be highly emotive. Particularly when contrasted with the grindingly abrasive and ultimately polishing actions of ice, sea, wind and rain: nowhere better illustrated than in the works of Henry Moore.

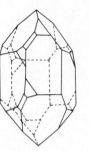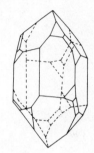

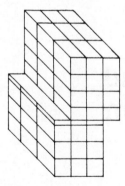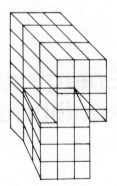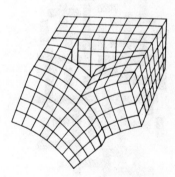

Top right: Right handed and left handed quartz crystals.

Edge, screw and mixed dislocations.

243

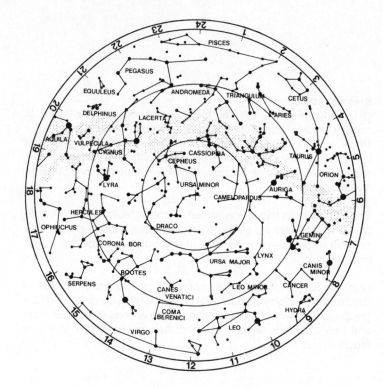

Polar projection of the northern hemisphere of the sky, centred close to the Pole Star.

Above: Vertical and horizontal composition from Theo Van Doesburg (1916).

13 Energy and equilibrium

The hidden harmony is better than the obvious.

Fragments, Heraclitus (*c* 500 BC)

The conservation of energy

Man assumes, and observes, balance in the universe. The conservation of energy postulates that no energy is lost and none is gained. It can be changed only from one form to another, one location to another, while its total remains a constant.

This law has been axiomatic in the evolution of the sciences. However the comparative ease with which energy can be transferred requires a neat balance of opposing forces if any object or event is to persist or acquire longevity.

Within the atom, for example, the number of protons is electrically balanced by the number of electrons. One for one. If a surfeit or deficiency of electrons occurs, the atom becomes electrically charged, negative and positive.

The character of an element is decided by the number of protons in its nucleus. Hydrogen has one, helium has two, carbon has six and lead has 82. The number of protons in the nucleus gives the atomic *number* of the element, which must necessarily be integer: 1, 2, 3, 4, 5, 6 to 92.

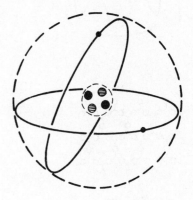

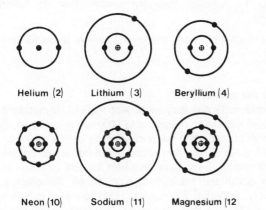

Helium (2)   Lithium (3)   Beryllium (4)

Neon (10)   Sodium (11)   Magnesium (12

The two orbiting electrons of the helium atom form a shell. The nucleus has two protons and two neutrons. The mass of the proton is 1836 times that of an electron, yet their electrical charges equate. The mass of a neutron slightly exceeds that of a proton and, when isolated, a neutron decays into a proton and a negative pion.

An electrically charged atom is known as an ion, positive or negative. The helium atom without its electrons is known as an *alpha* particle, and is therefore positively charged.

The diagrams show electron shells of six of the lighter elements. In elements with multiple electron orbits, the smallest orbits correspond with the lowest energy and these fill up first. The chemical character of an atom is chiefly determined by the number of electrons in the outermost shell.

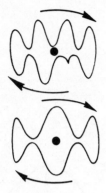

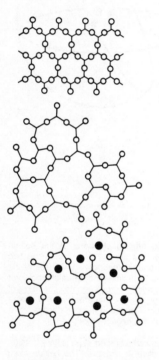

Top: Model of a two dimensional electron wave orbiting a nucleus of hydrogen. The first diagram is incorrect. The wave cannot be discontinuous.

Below: A graphical representation of:
The crystalline structure of silica.
The network structure of glassy silica.
Soda-silica glass.

Within the atom

Particles obey principles similar to magnetism; like poles repel, and unlike poles attract. Therefore protons normally repel one another.

Within the nucleus of a stable atom, the interproton repulsion is overwhelmed by *the strong nuclear force* that binds the protons firmly together with *neutrons*. The presence of neutrons explains why the atomic weights of elements do not correspond with their atomic numbers. The number of neutrons within the atomic nucleus of an element can vary, producing *isotopes*, for example, graphite, charcoal and diamond are isotopes of carbon. Each has six protons in its nucleus but the number of neutrons differs.

Every atom seeks equilibrium at the lowest energy level, giving off surplus energy as radiation. If it is positively charged electrically, it will seek electrons. If negative, it will gladly discharge electrons. But within the atom, the electrons must accept a hierarchy. By Pauli's exclusion principle in quantum theory:

No more than one electron in a given atom can have a given set of the four quantum numbers.

The quantum numbers represent energy levels. We may visualise them as wavelengths and orbits about a nucleus – with some similarity to a miniature solar system. Thus Pauli's principle ensures that each electron within the atom has *identity*, and status (see Chapter 1). Although they are similar, they are instantaneously different!

In a multi-electron atom, the lowest energy shells fill up first.

Within the nucleus

An atomic nucleus is very small; less than 10^{-15} metres in diameter. If an atom were to be magnified to 100 metres diameter, the size of a large concert hall, then the nucleus in its centre would be about the size of a grain of salt. The space of the hall would be defined by an electron cloud: the volume required for one or more electrons to revolve about the nucleus at high speed. An electron is never stationary. Although it occupies much space, it is very tiny. It has mass, but so little that the nucleus has some 99.99 per cent of the weight of an atom.

Nucleons are either protons or neutrons, locked together into a boiling cauldron that is the nucleus. The nucleons are whirling about within a sphere of only 10^{-15} m at 100 000 km per second. The proton has positive electrical charge, the neutron has none. Otherwise they are similar, although the neutron has slightly more mass. A neutron in a free state will decay in about ten minutes into a proton, after giving off one unit of negative electrical energy in the form of a negative pion.

The selection of elements described below is quite revealing. We can deduce that a nucleus of beryllium has four protons and five neutrons, iron has 26 protons and 30 neutrons, lead has 82 protons and an awful lot of neutrons.

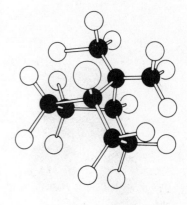

Element	Atomic number	Atomic weight	Melting point(°C)	Electron sub-shells				
				K		L		M
				1s	2s	2p	3s	...
Hydrogen	1	1.008	−259.2	1				
Helium	2	4.003	−270?	2				
Lithium	3	6.94	180.5	2	1			
Beryllium	4	9.01	1277	2	2			
Boron	5	10.81	2100	2	2	1		
Carbon (graphite)	6	12.01	3700	2	2	2		
Nitrogen	7	14.01	−210	2	2	3		
Oxygen	8	16.00	−219	2	2	4		
Calcium	20	40.08	838	2	2	6	2	...
Iron	26	55.847	1536	2	2	6	2	...
Lead	82	207.19	327.4	2	2	6	2	...
Uranium	92	238.03	3820	2	2	6	2	...

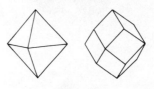

It is interesting to observe that hydrogen, oxygen, nitrogen and carbon, which are so important to life on Earth, are all of low atomic number. The high melting point of carbon may also be significant. As the surface of the primeval Earth cooled, carbon will have been one of the first elements to solidify. But, of course, its major service to us carbohydrates is its ability to link hydrogen, oxygen, nitrogen and trace elements into the complex molecules of earthly life.

This selection of elements also reveals the increase in atomic weight over atomic number. The atomic weight is a ratio quite distinct from the weight in grams.

Top: Model of carbohydrate.

Three natural crystal forms of diamond, which are lattices of carbon formed under great pressure.

247

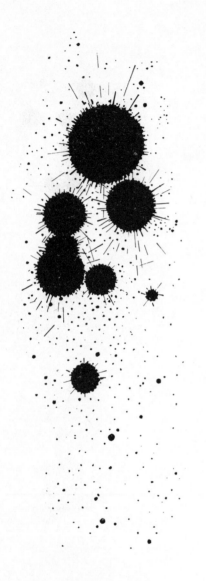

A search for symmetry

The principle of the conservation of energy implies balance in all interactions, from the largest at the intergalactic scale to the smallest at the elementary particle scale . . . with somewhere between them, the human scale.

To take a simple example: if we assume that the force of gravity permeates the whole material universe and that it is inversely proportional to the square of the distance between any two atoms anywhere, then two interesting propositions arise.

If the universe is homogeneous, then the long range forces in all directions balance out – by definition of homogeneity, they will be in equilibrium, forming a continuous forcefield or texture. Consequently only short range variations and perturbations in the field need be considered when studying the behaviour of a particle. The precise definition of short range will be conditional, in each study, upon the permissible tolerances.

The other proposition arising is that as two atoms touch, the gravitational force will maximise and crush them out of existence, unless the longe range weak gravitational forcefield is balanced by a strong short range repulsive force. Indeed such a force exists and permits atoms to assemble into molecules by sharing some of their electrons, while their nuclei have short range repulsion.

Observed on its larger scale the universe reveals a clustering of atoms to form stars, and of stars to form galaxies, it would not be unreasonable to anticipate the possibility of a clustering of galaxies. Sure enough, there is observational evidence of such clusters going back to the 11 000 nebular objects listed in J. L. E. Dreyer's *New General Catalogue*, in the 1890s, long before Hubble's discovery of their true nature. A typical rich galactic cluster appears to have three major components: galaxies, and a giant central galaxy and an enormous halo of hot gas studded with additional stars.

The bulk of the atoms in the universe is hydrogen. The hot stars radiate energy as this hydrogen is converted to helium in their nuclear furnaces. As stars cool, so the heavier elements are formed. The balance of forces is between implosive gravitation and explosive nuclear reaction. When nicely balanced, these forces permit the star a lifecycle as it radiates energy to finish as a lump of heavy elements.

248

If imbalance occurs, then the star may explode as a *supernova*, or implode to entrap its own radiation in a *black hole*.

Such an equilibrium of forces is *not* symmetry. On the other hand it is not chaos, and within the context of this essay it is regarded as *asymmetry* . . . a balance of dissimilar forces.

Symmetry

Symmetry requires mirror imagery, on the principle of the child's folded ink blots.

Folding is its essential property along an axis of symmetry so that the two halves make a perfect overlay. Thus a butterfly has one-fold symmetry.

Superficially, the human being has one-fold symmetry based upon duality. There are obvious functional advantages in the possession of two legs. Three would involve complex skeletal and muscular problems tending to impede rather than improve mobility. Although the kangaroo has a fast turn of speed on the plain, he is handicapped when climbing trees.

Similarly, we are two eyed, two handed, two eared. Yet the distribution of internal organs is asymmetric.

The eye seeks and recognises the singularity of a symmetrical pair.

249

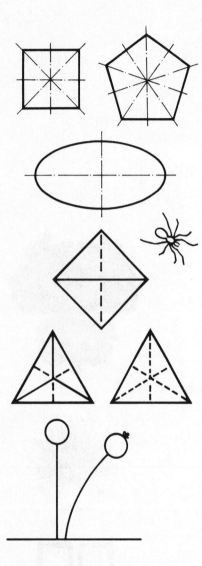

It seems that symmetry is a useful means of combating a dominant force, such as gravity. It is a unidimensional clasping, gripping of its own centre. Symmetry is therefore essentially introvert, egocentric, finite and independent: ideally suited to a palace, of creature or God.

It is reasonable to anticipate that wherever in this universe life evolves on the surface of a massive ellipsoid like the earth, the advanced forms will have one-fold symmetry. They will probably have two eyes, two hands, two legs with which to move in one direction at a time. Ears and nostrils? Well that will depend upon the atmosphere in which they originate!

Symmetry is the stuff of paradise: the home of Plato's perfect, regular solids.

A straight, uniform and finite line has symmetry about its midpoint.

A finite curved line can have symmetry; and asymmetry!

A shape can have multifold symmetry. For example, the square has four-fold symmetry, the pentagon has five-fold, the hexagon has six-fold symmetry. A circle is multi-fold, whereas an ellipse has two-fold symmetry.

A regular solid can fold: edge on, face on, vertex on.
The tetrahedron is 2, 3, 3 fold.
The cube is 2, 3, 4 fold.
The icosahedron is 2, 3, 5 fold.
The spiral and the helix are not symmetrical.

Symmetry can be used to convert a unidimensional vector into a two or three dimensional truss.

For example, gravity can be opposed by a single, vertical prop but the slightest eccentricity will cause it to gyrate and buckle.

The structure can be stabilised by a triangulation that is most economic when symmetrical and evolves into the familiar forms of roof trusses, bridges, arches and vaulting.

Folding of square, pentagon, ellipse, spider and tetrahedron.

Our senses are responsive to symmetry, recognising instantly that it has an independence from its environment. It may be a thing? Attention is drawn towards the axis. Symmetry thus has *focus* and possesses an internal force field.

It becomes essential to vectorial movement through any uniform fluid. A rudderless boat must be perfectly balanced if it is to follow a straight course. Any curvature or flaw in the line of its keel must be countered by a rudder, with consequent loss of energy.

Similar principles apply to all vehicles that are required to travel in a straight line.

Symmetry is thus associated with, and can be used to suggest, movement in the direction of its fold.

Asymmetry

The stillness, the poise, of perfect symmetry are not of the everyday world. Where the wind blows from one direction at a time, with a prevailing bias, in tenderness or fury, and every tree must flex its fibres to withstand the stresses of life, there we find asymmetry.

Similarly, the human being, right handed or left handed, but because he is one or the other, is not perfectly symmetrical. Only Gods can be! Absolute symmetry, in its very stability and self-sufficiency, tends to be superhuman and resistant to change. While we seek its security, we find a repetitive and invariant sameness to be lifeless.

So the human being seeks *variations within a theme of symmetry*: a sensitive balance of dissimilar forces . . . we seek an equilibrium, an order, that permits variety yet is not chaos. We seek asymmetry.

Trees on the English southern coasts usually lean to the north east, obedient to the prevailing wind.

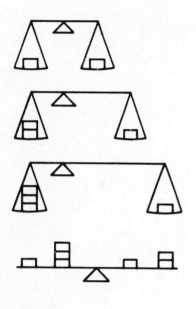

The Law of Moments

The moment of a force about a point is equal to the magnitude of the force multiplied by its perpendicular distance from the point.

On a uniform rod, unit weights can be balanced equidistant from the fulcrum. We have symmetry of loading, in terms of a force attributed to gravity.

If the downwards forces are each one Newton at distances of plus and minus four metres, then the anticlockwise and clockwise moments equate at 4 Nm. The rod is in equilibrium.

The rod can be kept in balance by adjusting forces and distances so that their product is a constant:

$$1N \times 4m = 2N \times 2m = 4N \times 1m = 8N \times 0.5m$$

Equilibrium can be maintained by balancing several forces about a fulcrum, such that the sum of the anticlockwise moments equals the sum of the clockwise moments.

Centres of energy

Given a set of forces and an assurance that equilibrium prevails, the human sense of balance is so finely developed that it directs us to their focus.

Most visitors to London, left freely to move, gravitate to Piccadilly Circus and Leicester Square. Most visitors to Paris find the banks of the Seine and Notre Dame. In New York, by tradition, it is Times Square. Is it still?

The Law of Moments can be demonstrated on a balance.

A group of similar objects direct attention towards their fulcrum, according to the Law of Moments.

All thriving, interactive conglomerates of forces develop centres of energy. The *inverse square law* tends to apply. *The centripetal force is inversely proportional to the square of the distance from the centre.*

It is the responsibility of a designer to ensure that the centre of energy of any organisation is where it should be.

This requirement is as relevant to an industrial organisation as to a city, town or village. As vital to a painting, building or symphony as to a multinational trading corporation or the kitchen of a domestic house.

All mechanisms have a centre of energy to which constituent elements contribute and refer. Every living cell and every atom has a nucleus. Recent developments in particle physics suggest that every nucleon may itself have a nucleus.

Foveal and peripheral awareness

Our senses, and our thought processes too, function through centres of energy. Brainy people are said to have *power of concentration*. By which is meant that they have developed their ability to focus both senses and mind upon a thought process. This *foveal* acuity can be of high definition, to be beamed like a searchlight on any tiny part of the surrounding, *peripheral* environment.

Peripheral awareness becomes progressively blurred as it recedes from the foveal zone and adjusts to an overall equilibrium. Repetitive stimuli are relegated to *background noise* and, like the ticking of *that clock*, are not heard until they stop.

Yet the peripheral zone is hypersensitive to sudden change. The human eye can detect unexpected movement at almost 90° to its central visual ray, or CVR. A flicker, caught by the corner of an eye, will cause the head to turn and invite foveal scrutiny.

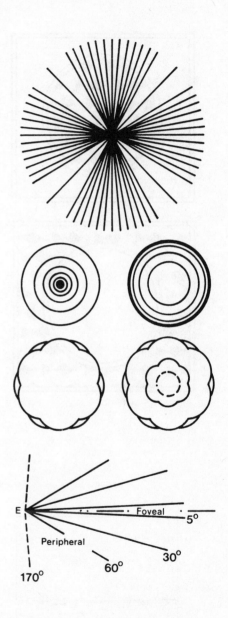

An alternation of foveal and peripheral experiences can be rhythmic and alive.

Working within a frame

A designer, working into a defined space, should recognise that both the space itself and the forces bearing upon it will develop centres of energy. These need to be clearly formed into a hierarchy so that an observer can move freely from one to another using both peripheral and foveal receptivity.

For example, the normal centre of energy of a rectangle is just above the geometric centre . . . this allows for effects of gravity. The natural place to mount a small drawing is on this centre. When the energy centres of both drawing and containing rectangle correspond, attention is focused upon the content of the drawing.

If the drawing is moved towards the edge of the rectangle it gains weight as a thing, a unit, a shape. Its moment about the centre of the rectangle increases and it needs balancing by one, but preferably two, additional drawings. Alternatively it can be balanced by the large expanse of blank, negative mount, which will assert its texture. Whatever the location of the drawing, an adequately bounded, or framed, rectangle will retain its centre of energy. As it is moved away from the centre of energy towards the edge of the rectangle, the drawing will appear smaller and heavier while the significance of its content will become subordinate to its overall shape.

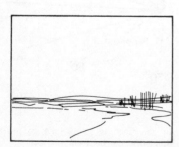

254

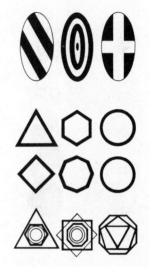

A design that inverts the desirable situation, filling the peripheral zone with fine detail and leaving the fovea blank, is disconcerting, even bewildering, and sometimes frightening.

In the hands of a great designer – Mondrian, de Staël, Rothko, Turner, Klee – the central void can be stressed until it appears to radiate energy. It then becomes the dominant element in the design, just where it should be, near the geometric centre.

Forming a language

As Descartes made clear, the mind, like the senses, prefers to focus only on one event at a time. But it can learn to comprehend a series of events by bringing them together into a cohesive, learned pattern to form a *language*.

The mind learns to hold the elements of a properly structured language in both peripheral and foveal zones so that particles are magnified in and out of the group instantaneously.

Using regular polygons, simple languages can be structured from AP, Pythagorean and other series.

Most languages, when arrayed in order, offer a rhythmic transition series or sensory structure.

A series of ellipses, arranged to balance according to the Law of Moments, assume a depth scale by size. The Law can also be applied to the depth dimension, with a fulcrum in the middle ground.

Three other members of the family are reminiscent of medieval shields.

The Pythagorean harmonic triads are found in Islamic structures, linking a dome to a square base. These can be related to the master series: 3, 4, 6, 8, infinity.

The φ series has an air of mystery.

255

Potential and kinetic energy

In mechanics, energy is considered in two general forms: *potential energy* that is held within a body by virtue of its location, temperature, even chemical state, and *Kinetic energy* by virtue of its velocity or rate of change.

A basic example occurs in an electron beam – so important in television and radio.

The potential energy of an electron will be eV where e is its charge in coulombs and V is the applied voltage to cause the acceleration of the electron.

The accelerating electron increases its kinetic energy at the expense of its potential energy and, if it is treated as a *particle*:

$$\tfrac{1}{2}mv^2 = eV \text{ when } m = \text{mass and } v = \text{velocity.}$$

A more common description of potential energy is of an object such as a ball resting precariously on a ledge. It possesses the *potential* to fall by virtue of its position. Energy in one form or another has been invested in it to get it up there.

The scale of textures affects the apparent size and distance of similar shapes.

If it is nudged so that the ball falls, the potential energy is progressively converted into kinetic energy such that $E = mv^2$.

At the end of its journey this energy is converted into heat, into further movement or deformation of the bodies in collision.

Concepts of potential and kinetic energy are fundamental to the fine arts. It is a great accomplishment in singing to take a melodic line up to a position of potential energy, and to hold it there, poised and ready to plunge like a kingfisher. And to wait while another is brought up to join it; and another; and another; until a monumental cluster of notes are permitted the final lunge into kinetic energy. The master of such an accumulation of potential energy was, and is, Beethoven.

It is *top weighting*. The optimistic, structuring of an art form until it appears to be on tiptoe in defiance and compliance with gravity . . . or whatever the dominant forcefield may be. *Building up to a climax!*

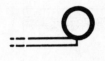

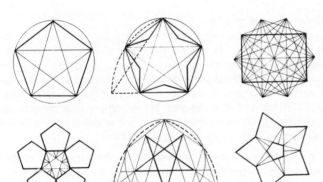

An alphabet of the pentagon.

257

Top weight

Memorable architecture is top weighted . . . whatever the period or culture. Until the new technologies of steel and prestressed concrete arrived the masonry of buildings was heavily based. Top weighting had to be achieved by the disposition of proportion, ornament and light. In Gothic cathedrals the light flows up to dominate the downward flow of masonry. In both Byzantium and Islam the surface enrichment, though opposed in motivation and manner, draws the eyes up to the arches and the vaulting.

And what is European Classicism if it is not about propping magnificently sculpted and weighted pediments upon tall columns.

Memorable paintings are top weighted. This is the crowning glory of Van Gogh's maize and corn fields. Most of the canvas is blown by the wind in the fore and middle grounds, while a strip of distant but finely detailed farmhouses, trees and human paraphenalia grips the top of the canvas.

Sometimes, as in the Dutch and East Anglian landscape paintings, the detailing of the sky becomes the top weight.

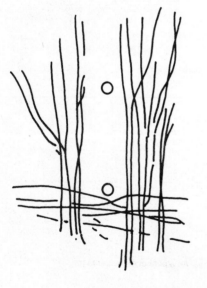

Sedimentary weighting

If a container of mixed aggregate, from broken flintstones and river ballast to fine sand, is placed on a vibrating table, the mixture separates out into sedimentary layers. It becomes graded so that the smallest and smoothest particles are at the bottom and the largest and most angular are at the top. Similar processes occur in water courses, rivers and tidal streams. *Hards*, where seamen may step ashore without muddying their boots, occur where the water velocity is sufficient to carry away fine clays and sands.

We are acutely sensitive to sedimentary layering, perhaps because of our origins in prehistory? Certainly its emotive possibilities go beyond obvious applications in architecture and landscaping to a structuring, by analogy, of graphics and music.

Considering the simplest case that can be rhythmic, a minimum of three sedimentary layers – light, medium and heavy; 1, 2, 3 – can be permuted into six possible relationships.

Experience, and tradition, teach that their orderly sequence is most readily understood and welcomed when sandwich effect is avoided. Reading from top to bottom, the series 1, 2, 3 is known as

258

architectural form, an unfortunate and misleading phrase derived from the bottom weighting of masonry, necessary to its stability.

The series 3, 2, 1 is known as *graphic form* and is a time honoured layout for newsprint. Most tabloid newspapers are emphatically graphic in the presentation of their headlines and subheadings. But when recognised as an interpretation of top weighting, their methods are basically similar to those of fine artists who seek monumentality in their works.

Other layouts, in which the lightest or heaviest layer is in the middle, are difficult to handle with conviction. They succeed best when the decision to form a sandwich is clear and uncompromising.

The problem of clarifying a sensory structure can be eased by putting the trio into dynamic, harmonic or GP series and then linking them through another dimension. Texture, line or a prop or plinth are useful unifying agents.

The moon effect

It is generally agreed that objects appear smaller and heavier as they move upwards. The *moon effect* can be tested with a torchlight on a dark night and, sure enough, the light disc appears to get smaller and more intense as it rises.

This effect has immediate graphic, sculptural and architectural applications. Typefaces at the top of a page of a newspaper need to be larger than those lower down. On the face of a building or in civic sculpture, the raising of objects above eye level will reduce their apparent size and due allowance for this must be made.

If a grid, an uncompromisingly repetitive though rhythmic grid, is provided, the eye-brain complex makes due allowance for height and perspective and recognises the continuity of the scale into the distance, both vertically and horizontally. The *moon effect*, therefore, is applicable only to isolated sensory stimuli.

Note: Given adequate clues, the human facility for making due allowance for effects of perspective permits the designing of architectural elevations by orthogonal means. Planar proportions that are harmonic on the drawing board will remain so in the structure, provided effects of *overlapping* are taken into consideration. This means also that proportions in elevations are expressions of the plan.

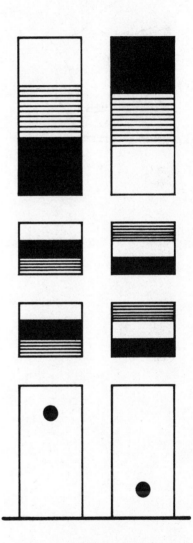

Despite interference from elsewhere on this page, the black disc on the left should seem smaller and more intense than that on the right. Provision of a strong ground line is essential to the moon effect.

Catastrophe theory

Catastrophe theory was developed by mathematician, René Thom, as a general theory of morphogenesis (the changing form of things). The growth of an organism is seen as a series of gradual changes triggered by, and in turn triggering, sudden jumps in the biochemistry.

Catastrophies, involving sudden change from one state of equilibrium to another, as stress and strain build up, are familiar to all of us, emotionally and physically. A unidimensional catastrophe can be plotted geometrically by the *introduction of an additional dimension*.

The path marked by a ball rolling down a corrugated graph paper would reveal a gap when the paper is later flattened.

A stiffened metal panel, subjected to a prod, can clank suddenly from convex to concave. The hyperbolic umbilic governing its strength was discovered by G. W. Hert, after Michael Thomson.

Cusp catastrophies occur in snowflakes and inkblots.

The freezing of energy

In some art forms, such as music and cinema, kinetic energy can be employed to express its own dynamic. There are few film directors who can resist a good car chase. Similarly intermittent acceleration is basic to the innovatory music of recent history, including the popular forms of *ragtime*, *jazz and rock*.

Quite apart from the obvious expression of kinetic energy in the mechanics and electronics of contemporary *kinetic arts*, static forms of painting, sculpture and architecture can freeze kinetic energy during the process of their creation. The *act* of casting, carving, moulding and placing materials can be clearly recorded in the substance and surfaces of the product. Similarly, even in that most abstract of arts, music, the playing of a musical instrument can inscribe the peculiar energy of the act of plucking, blowing or striking into its sound such that it is rendered unique or concrete. These arts lay stress upon the manipulation of materials and the instruments of communication, upon craftsmanship and crafts, old and new. Inevitably this has led many twentieth century artists to an interest in folk arts and foreign forms which previously might have been classed as *primitive*.

Cusp catastrophe model.

Opposite page: Drawing of a gaseous nebula taken from a photograph published by the Lick Observatory, contrasted with an impression of a hand.

260

The *working* of a material can convert kinetic energy into potential energy as an aesthetic process; just as the energy expended in lifting a one kilogramme weight to a height of one metre invests it with one kgm of potential energy.

Like any small boy who scribbles on a wall that 'Johnny was here', so the gestures of talented individuals can record, on behalf of all of us, that 'we were here'.

One of mankind's first artistic gestures was to cover his hand with charcoal and press it on to a cave wall: 'I, man, was here!'

The record of the craftsman's gesture in the design and production of any object establishes its scale and its humanity. Kinetic energy is thus invested in the product, augmenting its *presence*.

Abstract expressionism

Two million years ago an ancestor or cousin, Australopithecus, made simple stone tools by putting a cutting edge on to a pebble. Those tools are our first examples of *frozen actions* or gestures, an art that evolved into the sophistication of a Rubens, Delacroix and Pollock.

Abstract Expressionism ebulliently asserted post-war individual freedom during the 1950s, as *Action Painting* or *Tachism*, to become the first truly international art form since the flintstones. Influenced by *Dada* and *Surrealism*, it explored subconscious responses to configurations of dots, dribbles, shapes, textures and juxtaposed materials as a means of instantaneous communication . . . a visual music! Abstract expressionism exploited heuristics and programmed chance, using, in its poetry, both analogy and metaphor (ref: Chapter 15, 'The Design Spectrum'). Many of the illustrations in this book are expressionist.

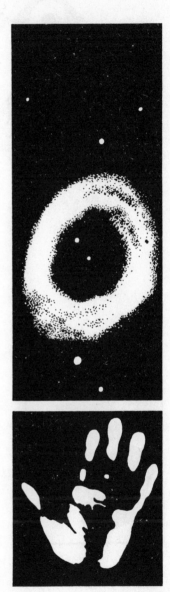

Constructivism

Parallel with *Expressionism*, a major design form of the twentieth century is Constructivism, devoted to the assembly of an intellectually emotive language. While at the hand of a Gabo, a Victor Vasareley or a Ben Nicholson its poetry enjoys analogy and metaphor, its strength is based on scientific methodology, inductive and deductive reasoning (ref: 'The Design Spectrum', Chapter 15). This continuing exploration of sequential thought forms has embraced a number of major movements of the twentieth century.

Constructivism is thus devoted to the conscious organisation of all forms of energy, potential and kinetic, into enduring and memorable identities and things.

The geometric origins of Constructivism can be found in the work of Pythagorus and its philosophy was prepared by Plato.

I do not now intend by beauty of shapes what most people would expect, such as that of living creatures or pictures, but . . . straight lines and curves and the surfaces of solid forms produced out of these by lathes and rulers and squares . . . These things are not beautiful relatively, like other things, but always and naturally and absolutely.

A basic concept, associated with Malevitch, in the search for a maximum expression of energy with minimal means. Constructivism, by name, originated in Russia but is now international.

Constructivism, and its complement, Expressionism, are thus the media of a search for a philosophy in this twentieth century that is commensurate with current technology and scientific discovery. Their *abstraction* permits the use of graphic forms as a means of research comparable with, though less stimulating and more contemplative than, music. The motivation of this book is, therefore, constructivist.

262

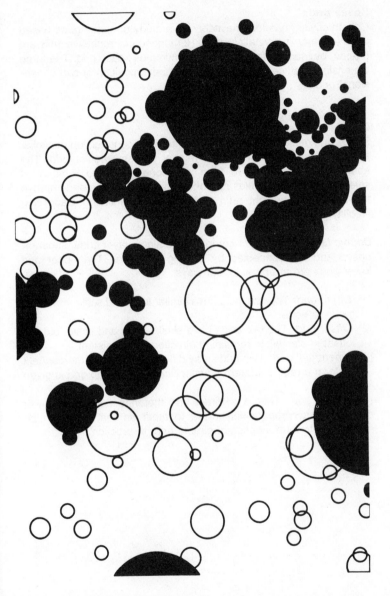

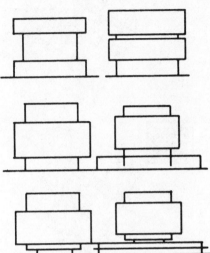

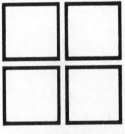

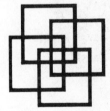

A meticulous hierarchy expressed through a maximum interpenetration of simple forms invigorates a structure.

263

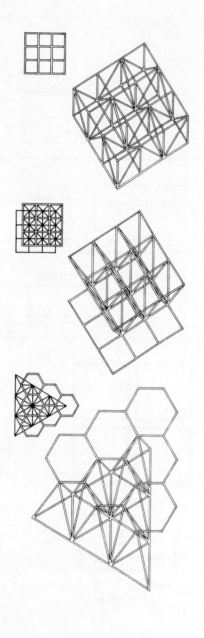

Space grids

Constructivism has led, inevitably, to a study of space grids based upon research in crystallography. Homogeneous, repetitive units are braced, by triangulation, to form a continuous space grid. The three dimensional lattice is formed by the superimposition of two dimensional grids.

Double layer space grids

Space grid geometries have evolved from the construction of similar pyramids upon the nodes of a regular or semi-regular grid. The apexes are connected to form a second grid. The removal of selected pyramid modules can offer internal openings and improve the strength to weight ratio of the system, while not sacrificing stability.

Double layer space grids comprise two single layer grids, superimposed and interconnected by bracing members. The upper and lower grids are arranged in four ways:

(1) *Direct grid:* The two grids have similar form and scale, matching node to node.
(2) *Offset grid:* The two grids have similar form and scale, but are offset in plan while remaining directionally consistent.
(3) *Differential grid:* Two grids may differ in design yet interconnect to form a regular pattern. In specifications, the top grid is given first.
(4) *Lattice grid:* This is a direct grid that has upper and lower members comparatively close together so that they can be braced to form a series of girders prior to erection.

The most convenient forms of lattice grid are direct or offset.

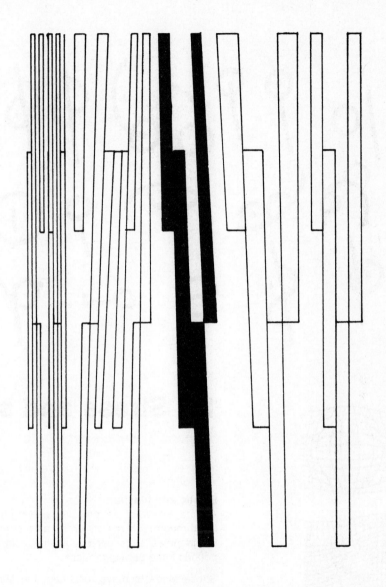

Studies for Kinetic Murals

14 Stress and strain

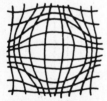

Variations on a theme of dot, line and circle.

Elastic and plastic

A force, tensile or compressive, bearing upon an object is transmitted through its fibres, its grain, as a stress, measured in so many kilogrammes force per square metre of cross section, kgf/m^2, or pounds force per square foot.

Stress tends to move, or *strain*, the fibres, crystals, granules or molecules and cause them to slide over one another into a deformation of the material. If the stress is within the *elastic limit* of the material, then the deformation will be temporary and the object will resume its original shape when the force is removed.

266

In the arts, elasticity is usually expressed by attenuation or flexure of a previously established grid: eg, a square pattern becomes a diamond pattern. Similarly, flexed and bent lines can appear elastic when they are roughly hyperbolic but not turned through more than 45°.

Plasticity occurs in two forms. It can display the faults, schisms, dislocations, crystalline fractures and slip planes of hard materials or the malleable lattices, folds and lumps of fabrics, plasticine and modelling clay.

Regular polygons represent matter in its coldest state, whereas it is usually more energetic in plastic, viscous, liquid, gaseous and volatile forms in which particles readily inflect, deflect and jostle one another.

Positive form

Whatever the intrinsic properties of a form may be, its reception by our sensory equipment may be distorted by one or other of the many factors that we have considered. For example, an isolated regular polygon, such as a geometric square, meticulously ruled and cut from plane board, is not necessarily felt and seen as a true square. The straight edges can seem slightly curved and concave. The four corners have more energy than the sides and attract attention. Also they are arrows, pointing outwards and confirming the concavity of each side.

To convert an engineer's square to a sensory square, the concavities can be opposed by *positive stressing*. Internal pressure, introduced as a uniformly distributed load, can appear to inflate the square. If the corners are pinjointed hinges, the sides become parabolic.

If point loads are used, one per side, then each side tends to become hyperbolic, its acuity dependent on the elasticity of edges. In some circumstances a better curve for countering an apparent concavity of form can be a very flat cycloid, like a five centred arch. In the extreme, this can convert a geometric rectangle into a superellipse.

Positive stressing of the geometric square could be achieved by the application of negative forces. External pressure applied diagonally to compress the hinged corners would again convert the sides into positively stressed curves.

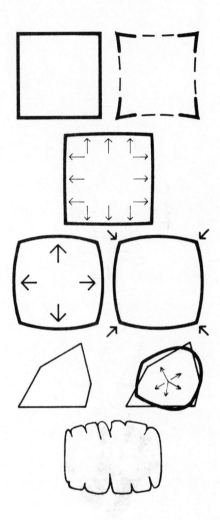

Positive form can be introduced into any polygon or polyhedron by regarding it as a closed skin subjected to internal expansion.

The positive rectangle can approach the superellipse, reminiscent of the *Desmid*, an algae of about 0.5 mm (0.02 inch) diameter.

267

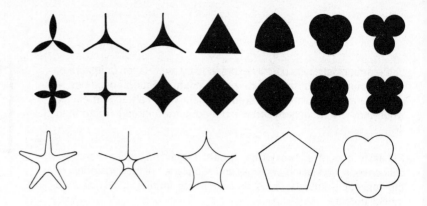

Positive and negative stressing

Positive and negative pressures applied to straight edged polygons and polyhedra convert them from the crystalline forms of rocks and earths to the positive and negative, male and female, expressions of life.

The rate of change of curvature reveals the distribution and the relative intensity of internal and external stress and strain, from soft and gentle to cruel and violent.

It can be employed progressively to modulate, by stages, from one shape to another. Modulation sets up a structural series that echoes the mutative processes of nature.

An equilibrium achieved by balancing the internal and external forces along a continuous boundary will reveal the qualities of the skin. Whether it is of constant length or is ductile will affect both the area and the shape.

In the case of the square, a perimeter of constant length must pull the corners inwards, as the sides flex outwards. If the corners are fixed and immoveable, then the square will appear to maintain its rigid shape until it bursts. Even so, some slight positive curvature can be expected immediately prior to the explosion.

Under normal conditions of plasticity, if the internal and external stresses are not balanced, the form will either expand or contract until equilibrium is achieved. The strain absorbs the stress. When the body is elastic, the strain converts kinetic into potential energy . . . like drawing the string of a longbow, or winding the spring of a clock, or charging an electrical condensor, or filling a balloon with hot air . . . and it looks to be alive.

The positive forms of living creatures express the internal pressure of their circulatory systems.

Concavity and negative forms are associated with elastic orifices, suction, closure and decline.

Positive and negative forms can be combined to form limbs.

268

Boundary, skin and lip

A body is motionless, in equilibrium, when all the forces, internal and external, equate to nil along its boundary and at its centroid.

An imbalance of forces can cause rotation when the resultant is non-radial (does not pass through the centroid) and forms a *couple* with the inertia of the body.

When a resultant is radial, the body can take off, like a rocket or a jet engine. Alternatively, imbalance of forces can be absorbed into the body, as strain or deformation, until the elastic and plastic limits are reached and the body disintegrates. The form of a malleable body thus reveals the forces bearing upon it.

The asymmetric deployment of forces can be used to change one geometric form into another. The intermediate elements comprise a formal series or structure.

It follows that for a shape to assume constancy it must be *closed* and possess a *skin*, or comprehensible boundary. An open form, with even the tiniest of openings, invites entry and permits a continuity of inside and outside space. *Open plan* design permits free flow between outside and inside, yet demands both internal and external skins.

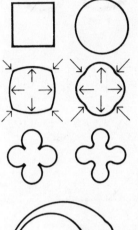

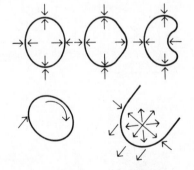

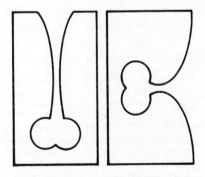

An unclosed form is in a state of change, opening or closing, sucking or pouting.

269

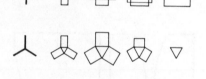

The differential stresses set up about an opening usually modify the skin to form a lip. This is as true of volcanoes and meteoric craters as of the functional orifices of animals. Similarly, the punctuation of changes of state, such as window frames, doorways, bearings and edging strips are as expressive in painting and music as they are necessary in architecture and mechanics.

A duality of explosion and implosion

A reversal of direction, in space or time, is implicit in the duality of explosion and implosion. This can be explored graphically as a principle of basic design that is applicable in other arts.

For example, a finite straight line can be transformed into its two dimensional form and thence into its linear dual by applying compressive and tensile forces.

Similarly, more complex forms such as superpolyhedra can be directed through a modular structure to arrive at their duals. In the diagrams the applied forces are linear and uniformly distributed for simplicity's sake; however this need not be the case. In the age of Computer Aided Design (CAD) that is arriving, complex modes of transposition and modulation become accessible from linear to volumetric; radial to circumferential; open to closed.

Change from one form to another is shown by transition forms. This technique can relate a shape to its dual, eg, a dual of a horizontal line is a vertical line. Their duality can be resolved spacially into a square.

Similarly, the dual of a square is a linear cross: the dual of a nought is a dynamic cross.

Stress patterns likewise reveal an opposition of tension and compression patterns in radial and circumferential forcefields; like cracking patterns.

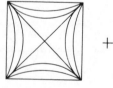 + 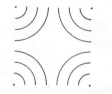 =

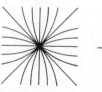 + 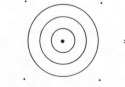 =

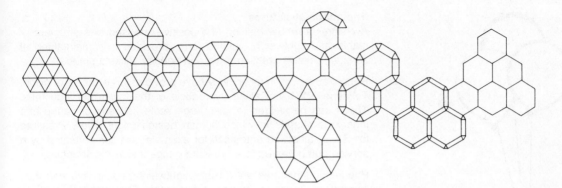

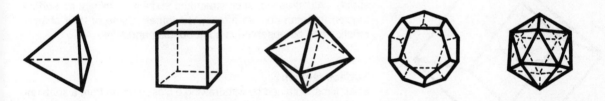

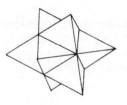

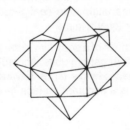

Top: A transition from a triangular grid to an hexagonal grid.

Bottom: Interactive dualities in Platonic solids:
(a) Two tetrahedrons
(b) A cube and an octahedron
(c) A dodecahedron and an icosahedron.

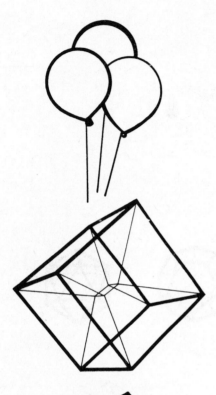

Pneumatic structures

A children's rubber balloon is a positive stressed skin structure of stable and lightweight volume form, provided it is maintained at constant relative pressure ratio and nobody sticks a pin in it.

Recent advances in technology have provided large sheets of nylon, Terylene, PVC and allied byproducts of the fossil fuel industries. These can be welded to form large scale balloons of varied and ingenious shapes in which human beings might dwell. Pressure losses, at airlocked entrances for example, are compensated by a service pump geared to a pressure gauge inside the structure.

Pneumatic structures are flexible, lightweight, collapsible and thus comparatively easy to transport and repair. Their usage is likely to increase wherever their advantages overcome their vulnerability to puncture and the service pump can be provided with a constant fuel supply. All stressed skin structures exhibit a minimum surface tension that can contain the applied forces. Some of their characteristics can be observed in soap bubbles and films.

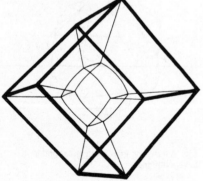

Surface tension

Soap films, obtained by withdrawing a closed frame from a soap and water solution, were first investigated by Joseph Plateau (1801–1883). Planes of soap solution have the property that only three can intersect along an edge at an angle between them of 120°.

The tension in the films draws them towards minimum surface area. Sometimes alternative configurations are formed by either fundamental or local minima.

The thickness of a soap film in thermodynamic equilibrium is between 30 and 70 Angstrom units. According to Helmholtz, the free energy F in a system always tends towards a minimum. Therefore $F = TA$, where T is a constant surface tension and A is the surface area.

If air is trapped in the system, producing a bubble, F has a contribution, $F°$, from the bubble: $F = TA + F°$.

Models based on soap films have many practical applications in the investigation of minimum surface areas. All organisms exhibit these properties in varying degree; however they are displayed in purest form in the skeletons of micro-organisms such as *Radiolaria*.

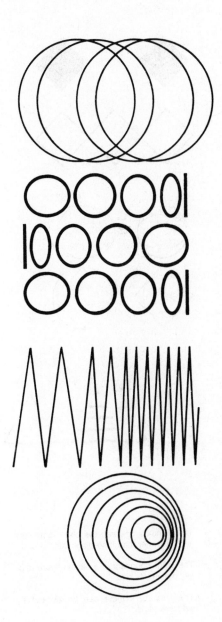

Reciprocal forces

The duality of forces is expressed by movement and change. Reciprocity of movement recognises that as I move towards A, A moves towards me. Movement is always relative. Yet the two activities can precipitate opposite emotional qualities. My movement is active, by *my* energy, with A as target. On the other hand A's movement renders me passive, as its target.

These can be very different experiences.

The boat and tide story can illustrate another source of illusion. Given a 4 mile stretch of placid water above a lock, a round trip in a 4 mph rowing boat will take 2 hours. If a 2 mph current flows when the lock is released, the round trip will take longer. The assistance of a fair tide is not as great as the hindrance of a foul tide – as any boatman will tell.

With the current, the 4 miles take $\frac{2}{3}$ hours.
Against the current, the 4 mile trip takes 2 hours.
Total time $= 2\frac{2}{3}$ hours.

The Doppler effect

The Doppler effect is an example of the effect of the movement of a radiating body on the wavelength of radiations. A train whistle or siren has a higher pitch as the train approaches than when it recedes. The wavelength of radiations is compressed ahead of the train and expanded behind it.

Light is also obedient to this effect so that light received from an approaching body has a *blue shift* and from a receding body a *red shift*. Observation that the red shift in light received from distant galaxies increases with distance, has led to theories of an expanding universe that originated in a big bang.

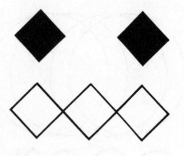

Optical illusions

The recognition of *things* creates a figure and ground relationship (see 'Foveal and peripheral vision'; while focusing on the object, the background is out of focus).

We judge the size of an object by direct comparison of the figure and ground scales and this can be a source of illusion.

Similarly the desire for closure, usually necessary to the recognition of an object, can lead to illusory assumptions. This is most common in the case of overlapping when it can be falsely assumed that part of a continuous form is obscured from view.

The recognition of a closed form is so intense that it seems to condense. The intervals seem proportionately to increase. In a regular line of buttons, their spacing will seem greater than it actually is, unless they are touching.

The perception of depth is not entirely dependent on bifocal vision. This faculty is supplemented by seven secondary factors: superposition or overlapping; comparative size in perspective; shadow projection; atmospheric perspective that blues and greys distant objects; height on the picture plane; filled and empty distance; and parallax of movement.

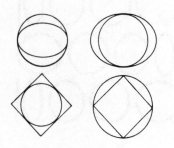

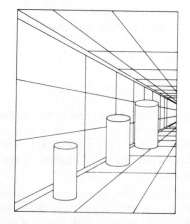

The distance between the black diamonds seems longer than their diagonals.

The outer boundary of a closed figure usually defines its size.

The concept triangle can be evoked by selected parts.

Bottom right: Spacial illusion derived from work by Ames.

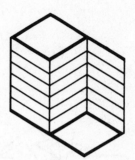

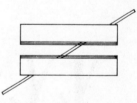

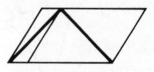

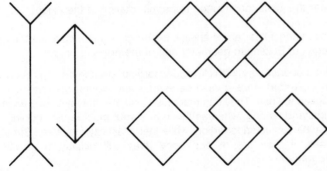

Top left: Chevron grids affect superimposed lines and can lead to moiré effects.

Top right: Thiéry's figure demonstrates a visual ambiguity arising from a lack of vanishing points.

The Sander Parallelogram distorts the apparent dimensions of an isosceles right angled triangle.

Lines and edges inflect to one another as they approach and cross.

The three overlapping squares actually comprised one square and two L's.

Bottom left: The Müller-Lyer illusion.

275

Flexure

Any two stimuli, brought into juxtaposition, affect one another. They inflect or deflect to a common force field, physical, sensual or emotional.

For example, the branches of a tree diminish in section according to their loading. It is therefore very difficult to draw a tree, however improbable, with branches that get thicker towards the top. The product asserts a strange, supernatural vigour. Sometimes this property can be suggested visually by putting the subject into extreme perspective, offering a close-up, end-on view.

Normal tree branches are, like the limbs of most living things, cantilevers capable of dealing with considerable bending and tortional or twisting moments. These tend to be greater at the junctions which are strengthened by additional flowlines of fibres.

The skeleton of a vertebrate reveals a similar thickening of the bones near the joints, augmented to permit rotation of the hinges.

These principles can be applied to energise and *bring to life* the hard edges of Euclidean geometry and of the drawing board.

Lines should vary in thickness according to their loading. Even the principle that struts should be shorter and stouter than ties can be applied to lines. They can recognise also that the joints of a tie must withstand tearing, whereas those of a strut must resist buckling. All may be subjected to tortion, while their elasticity may vary. But at all times, if they are of one body, they will display continuity of programme.

These conditions can be extended into all aspects of human communication and design, even including the design and selection of type faces.

276

Tensile structures

Structures predominantly based on tensile members offer big savings in self weight and lend themselves to lightweight and long span conditions. A uniformly distributed load can be supported by a hanging, catenary chain one thirtieth the cross section of a simply supported beam.

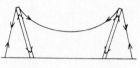

The chain can have the disadvantage of deformation under a superimposed point load. Its depression immediately under the load is compensated by elevation elsewhere in the chain.

Such deformation can be minimised by linking suspension cables to tensioning cables, converting them into a series of straight lengths. The tensioning cables need not be parallel in plan to the suspension cables. They are often most convenient at right angles in plan, but could be devised on a semi-radial principle.

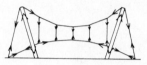

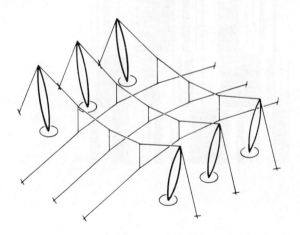

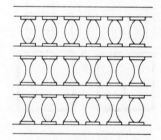

The compressive strength of most constructional materials exceeds their tensile strength; therefore, the failure of a strut is usually due to buckling or gyration. In most cases the slenderness ratio of effective length to minimum diameter of a strut at mid-span should not exceed 20:1.

The squeezing and elongation of materials is a basic design expression, nowhere better explored than in Baroque architecture of the eighteenth century and, more recently, abstract expressionism of the twentieth century.

277

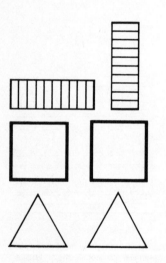

Sliding a pattern along a series of slip planes imparts energy.

The square and the triangle on the left have been slightly reduced in height.

The rectangles have the same geometric dimensions, yet the vertical rectangle seems longer.

Verticality is exciting

Some human dimensions command more energy than others. Looking upwards is more tiring than looking down. Verticality generally is more energetic than horizontality. A stimulus thrusting towards one is more energetic and aggressive than a similar stimulus moving away. Moving into a situation is usually less tiring than backing away. These experiences affect our perception. A measured, geometric square, stood on edge, seems too tall. To become a sensory square it can need a reduction of as much as a twentieth in its height.

278

Experiment will reveal that any regular polygon needs similar adjustment to transform a geometric shape into a sensory image. Most people, asked to stride a slope of 1 in 10, will regard it as quite steep. It is the maximum allowed in most driveways for safe use of motorcars. Yet it represents an angle to the horizontal of less than 6°. Because of its demands on our energy in dealing with gravity, we take it to be steeper than in fact it is.

Certainly verticality can be used to transform a small and uninteresting garden. For the cost of fa few cubic feet of topsoil, the garden can be terraced excitingly on to, say, three levels. With risers of no more than a foot, it will put more interest into the garden than twice the planting in the plain.

Distance by impediment
Most journeys are measured by the energy needed to traverse them. Distances are judged accordingly. Visually it is less tiring for the eye to follow a smooth than a serrated or intermittent line. Consequently the former seems shorter. Similarly any path filled with impediments and matters of diverse interest will seem longer than an uninterrupted and invariant passage. Experiment also shows that the eye learns to travel along the upper edge of a line in preference to the lower edge.

Top: The energising of a surface by apparent rotation of a square was devised by Victor Vasareley.

A serrated upper edge of a line lengthens the journey.

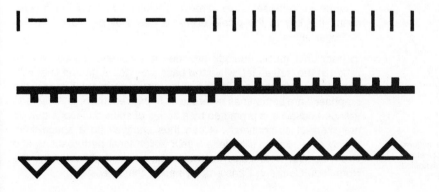

A minimal outline is sufficient to suggest familiar things. The silhouette of St Peter's, Rome, is dominated by Michelangelo's dome (built between 1546 and 1581).

The silhouette

When objects are subject to gravity or are otherwise attached to a deck, the silhouette is more significant than the ground line. Memorable works of art have memorable silhouettes, whether they be architecture, sculpture, painting or, by analogy, writing and music. Whenever identity can be encapsulated by the plot, the plan, the theme, the outline, it will command a silhouette.

In a large construction the silhouette of the ground floors, entrances, exits and more intimate areas can take precedence over the structure as a whole (see 'Foveal and peripheral vision') and thus become its representative. The microcosm becomes the macrocosm: the key to the whole universe may well be hidden in one hydrogen atom.

In traditional music, melody provided a silhouette, usually established in the treble clef, while the bass provided a ground line, with periodic counterchange. In contemporary experimental music, the emphases are sometimes reversed. A highly repetitive, textured and grouped baseline is promoted by a series of small mutations that do not interrupt its continuity. It can thus encapsulate a space-time, acting as a skin or silhouette within which local perturbations and even isolated notes can command attention. Architecturally, the Pompidou Centre in Paris employs such characteristics.

280

Scanning and perception

The scanning and perception of an area, and thus a volume, depends on two activities. Exploration of the closed silhouette describes a perimeter to give it shape, while a scanning of the content reveals an internal space.

The two activities can occur independently. The quality of a line, hard or soft, lost and found, can be merely recording the random movement of, say, a pencil point that makes no conscious claim upon area.

Similarly, the textural and structural elements of a space can be surveyed to reveal an intrinsic scale and intensity of energy. Is it close or open packed? Has it a dimensional or polar bias? Without necessarily revealing a shape or boundary.

The perception of area, volume and movement is a complex activity in which the space and its boundary are interdependent and the quality of one affects the other. The boundary becomes a skin. The space becomes a shape.

In the example, top right, the apparent shape of the rectangles is influenced by their content.

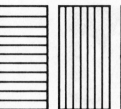

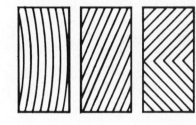
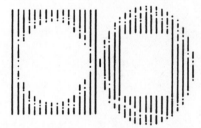

Left: Which ellipse appears largest? Which claims precedence?

Endotropic treatment, a favourite painter's device, loses the corners of a rectangle and emphasises the centre.

Exotropic treatment emphasises the edges.

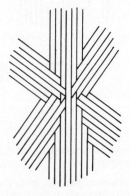

The aim of our theoretical work is always, in one form or another, the organisation of differences into unity, the combination of organs into an organism . . . .

The analytical approach is useful to us because it makes us familiar with the parts and the way they work together. A work, however, is not primarily a product, a work that is, but first and foremost genesis, work in progress. No work is predetermined; every work begins somewhere with a motif and outgrows its organ to become an organism. Likewise structure, which is what we are aiming at here, does not spring up ready-made, but is developed from interior and exterior motifs into its parts and thence into a whole . . . .

In summing up we may say: something has been made visible which could not have been perceived without the effort to make it visible.

from *The Sixth Exercise*
given by Paul Klee
at the Bauhaus, 3 July 1922
from *Paul Klee Notebooks*
Volume 1: The thinking eye

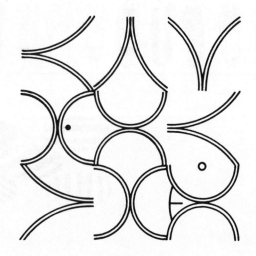

282

15 Dramatisation

We are so made that we can derive intense enjoyment only from a contrast and very little from a state of things.

Civilization and its Discontents, Sigmund Freud
Translated by James Strachey

Drama and antidrama

Dramatisation is the process of making an experience more exciting, vivid, emotionally stirring and memorable. This is visually achieved by emphasising some aspects of an experience at the expense of others. Selection, abstraction and hierarchy are of its essence: and these to be reordered, grouped and juxtaposed to maximum effect. Overemphasis, *hamming it up*, leads to the exaggerations of satire, cartooning, melodrama and farce.

The converse of drama, antidrama, is the predictable, invariant mishmash of everyday life that leads everywhere and gets nowhere. It is the greyed inconsequence of peripheral events. Antidrama should not be confused with the studied understatement, the unrepentant modesty of the true gentleman, for this is a product of drama. Understatement is most effective when in stark contrast with a highly charged force field. The calm sufficiency of the born leader is most dramatic when confronting, like Columbus, the inadequacy of his cringing, fearcrazed crew! Drama is a communication of contrast and change, of conflict, collision and rivalry, both crude and subtle, whereas antidrama is an unrelenting repetition that leads through boredom to apathy and oblivion.

In an urban society, which by its sheer size and evolving technology is largely insulated from even the seasonal changes of nature, the sense of social antidrama can be profound. Unfortunately, much of the drab utilitarianism of urban existence has come to be associated with the design philosophy of functionalism. But this is unjust to what has been a most important influence on modern design.

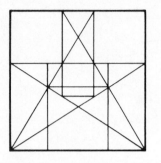

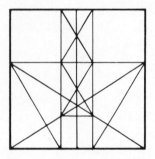

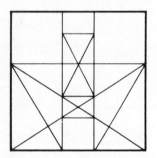

Functionalism

The idea that a design should fulfil required functions to maximum efficiency, unprejudiced by past practice, opinion or fashion, has achieved massive successes, particularly in the design of multiples and mass production. Le Corbusier's opinion that *a house is a machine to live in* is no longer disputed; just as planners now regard a town as a machine to live in. Failures in the application of Functionalism have derived from an incorrect definition of 'live in'. Functionalists have not always given sufficient priority to man's joy in his senses, and the need for enrichment and ornamentation of his environment. Appropriate sensory requirements, a hint of *unique to me*, should be included in the design criteria of every object to be used by mankind.

As its title suggests, Functionalism tends to reduce a problem, and its solution, to bare essentials. A simplistic analysis and synthesis of functions is pursued and this tends to eliminate the interlocution, the din and the vigour, the extravagances and the variety that casual solutions might offer.

Attempts to order, regulate and to 'tidy up' the apparently haphazard configurations of nature can themselves be regarded as natural processes. Their occurrence seems to be cyclic and may well express the evolution of levels of consciousness.

Decompositions of the square.

Right: Permutation on a theme of 'S' in which both positive and negative elements are permuted.

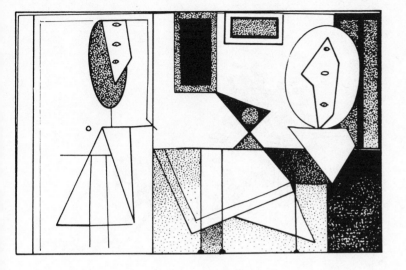

Levels of consciousness

Most cultures recognise three broad stages of development, in both the individual and the group:

(a) *Primitive response to nature*: Nature is accepted as containing all systems of order and mankind attempts its interpretation by immediate response to its stimuli. The process can involve great technical skill.

(b) *Conscious order*: By means of number, geometry, language and reason mankind seeks to impose an intellectual order on his observations of nature. Working through the design spectrum (discussed later in this chapter) he seeks algorithms and risks being entrapped by them.

(c) *Superconscious order*: A few privileged mortals (artists and scientists alike) have worked through stage (b) to emerge with a hypersensitivity to the interrelated principles involved. They commune with the subtleties of organic growth and decay and work with an intuition of a higher order than in stage (a).

Top left: The Studio (1927–29) by Picasso.

A tree of star hexagons.

285

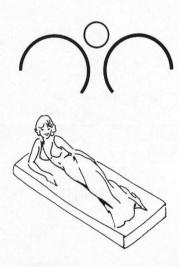

A Dickensian Christmas; a setting sun; a dainty damsel.

Emotive fragments

Our emotions are aroused by *symbols* and *associated ideas* that can be classified as emotive fragments. These can be local family and club emblems and songs such as those to be heard in soccer stadia. Or they may be national anthems, flags and romantic notions, like the English thatched cottage under a spreading chestnut tree. Every group of human beings has a set of agreed emotive fragments.

Beyond these, at a deeper level, images exist that can trigger emotions in *all* mankind. It is these that modern art, and science, is seeking. Julian Huxley, the biologist and writer, believed that the intellect is the sum of all emotions. If so, then the intellectual enrichment of the forms and surfaces of our general environment will also offer emotional stimulation. Similarly, the dramatisation of emotive fragments can stimulate the intellect.

The enrichment of forms and surfaces acts as a social catalyst. Its traditional use as ornament on and in temples, churches, stadia and other public buildings serves to integrate the social and personal roles of every citizen. Its neglect has imperilled both the culture and the respect for social order in many contemporary towns and cities. Inside the home it continues to express the status and intimate preferences of the occupants.

286

The competitive pressures of the market place have restrained industrial designers from the austerities that afflicted architects. Most successful businessmen recognise that sensuality, not always of the most edifying quality, positively affects their sales. Fortunately their customers are becoming more sophisticated and the styling of motor cars, typewriters, telephones and the like is now as critical as their engineering properties.

The design spectrum
The solution of problems is approached by seven broad methods, often referred to as the design spectrum.

(1) *Ratio and proportion:* simple comparisons of number, size and quality (Herbin, Rothko, Kline).
(2) *Induction:* reasoning from the particular to the general (Van Gogh, Cézanne, de Staël).
(3) *Deduction:* reasoning from the general to the particular (Miró, Moore, Pasmore).
(4) *Analogy:* partial similarity. If things agree in one particular, they may agree in others (Klee, Mondrian, Matisse).
(5) *Metaphor:* substitution of objects or actions that emphasises selected characteristics (Chagall, Gauguin, Magritte).
(6) *Heuristics:* The exploration of chance; discovery by trial and error; nature's method (Klee, Pollock, de Kooning).
(7) *Algorithm:* computation by prearranged steps intended to solve a specified problem (Seurat, Monet, Vasareley).

These processes are used by scientists and artists alike. The painters listed are examples of the *dramatisation of the methods*. Although they may not have used the above terminology, their written statements confirm the evidence in their work. In fact, therein lies the key to their achievements, for a work of art is the solution to a problem. It has differed from science in that the solution has also been the problem. This is no longer the case: scientists today are facing a similar dilemma!

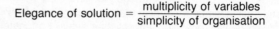

$$\text{Elegance of solution} = \frac{\text{multiplicity of variables}}{\text{simplicity of organisation}}$$

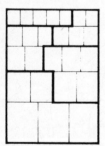

This is derived from a Fechner-Birkoff formula for assessing works of art. It has, today, been adapted to measure the effectiveness of *operational research*. Our journeys on the whiteboard suggest that it holds the key to our concepts of beauty. The formula attains a high mark when a diversity of *variables* is woven into a unified design.

The methods of the design spectrum can be subdivided into two groups, pivoting about *ratio and proportion* to form a cross:

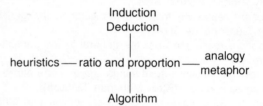

Vertical thinking

Vertical thinking is an alternation of the processes of deduction and induction to find and prove algorithms that hold true for all known applications. When new information arrives that cannot be satisfactorily accepted by the existing algorithm or *model*, then it must be adjusted or a search for a more comprehensive algorithm commences.

Vertical thinking is, therefore, the major tool of the mathematician, the philosopher and the scientist.

The following problem solving technique is derived from the practice of work study and management consultancy. To be successful it should be applied in meticulous detail. Even so its application is not reserved to science and technology. Though he may not know it, it is broadly the procedure of a creative artist who seeks to redefine his *criteria of success*, perhaps over the period of his lifetime.

A set of 25 rectangles can be grouped, for comprehension and variety, into 3, 4, 5, 6 and 7.

The sequence can be row by row, with bonding into groups of five. Overall unity can be reaffirmed by reasserting *similar* rectangles.

Stage 1 A Define the problem
B Simplify definition of the problem
C State criteria of success
D Put criteria into hierarchy
E Define critical criterion of success

Stage 2 F Redefine the problem, from Stage 1 findings
G Define the parameters
H Reconsider the criteria of success and their hierarchy

Stage 3 J Subject findings to critical examination
K Repeat the procedure for each emergent detail, as for the whole.

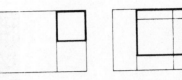

Critical examination procedure (*Stage 3, J above*)

A State the activity
B Why is it necessary?
C How is it to be performed?
D Can it be eliminated?
E Can it be combined with another activity?
F Can it be done at a different time?
G Can it be done at a different place?
H What is its hierarchic significance?

Horizontal thinking
One flaw in the techniques of vertical thinking is that they proceed from the known into the unknown. They are built on axioms that may or may not be universally true, and can carry false assumptions with them. Consequently it is possible, even likely, that their observations may have a built-in bias that is the more confining because it is unconscious. It is as though the information, induced and deduced by the techniques, were observed through tinted spectacles that obscure certain types of information.

A rectangle is subdivided into one large and two small squares such that the overlap is at constant width. As the two small squares grow so the trio reaches a peak of energy and declines into a single large square.

Throughout the transition the area of total overlap becomes foveal.

A computer programmed graded distribution in which the detail is random.

Below: A chance configuration of black squares. Each has a free choice from four locations within the grid.

Our means of removing such spectacles is by way of horizontal or *lateral thinking* (see the works of Edward de Bono). The conscious use of analogy, metaphor, playing a hunch, brainstorming, sheer chance, trial and error or heuristics are the stuff of the *think tank*, where lively minds, well versed in vertical thinking, strike imaginative sparks one from another. For history reveals, time and again, that while vertical thinking can bring our full intellectual powers to bear upon a problem and thus to consolidate a position, it is chance that causes us to stumble upon it (both the problem and its possible solution) in the first place. But is it chance? Could it be an incident in a Masterplan that we do not yet comprehend?

Nature uses heuristics. But, as we observe it, nature is not evolving completely at random. Its use of mutation and chance seems to occur within restraints; within an algorithm that we are still trying to decipher. Certain axioms seem self-evident. The first being survival: of the individual, the group, the species, of life itself. Of the big bang? Of chance?

Certainly nature's use of chance, by accident, incident or mutation, is therefore selective and subject to sensitive principles of a physical, chemical, organic and (many of us suspect) a spiritual, balance: a universal ecology.

290

Chance

The conscious exploitation of random configurations is an essential and exciting technique in both modern art and modern science.

But chance without restraint is *chaos*. A *bedlam* in which its disordered assault upon the senses becomes *repetitious*. To achieve coherence, therefore, the designer must state his parameters, his criteria of success, as precisely and restrictively as possible, before setting up conditions that exploit chance variations on a theme. This is the essential condition for all forms of extemporisation, as exemplified in jazz music.

Stravinsky commented in *Poetics of Music*:

My freedom thus consists in my moving about within the narrow frame that I have assigned myself for each one of my undertakings. I shall go even further: my freedom will be so much the greater and more meaningful the more narrowly I limit my field of action and the more I surround myself with obstacles. Whatever diminishes constraint diminishes strength. The more constraints one imposes, the more one frees one's self of the claims that shackle the spirit.

It can be argued therefore that the restraints of Functionalism, if prepared with the genius of a Stravinsky, a Mondrian, a Nervi, a Lloyd Wright or a Corbusier permit magnificent freedom within each disciplined field.

Algorithm

The antithesis of chance is an ordered structure, repetitious and predictable: an algorithm.

A waveform such as 1 2 4 3 5 6 8 7 9 10 12 11 remains peripheral. So does 134213421342, the conventional firing order of a four cylinder internal combustion engine. This sequence was selected to reduce the likelihood of *standing stress waves* in the body of the engine.

Once the engine is running smoothly, a backfire can be dramatic. Timed to occur just when you are selling a car, a backfire can be memorable! It is a *violation of expectation*.

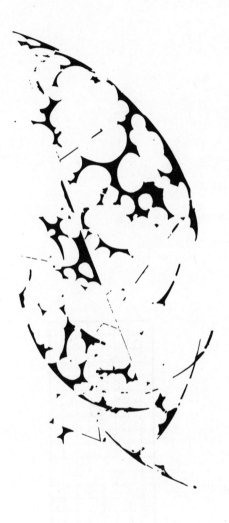

An ageing leaf, suggested by random blobs upon a shape evocative of a leaf.

291

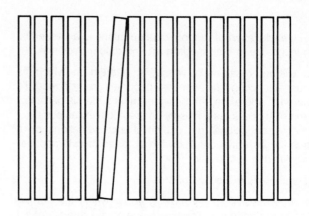

Violation of expectation

Violation of expectation can occur in both melodic and harmonic lines; however it is subject to certain restraints.

If a pattern of anticipation is to be disrupted, it must first be established. The pattern must suggest a capacity to continue after the violation, if only as an echo. Therefore, to have meaning, the disruption must share at least one dimension with both the structure and the observer.

Drama can be produced by juxtaposing the ordinary with the extraordinary, the usual and the unusual. In science fiction, for example, two forms of confrontation are available.

Either quite normal people, like the neighbours nextdoor, are transported into extraordinary circumstances, or a routine everyday humanoid way of life is invaded by strange creatures possessing extraordinary powers.

Although the experiences of strange creatures in a strange setting may be highly imaginative, they become dramatic only when we can identify with them emotionally. Science fiction thus illustrates a principle of all drama: it is a confrontation between normality and abnormality, security and insecurity, known and unknown, to be or not to be! Drama is a meeting and a rivalry of human antitheses.

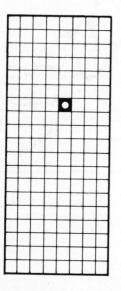

In a series, just one item has more energy than its colleagues and emphasises their inertia.

Dada

Dada is an event that took place between 1916 and 1922 releasing such creative energies that its reverberations and influences remain part of our daily lives: particularly among the young at heart and the rebellious. Dada claimed to be a nihilist reaction to the positivist disciplines of Traditionalism, Expressionism, Cubism and Futurism. Yet in both its anti-art and anti-dada stages it makes a positive contribution to modern art. Its manifestation, in neutral Switzerland during the First World War, rapidly spread through post-war Europe as a declaration of personal freedom. To this end, every object, every thought, everything idolised and admired was turned on its head, mocked and misplaced.

Johannes Baader later wrote:

Dada was a state of mind feverishly exalted by the freedom virus, a unique mixture of insatiable curiosity, playfulness and pure contradiction.

And Marcel Duchamp claimed:

If I say it is a work of art, it is work of art.

Therefore a urinal or a bicycle wheel, presented as an *objet d'art*, at a suitably exorbitant price, became a desirable *objet d'art*.

Of course the principle is open to exploitation. That was the point of Dada's challenge to all established values. Dada was an assault upon hypocracy and humbug. It also exploited the means of asserting hypocracy and humbug, creating its own contradiction.

Dada released an amazing fount of creativity that had been largely repressed by the ethics of previous centuries. To quote Hugo Ball:

It was an adventure even to find a stone, a clock movement, a tram ticket, a pretty leg, an insect, the corner of one's own room; all these things could inspire pure and direct feeling. When art is brought into line with everyday life and individual experience, it is exposed to the same risks, the same unforeseeable laws of chance, the same interplay of living forces. Art is no longer a 'serious and weighty' emotional stimulus, nor a sentimental tragedy, but the fruit of experience and joy in life.

Copies of a famous wash drawing by Hans Arp (1916); and a phonetic poem by Man Ray (Paris, 1924).

293

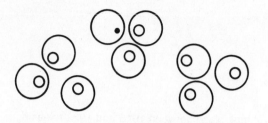

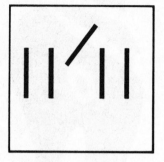

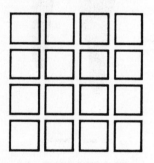

Odd man out

Changing the order or magnitude of just one term in a series is a violation of expectation.

In the kingdom of the blind the one-eyed man is king . . . but he is usually very lonely . . .

Any unusual incident in a peripheral series will attract attention. Dada consciously explored chance configurations of visual and aural signs, symbols and images, in both deed and word. Duchamp and Man Ray attempted to anaesthetise judgement and choice when exhibiting *found objects*. Their poetry emerged from *found words and phrases*. By the random selection of single items, they drew attention to the multitude of peripheral experiences that form the texture of life itself.

Yet they failed to achieve absolute chance. In *Lieschen*, Kurt Schwitters finds:

There is no such thing as chance. A door may happen to fall shut, but this is not by chance. It is a conscious experience of the door, the door, the door, the door.

Surrealism

Surrealism was inspired by the Freudian exploration of dreams and launched, in 1922, by André Breton into the intellectual ferment caused by *Dadaism*. The world of dreams, with its irrational juxtaposition of images, challenged the constructivist endeavour to build a new, modern, geometry. From the first, Surrealism was theatrical. To quote Lautréamont:

Beautiful as the chance encounter of a sewing machine and an umbrella upon an operating table.

Its use of analogy and metaphor exploited a simplistic emotive imagery that could be readily interpreted. The use of inversions of hierarchy, anecdote and paradox by de Chirico, Magritte, Ernst, Dali and many others in painting quickly found expression in the cinema and all forms of commercial promotion and later in 'pop' art, 'pop' records and 'pop' posters.

294

Biomorphic forms

At poetic levels the subtler ironies of Dada guided the geometry of Constructivism into the biomorphic imagery of Arp, Picasso, Klee, Miró, and, of course, Moore. In Moore's work flintstones, ground and chipped by sun and sea, are married to bones that have strained to flesh, sinew and muscle, to breed *positive* forms. Creatures, men and women and things, of bronze and marble, breathe the same air as we do. They do not illustrate or copy familiar images, but live their own independent lives according to their own programmes. The artist has thus become a God, privileged to breathe life into otherwise inanimate material, paint, clay, metal or stone.

The making of things

Modern art is motivated by the idea of *art for creativity's sake*, energising an intrinsic life force and asserting independence of both artist and observer. The artist is involved in the manufacture of things, individual things: like the works of Modigliani, or Kupka, or de Kooning, de Staël, Matisse, Moore, Braque, Miró, Picasso, Bacon, Rothko, Newman, Kline . . . . . Vasareley!

Modern art is directed at a public largely untutored in the fine arts amidst a rapid expansion of the means of communication. Attempts to energise old materials by bringing them together in new ways compete with experiments in new materials, such as electronics and rapid hardening plastics. Inevitably, novelty is confused with genuine innovation. Only the passage of time is revealing a broad evolutionary stream that springs from Constructivism and is nourished by various forms of Expressionism, such as Dada and Surrealism.

Dramatic configurations

The use of logic in modern art is multifaceted. Herbert Read described Constructivism as an 'Art of Determined Relations'. Neoplasticism dispensed with all curvature while Cubism was contrasting it with straights. Purism was an exercise in reason and even the Dadaists arrived at their apparent absurdities by a process of rational thought. Modern art has been quite self-conscious in its exploration of psycho-physical data and its use of dramatic purpose. It has thus, even in its periodic rebellion against itself, built an academism.

295

Biomorphic forms arranged to suggest the rich, linear tangencies of *Art Nouveau*.

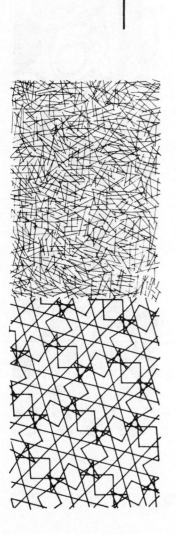

The exploration of dramatic configurations has revealed possibilities that are so many and varied that any list would be incomplete, if only for lack of tomorrow's development. However certain basic principles have emerged and a selection from these are discussed.

Proximity was discussed in Chapter 4, in terms of events, intervals and clustering. It can also be considered in terms of the observer's situation. Is he remote, viewing from a safe distance, or really involved?

The remote view reveals the degree of isolation of a cluster in the vastness of space; like a fly on a blank wall. As it is approached, its shape, then major, then minor subunits can be discerned progressively until it is under close scrutiny, from a safe distance. Although it may fill both our physical and mental viewing frames, we remain detached from it and have not entered the cluster.

If we get sufficiently close, the experience can be memorable, but for high drama we need to summon our courage to enter the cluster. Touch it, taste it, feel it. Such intimacy requires careful selection of a detail that is representative of the whole. When the microcosm presents an experience of the macrocosm, it is dramatic indeed.

Like man's first steps upon the Moon. For centuries we had studied the Moon through telescopes and, latterly, from satellites. But no previous experience compared with the handling of real Moon rocks, in situ, and their subsequent journey to Earth.

Analogous situations in our everyday lives are too obvious to require further comment, other than that they, too, have dramatic potential.

Sun and satellites – the juxtaposition of large and small, like medieval dwellings clustered about the foot of a towering chateau or cathedral; or like ducklings seeking the protection and domination of their mother. To provide a dramatic contrast that is also a unity, the sun must be truly dominant and its satellites must be a family that shares a common property of shape and size: just like an atom or a solar system.

The near miss is exciting; even shocking. And so is that instant of anticipation when it seems that two bodies must collide, brutally, and one is helpless to stop it. Yet for the moment there is still hope, a desperate hope of a near miss. Or like the boulder, poised precariously on the very edge of a cliff so that the slightest puff of wind will bring it crashing down. Or that moment that all warriors know, the hush that seems to silence the wind itself, as the day of battle dawns.

The prod is not to be confused with the *caress* which gently brushes a surface. Whereas the former invades territory, the latter respects boundaries. They can thus be suitable adversaries for a dramatic confrontation.

The *embrace* can be taken to extremes. It can be a clasp that grips and devours and from which there is no escape. Or it can be an offer of shelter, of friendship, a port in a storm.

297

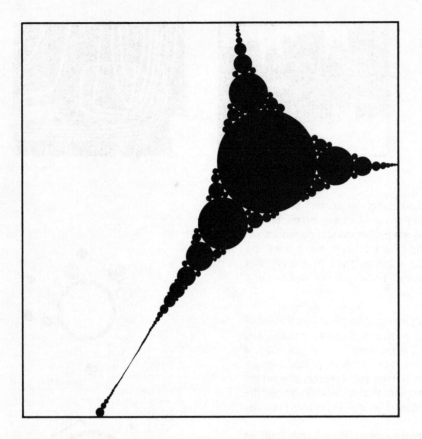

The *Apollonian Gasket*, attributed to Apollonius of Perga, is bounded by three large circles tangent two by two. A dominant circle is inserted, tangent to the three arcs of the circular triangle. Progressively smaller circles are inserted, generation after generation. At each generation the unfilled, negative area between the circles is the Apollonian Gasket.

Similarity groups tend to be more unified than *proximity* groups, and they can be set in *competition*.

The alternation of stretching and squeezing can be rhythmic. It can be used to dramatise the competition between proximity and similarity.

Dramatic potential can be found in any challenge to an established normality. A man doing a handstand in the town centre is likely to arouse interest. Five men doing handstands are likely to be regarded as a conspiracy against the public interest. Their relationship with the community has considerable dramatic potential. Just like the cube standing on a vertex, discussed in Chapter 7.

298

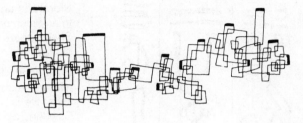

Catastrophe, as discussed in Chapter 13, can be linked with inevitability, to assert dramatic power.

Once a repetition has been observed to flow, it can be dammed like a river, building up the pressure until it becomes irresistable and the dam bursts.

Hit and rest

Repetition dulls receptivity (as discussed in Chapter 3). Even the most exciting events require a period of rest in which their reverberations may subside, before they are repeated. The interval permits time for contemplation and anticipation.

Rhythmic grouping procedures organise the alternation of hits and rests. Robert Mitchum, the Hollywood film star, once described his films as:

A sequence in which they knock me down and I get up. Then they knock me down, I think it over and get up. So they knock me down and I shake my head and I get up. So they knock me down . . .

In a first-rate film this happens *plenty* of times. The designer's problem is to devise sufficient variety of ways to knock him down, revive him and weave a pattern of rests between the peaks of conflict.

Ian Fleming's James Bond stories each contain about thirteen peaks, offering plenty of excitement. A major triad of characters comprises Bond, the Master Villain, the primary Girl Friend. The secondary triad comprises a rival agent, a vicious hit-man for the opposition and a series of pretty girls. Ancillary triads are formed at the headquarters of both Bond and the Master Villain.

Copy of a pen drawing by Paul Klee (1917).

299

Hierarchy and number

In any memorable play the characters are scaled. It is the genius of Shakespeare that his plays offer plenty of fully written parts to a band of players.

In *Macbeth*, for example, the organisation of numeracy of players, hits and rests, is magnificent. Duncan, King of Scotland, has two sons. He is murdered by Macbeth, Thane of Glamis (and later of Cawdor), so that Macbeth can claim the kingdom. *Seven* other thanes figure in the story, of which Banquo and Macduff hold key roles. Banquo is a passive symbol of friendship betrayed. Macduff is an active instrument of righteous vengence. Of the two wives, Lady Macbeth is active and Lady Macduff is passive.

Three weird sisters, *three* other witches and *three* murderers figure in the plot to provide on-stage movement.

The contents of the witches brew has a touch of *Dada*. The second witch's contribution is, for example:

Fillet of a fenny snake
In the cauldron boil and bake;
Eye of next, and toe of frog,
Wool of bat, and tongue of dog,
Adder's fork, and blind-worm's sting,
Lizard's leg and howlet's wing,
For a charm of powerful trouble,
Like a hell-broth, boil and bubble.

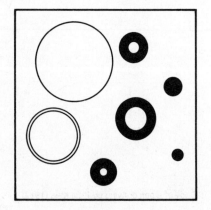

Counterpoint

Ultimately drama resolves into the juxtaposition of antitheses. Though they are interdependent, the head and tail of a coin battle for supremacy.

In counterpoint, two contrasting themes which share a common space-time scale discuss, compete, debate, argue, fight for their points of view. Each must be a convincing contender and although the conflict may be resolved in the favour of one, the other cannot be obliterated.

When the coin comes to rest head up, the tail must be underneath! One sustains the other. As one rises the other declines and the discourse is maintained through variations upon the two themes and alternation of supremacy.

Drama, counterpoint can be enriched beyond bald competition between two themes by the use of transitions and interweaving sub-plots.

The scenario

Everything designed by man, actively by the making of a thing or passively by the comprehension of signals, acquires a scenario. Its locality, outline and centroid may define a town centre, a kitchen, a command module or a cassette player, but within it a hierarchy of players and activities will emerge. The enrichment of the master plot by interweaving sub-plots renders it significant and memorable.

The *cassette player* becomes a *music centre*!

The fulfilment of expectation

It is not possible to predict the unimaginable. Therefore any expectation is a projection into the future of past experiences or a combination of past experiences. And to be anticipated these should have a capability of fulfilment, if only as fantasy.

It then becomes a dramatic possibility to violate the anticipation. A subsequent fulfilment becomes the happy ending. Alternatively the violation can be inverted; like a black comedy, or the assertion of a stark revenge or retribution.

Above: Chartres Cathedral: north rose window and west rose window.

Opposite page, top left: Copy of ancient Egyptian writing, *c* 1450 BC.

Useless information

Perhaps the essential clue to dramatisation was given in the discovery that *new born babies enjoy solving problems*. We enjoy mysteries, so long as they do not threaten our person. Better still, we enjoy solving mysteries: and if we cannot solve them then, when the auspices are right, they can acquire the aura of magic. To this end, disguise can be part of nature's game. But it must not be false; that would be downright cheating and nature cannot cheat. Nature misleads to a purpose, like the use of camouflage to deceive predators.

Nature's mysteries frequently stem from ambiguities and extremes of scale: for example, an x-ray scanner is needed to show that over 99 per cent of solid matter is empty space.

Yet *we* have been programmed to be curious, to question, to probe and to seek to solve riddles. And as part of that process, we attempt to imitate and parallel nature's wonders and its creativity. To this end there can be no such thing as useless information. Each item can reveal some facet of nature's purpose and can become a spur to our imagination. If it appears useless then we have not yet understood its function in the order of things: it is not yet woven into a personally cohesive pattern of ideas and events.

Knowingness

Yet to function as designers, our priority is the need to comprehend a cohesive pattern that contains the problem we wish to solve. For at the moment of creativity, the designer draws upon a *knowingness*, an intuition either subconscious or superconscious that is a multi-dimensional encapsulation of both problem and solution. Momentarily these two become one. The problem is the solution. The solution is the problem.

Overall comprehension of this order requires either a complete assimilation of all relevant information on the lines described by Descartes, or an instant of penetrating insight that we may classify as a *Gift from God*. By either course we need a considerable background of information that may seem to be largely useless until the creative moment arrives. This is perhaps why many an ageing schoolteacher smiles benignly when his students demand: 'Why are you giving us this information? We see no use for it.'

This figure may suggest colour by ocular diffraction. If so, then it is possible for one form of communication (white and black, positive and negative light) to suggest the existence of another dimension (colour).

302

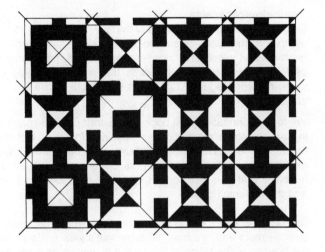

Knowledge is knowledge. Who can say what will or will not contribute to the solution of problems?

In 1896, as a 21 year old French medical student preparing a thesis for his MD degree, Ernest Augustin Clement Duchesne unmistakably demonstrated the antibacterial action of *Penicillium* (see *Scientific American*, November 1978) and recommended that further research might lead to new developments that could prove directly applicable to prophylactic hygiene and therapy.

This pioneering work was ignored by his contemporaries and when Alexander Fleming first noted, by chance, the antibacterial action of *Penicillium* mould in 1928, he was completely unaware that his discovery had been anticipated. In 1945, after sharing with Chain and Florey the Nobel prize for physiology and medicine, Fleming, in a speech given in Lyon, paid generous tribute to the work of Duchesne, which by then was known to him.

For nigh on fifty years *Penicillium* had been useless.

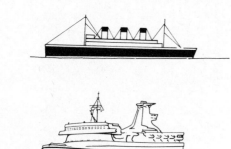

Technological scales

Similarly, it seems only yesterday that we romantics were vigorously defending the vast technological resources invested in space research and travel. The critics argued that the space probes were a useless waste of money in words that were amazingly similar to those recorded against Columbus some four and a half centuries earlier.

Yet today information sent back from extraterrestrial space is unveiling an awesome picture of our physical universe. Not only of its fastnesses and vastnesses but also of the minute detailing of existence upon our own planet: its climatic patterns and the plate tectonics that give rise to earthquakes, volcanoes, fold mountains and the oceanic ridges.

But perhaps more important, at this time when the infancy of our species must end, we have an astronaut's view of Earth rise above the horizon of the Moon to teach us that we live on a tiny island in a vast ocean of energy, space and time.

Meanwhile the massive technological 'spin-off' from the space programmes promises to change our social and working lives completely during the next two decades. The age of microelectronics, automation and biological engineering has arrived. These technologies carry their own intrinsic scales which are not human yet can render unprecedented service to mankind. It is therefore more than ever essential that we modulate our human scale through all the new processes of social order that are about to dawn.

And from a few basic observations we have learned that even *all* may be relative.

Ships embrace their own scenario, the sea; and so do motor cars and teapots. We find it odd, even offensive, if a boat looks like a teapot and at best quaint when a teapot looks like a boat.

Right: The Vauxhall *Chevette* looks what it is: a nippy, small family hatchback saloon car.

Total space

The idea of total space no longer sounds strange to the European whose once implacable materialism has been subjected to both Dada and contemporary science. Oriental philosophies have long been conscious of the ultimate duality of awareness. Just as up cannot exist without down, left without right, hot without cold, so existence is a condition of non-existence, space of non-space, being of non-being. It is interesting to learn that nuclear scientists are now seeking the particles necessary to anti-matter and may have found some of them.

Flux and the echo sounder

Form thus becomes a condition of non-form and, however stable it may seem, all that can be observed in our universe is the existential process of change from one state to another. If this is viewed with an optimism that assumes and seeks ultimate order, then the artist, the technologist, the scientist, each in his way a designer of things, are embarked upon a common voyage.

Upon the vast ocean of the *whiteboard*, each is a navigator in need of a chart, a bell and the joy of discovery!

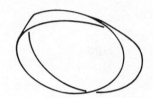

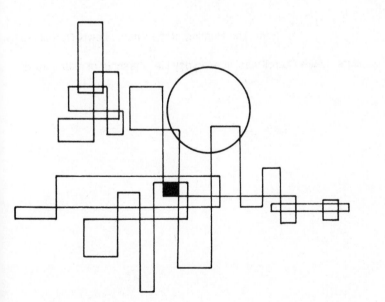

The two enantiomorphic polyhedrons are exactly alike in all geometric properties yet they are *not* identical.

The mobius strip has a *single* continuous surface.

The Klein bottle has a single continuous surface that passes through the bulb to connect inside with outside.

A finite area needs no more than four colours to distinguish the boundaries of its subdivisions, no matter what the configuration.

305

The Bellman himself they all praised to the skies —
Such a carriage, such ease and such grace!
Such solemnity too! One could see he was wise,
The moment one looked in his face!

He had bought a large map representing the sea,
Without a vestige of land:
And the crew were much pleased when they found it to be
A map they could all understand.

'What's the good of Mercator's North Poles and Equators,
Tropics, Zones and Meridian Lines?'
So the Bellman would cry: and the crew would reply
'They are merely conventional signs!'

'Other maps are such shapes, with their islands and capes!
But we've got our brave Captain to thank'
(So the crew would protest) 'that he's bought us the best —
A perfect and absolute blank!'

This was charming, no doubt: but they shortly found out
That the Captain they trusted so well
Had only one notion for crossing the ocean,
And that was to tingle his bell.

from 'The Hunting of the Snark', Lewis Carroll (1876)

Note: Lewis Carroll was, in everyday life, a teacher of mathematics.

People

Alberti	1404–1472	Sculptor, architect
Alexander the Great	356–323 BC	Greek soldier, monarch
Apollonius	c 250 BC	Greek mathematician
Archimedes	287–212 BC	Greek mathematician
Aristotle	384–322 BC	Greek mathematician, philosopher
Arp, Jean	1887–1966	Artist
Bach, Johann Sebastian	1685–1750	Composer
Bacon, Francis	b. 1909	Painter
Ball, Hugo	1886–1927	Painter, poet
Balla, Giacomo	1871–1958	Painter, sculptor
Beardsley, Aubrey	1872–1898	Draughtsman, painter
Beethoven, Ludwig van	1770–1827	Composer
Birkhoff, George David	1884–1944	Scientist
Boccioni, Umberto	1882–1916	Painter, sculptor
Breton, André	1896–1966	Painter, poet
Bronowski, Jacob	1908–1974	Mathematician
Brianchon, Charles	1783–1864	Mathematician
Bright, Greg	b. 1949	Writer
Brunelleschi, Filippo	1377–1446	Sculptor, architect
Buckminster Fuller, Richard	b. 1895	Geometer, architect
Canaletto, Antonio	1697–1768	Painter
Carroll, Lewis	1832–1898	Writer, mathematician
Caruso, Enrico	1873–1921	Singer
Cézanne, Paul	1839–1906	Painter
Chagall, Marc	b. 1887	Painter
Chevreul, M. Eugène	1786–1889	Chemist
Columbus, Christopher	1446–1506	Navigator
Copernicus	1473–1543	Astronomer
Dali, Salvador	b. 1904	Painter
Dante Alighieri	1265–1321	Poet
de Bono, Edward	b. 1933	Writer
de Capelle, Jan van	1600–1682	Painter
de Chirico, Giorgio	b. 1888	Painter
de Kooning, William	b. 1904	Painter
Delacroix, Eugène	1799–1863	Painter
de Staël, Nicholas	1914–1955	Painter
Desargues, Gérard	1593–1662	Geometer, engineer
Descartes, René	1596–1650	Mathematician, scientist
Dickens, Charles	1812–1870	Writer
Disney, Walt	1901–1966	Draughtsman, cinema designer
Duchamp, Marcel	1887–1968	Artist
Dürer, Albrecht	1471–1528	Mathematician, artist
Einstein, Albert	1879–1955	Mathematician
Ensor, James	1860–1949	Artist

Ernst, Max	1891–1976	Painter
Euclid	330–260 BC	Greek mathematician
Euler, Leonhard	1707–1783	Mathematician
Fechner, Gustav	1801–1887	Scientist
Fibonacci (Leonardo of Pisa)	1170–1230	Mathematician
Fleming, Ian	1908–1964	Writer
Francesca, Piero della	1420–1492	Painter
Freud, Sigmund	1856–1939	Psychoanalyst
Gabo, Naum	1890–1977	Sculptor
Galileo	1564–1642	Astronomer, mathematician
Gaudi y Cornet, Antoni	1852–1926	Architect
Gauguin, Paul	1848–1903	Painter
Gauss, Karl Friedrich	1777–1855	Mathematician
Gershwin, George	1898–1937	Composer
Gleizes, Albert	1881–1953	Painter
Gris, Juan	1887–1927	Painter
Gropius, Walter	1883–1969	Architect
Guillotin, Joseph	1738–1798	Physician
Helmholtz, Hermann Ludwig F. von	1821–1894	Mathematician, scientist
Hepworth, Barbara	1903–1975	Sculptor
Heraclitus	c 535–475 BC	Greek philosopher
Hertz, Heinrich	1857–1894	Mathematician
Hobbema, Meindert	1638–1709	Painter
Hofmann, Armin	b. 1924	Draughtsman, designer
Hubble, Edwin	1889–1953	Astronomer
Hogarth, William	1697–1764	Painter
Hipparchus	146–127 BC	Greek mathematician
Huxley, Julian	1887–1972	Biologist, writer
Jones, Inigo	1573–1652	Architect
Jung, Carl	1875–1961	Psychologist, analyst
Kandinsky, Wassily	1866–1944	Painter
Kepler, Johann	1571–1630	Astronomer
Khayyam, Omar	1050–1132	Mathematician, poet
Kirchner, Ernst Ludwig	1880–1938	Painter
Klee, Paul	1879–1940	Painter, teacher
Kline, Franz	1910–1962	Painter
Kupka, Frank	1871–1957	Painter
Lasdun, Denys	b. 1914	Architect
Le Corbusier (Charles-Edouard Jeanneret)	1887–1965	Architect, engineer, artist
Léger, Fernand	1881–1955	Painter, sculptor
Leibnitz, Gottfried W.	1646–1716	Mathematician, philosopher
Leonardo da Vinci	1452–1519	Artist
Lissitski, El	1890–1941	Painter, sculptor
Lorrain, Claude	1600–1682	Painter
Lycophron	c 260 BC	Greek poet
Mackintosh, Charles Rennie	1868–1928	Architect, designer, painter
Magritte, René	1898–1967	Painter
Malevitch, Kasimir	1878–1935	Painter
Manet, Edouard	1832–1883	Painter
Marinetti, Filippo Tommaso	1876–1944	Writer

Marlowe, Christopher	1564–1593	Writer
Masaccio, Tommaso di Ser Giovanni	1401–1428	Painter
Matisse, Henri	1869–1954	Painter
Mendel, Gregor Johann	1822–1884	Botanist
Mercator, G. K.	1512–1594	Geographer, astronomer
Metzinger, Jean	1883–1956	Painter
Michelangelo Buonarroti	1475–1564	Artist
Milton, John	1608–1674	Writer
Miró, Joan	b. 1893	Painter, sculptor
Mitchum, Robert	b. 1917	Actor
Modigliani, Amedeo	1884–1920	Painter
Mondrian, Piet	1872–1944	Painter, writer
Monet, Claude	1840–1926	Painter
Moore, Henry	b. 1898	Sculptor
Morris, William	1834–1896	Designer, writer
Mozart, Wolfgang Amadeus	1756–1791	Composer
Münch, Edvard	1863–1944	Painter
Napier, John	1550–1617	Mathematician
Nervi, Pier Luigi	1898–1979	Engineer, architect
Newman, Barnett	1905–1968	Painter
Newton, Isaac	1642–1727	Mathematician, scientist
Nolde, Emil	1867–1956	Painter
Northrop, Eugene P.	1908–1969	Mathematician
Ozenfant, Amédée	1886–1966	Painter, writer
Palladio, Andrea	1518–1580	Architect
Pappus	c 320 AD	Greek mathematician
Pascal, Blaise	1623–1663	Mathematician, philosopher
Pasmore, Victor	b. 1908	Painter
Pauli, Wolfgang	1900–1958	Mathematician
Philolaus	c 450 BC	Greek mathematician
Picabia, Francis	1879–1953	Painter
Picasso, Pablo	1881–1973	Artist
Plateau, Joseph	1801–1883	Mathematician
Plato	427–347 BC	Greek mathematician
Pollock, Jackson	1912–1956	Painter
Poussin, Nicholas	1593–1665	Painter, geometer
Ptolemy, Claudius Ptolemaeus	90–168 AD	Astronomer
Pythagoras	582–507 BC	Greek mathematician
Ray, Man	1890–1976	Photographer
Read, Herbert	1893–1968	Writer
Rembrandt, H. van Rijn	1606–1669	Painter
Renoir, Auguste	1842–1919	Painter
Riemann, Bernhard	1826–1866	Mathematician
Rietveld, Gerrit	1888–1964	Architect, designer
Riley, Bridget	b. 1931	Painter
Rodin, Auguste	1840–1917	Sculptor
Rothko, Mark	1903–1970	Painter
Rubens, Peter Raul	1577–1640	Painter
Ruskin, John	1819–1900	Writer, painter
Russell, Bertrand	1872–1970	Philosopher, mathematician
Ryan, Christopher	b. 1949	Writer

Schiller, Friedrich von	1759–1805	Writer
Schwitters, Kurt	1887–1948	Painter
Seurat, Georges	1859–1891	Painter
Severini, Gino	1883–1966	Painter
Shakespeare, William	1564–1616	Writer
Sierpinski, W.	b. 1912	Mathematician
Singier, Gustave	b. 1909	Painter
Stravinsky, Igor F.	1882–1971	Composer
Sullivan, Louis	1856–1924	Architect
Thom, René	b. 1923	Mathematician
Tintoretto, Jacopo	1518–1594	Painter
Toulouse-Lautrec, Henri de	1864–1901	Painter
Turner, J. M. W.	1775–1851	Painter
Uccello, Paolo	1396/7–1475	Painter
Van der Rohe, Mies	1886–1969	Architect
Van de Velde, Henri	1883–1957	Architect, designer
Van Doesburg, Theo	1883–1931	Artist
Van Gogh, Vincent	1853–1890	Painter
Vasarely, Victor	b. 1908	Painter
Vermeer, Jan	1632–1675	Painter
Verne, Jules	1828–1905	Writer
Veronese, Paolo	1528–1588	Painter
Vitruvius Pollio, Marcus	active 46–30 BC	Architect, writer
Wagner, Richard	1813–1883	Composer
Wells, H. G.	1866–1946	Writer
Wren, Christopher	1632–1723	Astronomer, architect
Wright, Frank Lloyd	1867–1959	Architect

Further reading

Aesthetics, psychology, ideas

Arnheim, Rudolph, *Visual Thinking*, Faber & Faber, 1970
Arnheim, Rudolph, *Entropy and Art*, University of California Press (USA), 1971
Arnheim, Rudolph, *Art and Visual Perception*, Faber & Faber, 1956
Arp, Jean, *On My Way: Poetry and Essays, 1912–1947*, George Wittenborn (USA), 1948
Asimov, Isaac, *A Short History of Biology*, Nelson, 1965
Asimov, Isaac, *Understanding Physics*, New American Library (USA), 1969
Banham, Rayner, *The New Brutalism*, Architectural Press, 1966
Banham, Rayner, *Theory and Design in the First Machine Age,* Architectural Press, 1960
Berne, M. D., *Games People Play*, Penguin Books, 1968
Beveridge, W. I. B., *The Art of Scientific Investigation*, Heinemann, 1972
Broadbent, D. E., *Perception and Communication*, Pergamon Press, 1958
Bronowski, J., *The Ascent of Man*, BBC Publications, 1973
Brothwell, Don R. (Ed) *Beyond Aesthetics*, Thames & Hudson, 1976
Brunes, T., *The Secrets of Ancient Geometry and Its Use*, Humanities Press (USA), 1967
Carver, Norman F. Jnr, *Form and Space in Japanese Architecture*, Shokousha, 1955
Clark, Kenneth, *Civilization: A Personal View*, BBC and John Murray, 1969
de Bono, Edward, *The Mechanism of Mind*, Penguin Books, 1971
de Bono, Edward, *Lateral Thinking*, Penguin Books, 1971
Descartes, René, *Philosophical Writings*, Open University Press, 1970
Eysenck, H. J., *Know Your Own IQ*, Penguin Books, 1962
Eysenck, H. J., *Uses and Abuses of Psychology*, Penguin Books, 1953
Foss, Brian M. (Ed) *New Horizons in Psychology*, Penguin Books, 1966
Foss C and Magdalino, P., *Rome and Byzantium*, Elsevier-Phaidon, 1977
Freud, Sigmund, *Outline of Psychoanalysis*, Hogarth Press, 1969
Freud, Sigmund, *The Interpretation of Dreams*, Allen & Unwin, 1955
Fry, Roger, *Vision and Design*, Penguin Books, 1937
Gamow, George, *Matter, Earth and Sky*, Macmillan, 1959
Gardner, Martin, *The Ambidextrous Universe*, Penguin Books, 1970
Gombrich, E. H., *Art and Illusion*, Phaidon Press, 1956
Gregory, R. L. and Gombrich, E. H. (Eds), *Illusion in Nature and Art*, Duckworth, 1973
Gregory, R. L., *Eye and Brain*, Weidenfeld & Nicolson, 1966
Gregory, R. L., *The Intelligent Eye*, Weidenfeld & Nicolson, 1970
Hawkins, Gerald S., *Beyond Stonehenge*, Arrow Books, 1977
Hebb, Donald O., *Textbook of Psychology*, W. B. Saunders, 1972
Hesselgren, Sven, *Man's Perception of Manmade Environment*, Dowden, Hutchinson & Ross (USA), 1977
Hitchcock, H. R., *In the Nature of Materials: 1887–1941 The Buildings of Frank Lloyd Wright*, Duell, Sloan & Pearce (USA), 1942
Hogg, J., *Psychology and the Visual Arts*, Penguin Books, 1969
Huxley, Aldous, *The Art of Seeing*, Chatto & Windus, 1943
Jones, Ernest, *The Life and Work of Sigmund Freud*, Hogarth Press, 1953–1959
Jung, Carl G., *Man and His Symbols*, Pan Books, 1978
Jung, Carl G., *Memories, Dreams, Reflections*, Fontana, 1967
Jung, Carl G., *The Psychology of the Unconscious*, Routledge & Kegan Paul, 1951
Klee, Paul, *The Thinking Eye*, Lund Humphries, 1961
Klee, Paul, *The Nature of Nature*, Lund Humphries, 1973
Koffka, Curt, *Principles of Gestalt Psychology*, Routledge & Kegan Paul, 1935
Lloyd, Barbara B., *Perception and Cognition*, Penguin Books, 1972
Lucio-Meyer, J. de, *Visual Aesthetics*, Lund Humphries, 1973

Mendelssohn, Kurt, *The Riddle of the Pyramids*, Thames & Hudson, 1974
Meyer, Leonard B., *Music, the Arts and Ideas*, University of Chicago Press (USA), 1967
Miller, G. A. (Ed), *Psychology*, Penguin Books, 1966
Miller, G. A., *Psychology of Communication*, Penguin Books, 1970
Burkhardt, Dietrich, *Signals in the Animal World*, Allen & Unwin, 1968
Oates, David and Joan, *The Rise of Civilisation*, Phaidon Press, 1976
Palmer, F., *Visual Awareness*, Batsford, 1972
Pendretti, Carlo, *The Notes of Leonardi da Vinci*, Peter Owen, 1965
Pierce, J. R., *Symbols, Signals, Noise: The Nature and Process of Communication*, Hutchinson, 1962
Reichardt, Jasia, *The Computer in Art*, Studio Vista, 1971
Reichardt, Jasia, *Cybernetics, Art and Ideas*, Studio Vista, 1971
Rhinehart, Luke, *The Dice Man*, Panther, 1972
Rowland, Kurt, *A History of the Modern Movement*, Van Nostrand Reinhold (USA), and Looking and Seeing (UK), 1973
Russell, Bertrand, *An Inquiry into Meaning and Truth*, Penguin Books, 1962
Saarinen, Eliel, *Search for Form*, Kennikat Press (USA), 1969
Spencer, Herbert, *First Principles*, Greenwood Press (USA), 1976
Thompson, D'Arcy Wentworth, *On Growth and Form*, Cambridge University Press, 1952
Tucci, G., *The Theory and Practice of Mandala*, Rider, 1969
Van Doesburg, Theo, *Principles of Neoplastic Art*, Lund Humphries, 1969
Vavilov, S. I., *The Human Eye and the Sun*, Pergamon Press, 1965
Wells, H. G., *A Short History of the World*, Penguin Books, 1922
Wertheimer, Max (Ed W. D. Ellis), *A Source Book of Gestalt Psychology*, Routledge & Kegan Paul, 1955
Whyte, L. L. (Ed), *Aspects of Form*, Lund Humphries, 1968
Wijsenbeek, L. J. F., *Mondrian*, Studio Vista, 1969
Zacharia, Sitchin, *The Twelfth Planet*, Allen & Unwin, 1977

Design and design theory

Albarn, Keith and others, *The Language of Pattern*, Thames & Hudson, 1974
Archer, L. Bruce, *Computers, Design Theory and the Handling of the Qualitative*, Royal College of Art
Archer, L. Bruce, *Systematic Method for Designers*, Council of Industrial Design, 1965
Bardesch, Mario Dezzi, *Frank Lloyd Wright*, Paul Hamlyn, 1972
Bates, Kenneth F., *Basic Design*, Constable, 1960
Battersby, A., *Network Analysis*, Macmillan, 1964
Bloomer and Moore, *Body, Memory and Architecture*, Yale University Press (USA), 1977
Boesigner, Willy (Ed), *Le Corbusier: Last Works*, Thames & Hudson, 1970
Borrego, John, *Space Grid Structures*, MIT Press (USA), 1968
Broadbent, Geoffrey and others, *Design in Architecture*, John Wiley & Sons (USA), 1973, 1975
Buckminster Fuller, R., *Synergettes: Explorations in the Geometry of Thinking*, Collier-Macmillan, 1975
Buckminster Fuller, R., *Utopia or Oblivion*, Penguin Books, 1970
Burns, Howard, *Andrea Palladio 1508–1580*, Arts Council of Great Britain, 1975
Campion, D., *Computers in Architectural Design*, Elsevier, 1968
Casson, Hugh, *Inscape: The Design of Interiors*, Architectural Press, 1968
Cox, H. L., *The Design of Structures of Least Weight*, Pergamon Press, 1965
Critchlow, Keith, *Order in Space*, Thames & Hudson, 1969
Critchlow, Keith, *Islamic Pattern*, Thames & Hudson, 1976
Cross, Nigel, *The Automated Architect*, Pion, 1977
Currie, R. M., *Work Study*, Pitman, 1959
de Sausmarez, M., *Basic Design: The Dynamics of Visual Form*, Studio Vista, 1967
Doblin, J., *One Hundred Great Product Designs*, Van Nostrand-Reinhold (USA), 1970
Duckworth, E., *A Guide to Operational Research*, Methuen, 1962
Farr, Michael, *Design Management*, Hodder & Stoughton, 1966
Fisher Cassie, W., *Structural Analysis*, Longman, 1957

Fowler, D. H., *Structural Stability and Morphogenesis*, Addison-Wesley (USA), 1976
Fry, Roger, *Vision and Design*, Chatto & Windus, 1920
Furman, T. T. (Ed), *The Uses of Computers in Engineering Design*, English Universities Press, 1970
Gasson, P. C., *Theory of Design*, Batsford, 1974
Gerstner, Karl, *Designing Programmes*, Tiranti, 1968
Gheorghin and Dragomir, *Geometry of Structural Forms*, Applied Science Publishers, 1978
Gibson, J. E., *The Design of Shell Roofs*, Spon, 1968
Ghyka, Matila, *Geometrical Composition and Design*, Tiranti, 1956
Goslett, Dorothy, *Professional Practice for Designers*, Batsford, 1972
Grillo, J. P., *Form, Function and Design*, Dover Publications (USA), 1975
Gropius, Walter, *The New Architecture and the Bauhaus*, Faber & Faber, 1965
Gropius, Walter, *Bauhaus 1919–1928*, Allen & Unwin, 1939
Gwilt, *Encyclopaedia of Architecture*, Longman, 1899
Hall, A. D., *A Methodology of Systems Engineering*, Van Nostrand-Reinhold (USA), 1962
Hambridge, Jay, *The Elements of Dynamic Symmetery*, Oxford University Press, 1912–1920
Harper, William Massie, *Statistics*, Macdonald & Evans, 1965
Hesselgren, Sven, *The Language of Architecture*, Applied Science Publishers, 1972
Civil Service Department, *Design of Forms in Government Departments*, HMSO, 1972
Hofmann, Armin, *Graphic Design Manual*, Tiranti, 1970
Humbert, Claude, *Ornamental Design*, Thames & Hudson, 1970
Itten, Johannes, *Design and Form* (Bauhaus), Reinhold Publishing Co (USA), 1964
Jones, Chris, *Design Methods*, Pergamon Press, 1962
Jones, Owen, *The Grammar of Ornament*, Bernard Quaritch, 1910
Kepes, Gyorgy, *Structure in Art and Science*, George Braziller (USA), 1965
Kepes, Gyorgy (Ed), *Vision and Values* series, Studio Vista
Kepes, Gyorgy, *Language of Vision*, Academy Editions, 1969
Kron, Joan and Slesin, Suzanne, *High-Tech*, Allen Lane, 1979
Lalvani, Havesh, *Transpolyhedra*, Havesh Lalvani, 1977
Le Corbusier, *The Modulor*, Faber & Faber, 1964
Leech, D. J., *Management of Design*, John Wiley & Sons (USA), 1972
Lesser, G., *Gothic Cathedrals and Sacred Geometry*, Tiranti, 1957
Makowski, S., *Space Structures*, Michael Joseph, 1965
March, Lionel and Steadman, Philip, *Geometry of Environment*, Methuen, 1974
Marks, R. W., *The Dymaxion World of Buckminster Fuller*, Van Nostrand Reinhold (USA), 1960
Matthews, W., *Mazes and Labyrinths*, Dover Publications (USA), 1970
Mayall, W. H., *Industrial Design*, Iliffe, 1968
Mischke, C. R., *Introduction to Computer Aided Design*, Prentice-Hall (USA), 1968
Nervi, Pier Luigi, *Aesthetics and Technology in Building*, Oxford University Press, 1966
Otto, Frei, Institute of Lightweight Structures, Stuttgart University, *IL6: Biology and Building – Soap Film Models*, Karl Krämer Verlag, Stuttgart
Otto, Frei (Ed), *Tensile Structures*, MIT Press (USA), 1973
Papenek, Victor, *Design for the Real World*, Thames & Hudson, 1972
Pawley, Martin, *Mies van der Rohe*, Thames & Hudson, 1970
Pehut, Wolfgang, *Expressionist Architecture*, Thames & Hudson, 1973
Pevsner, Nikolaus, *Pioneers of Modern Design from William Morris to Walter Gropius*, Penguin Books, 1960
Read, Sir Herbert and Martin, Leslie, *Naum Gabo*, Zwemmer, 1957
Redstone, L. G., *Art in Architecture*, McGraw-Hill (USA), 1968
Reekie, R. Fraser, *Design in the Built Environment*, Arnold, 1972
Reichardt, Jasia, *The Computer in Art*, Studio Vista, 1971
Robertson, Howard, *Principles of Architectural Composition*, Architectural Press, 1924
Rowland, Kurt, *Looking and Seeing* series, Ginn & Co
Scholfield, P. H., *The Theory of Proportion in Architecture*, Cambridge University Press, 1958
Siegal, Curt, *Structure and Form*, Crosby Lockwood, 1961
Sutton, I. (Ed), *The Twentieth Century*, Thames & Hudson, 1971
Tange, K., *Katsura Japanese Architecture*, Yale University Press (USA), 1972
Taylor, John F. A., *Design and Expression in the Visual Arts*, Dover Publications (USA), 1965
Vitruvius, *The Ten Books on Architecture*, Yale University Press (USA), 1972

Whyte, Lancelot Law (Ed), *Aspects of Form*, Lund Humphries, 1968
Wittkower, R., *Architectural Principles in Age of Humanism*, Tiranti, 1952

Fine art
Alley, Ronald, *Francis Bacon*, Thames & Hudson, 1964
Arts Council catalogue, *Bridget Riley*, Arts Council of Great Britain, 1974
Baljen, J., *Theo van Doesburg*, Studio Vista, 1974
Barrett, Cyril, *An Introduction to Optical Art*, Studio Vista, 1970
Barilli, Renato, *Art Nouveau*, Paul Hamlyn, 1969
Battersby, Martin, *The World of Art Nouveau*, Arlington Books, 1968
Bouleau, Charles, *The Painter's Secret Geometry*, Thames & Hudson, 1963
Bazin, Germain, *The Avant-Garde in the History of Painting*, Thames & Hudson, 1969
Benthall, Jonathan, *Science and Technology in Art Today*, Thames & Hudson, 1972
Bonnefoy, Yves, *Miró*, Faber & Faber, 1967
Bowness, Alan, *Gauguin*, Phaidon Press, 1971
Breton, André, *Manifestos of Surrealism*, University of Michigan Press (USA), 1972
Cooper, David, *Nicholas de Staël*, Norton & Co (USA), 1961
Cooper, David, *Toulouse-Lautrec*, Harry N. Abrams (USA), 1966
Davis, Douglas, *Art and the Future*, Thames & Hudson, 1973
D'Harnoncourt and McShine, *Marcel Duchamp*, Thames & Hudson, 1973
Diehl, Gaston, *Victor Vasareley*, Crown Publishers (USA), 1973
Dube, Wolf-Dieter, *The Expressionists*, Thames & Hudson, 1972
Dumur, Guy, *Nicholas de Staël*, Crown Publishers (USA), 1976
Erni, Hans, *Man the Artist, His Creative Imagination*, Macdonald, 1964
Evans, M. G., *Primer of Facts about Music*, Theodore Presser Co (USA), 1909
Fry, Edward F. (Ed), *Cubism*, Thames & Hudson, 1966
Gieure, Maurice, *G. Braque*, Zwemmer, 1956
Ginderstael, R. V., *De Staël*, Galerie Beyder, Basel, 1966
Gray, Steve (Ed), *Hans Richter*, Thames & Hudson, 1971
Grohmann, Will, *Art of Our Time*, Thames & Hudson, 1967
Habasque, G., *Cubism*, Zwemmer, 1968
Haftmann, Werner, *Painting in the Twentieth Century*, Lund Humphries, 1960
Hammacher, A. M., *Vincent van Gogh*, Spring Books, 1961
Herbert, E. L. (Ed), *Modern Artists on Art*, Prentice-Hall (USA), 1964
Hillier, J., *Hokusai*, Phaidon Press, 1955
Hofmann, Werner, *Gustav Klimt*, Studio Vista, 1972
Holt, Michael, *Mathematics in Art*, Studio Vista, 1971
Jaffe, Hans, *Klee*, Hamlyn, 1972
Jaffe, Hans, *Mondrian*, Thames & Hudson, 1970
Jaffe, Hans, *De Stijl*, Thames & Hudson, 1970
Kandinsky, Vassily, *Concerning the Spiritual in Art and Painting in Particular*, George Wittenborn (USA), 1976
Károlyi, Otto, *Introducing Music*, Penguin Books, 1971
Lassaigue, J., *Henri Matisse*, Skira, Geneva, 1959
Lebel, Robert, *Marcel Duchamp*, Trianon Press (USA), 1959
Leymarie, Jean, *Fauvism*, Zwemmer, 1959
Leymarie, Jean, *Impressionism*, World Publishing (USA), 1955
Loran, Erle, *Cézanne's Composition*, University of California Press (USA), 1963
Maillard and Elgar, *Picasso*, Thames & Hudson, 1956
Marcel, Jean, *The History of Surrealist Painting*, Grove Press (USA), 1960
Marnat, Marcel, *Klee*, Spurbooks, 1974
Martin, Marianne W., *Futurist Art and Theory*, Clarendon Press, 1968
Martin, Nicholson and Gabo, *Circle: International Survey of Constructive Art*, Praeger (USA), 1971
Messer, Thomas M., *Münch*, Harry N. Abrams (USA), 1970

Moholy-Nagy, Laszlo, *Vision in Motion*, Academy Editions, 1969
Motherwell, Robert, *The Dada Painters and Poets*, George Wittenborn (USA), 1951
Muller, J-E., and Elgar, Frank, *A Century of Modern Painting*, Thames & Hudson, 1972
Myers, Bernard, *Expressionism: A Generation in Revolt*, Thames & Hudson, 1957
Nash, J. M., *The Age of Rembrandt and Vermeer*, Phaidon Press, 1972
Overly, Paul, *Kandinsky*, Paul Elek, 1969
Panofsky, E., *Life and Art of Albrecht Dürer*, Princeton University Press (USA), 1967
Parola, René, *Optical Art Theory and Practice*, Van Nostrand Reinhold (USA), 1975
Perruchot, Henri, *Gauguin*, Perpetua Books, 1963
Popper, Frank, *Origins and Development of Kinetic Art*, Graphic Society, New York (USA), 1968
Raynal, M., *Cézanne*, Skira, Geneva, 1952
Read, Herbert, *Education Through Art*, Faber & Faber, 1961
Read, Herbert, *A Concise History of Modern Painting*, Thames & Hudson, 1959
Rice, David T., *Islamic Art*, Thames & Hudson, 1965
Richter, Hans, *Dada*, Thames & Hudson, 1965
Rickey, George, *Constructivism*, Studio Vista, 1967
Robertson, Brian, *Jackson Pollock*, Thames & Hudson, 1965
Roethel, Hans K., *The Blue Rider*, Praeger (USA), 1971
Rose, Barbara, *American Art since 1900*, Thames & Hudson, 1967
Roters, Eberhard, *Painters of the Bauhaus*, Zwemmer, 1969
Rowland, Kurt, *History of the Modern Movement*, Van Nostrand Reinhold (USA) and Looking and Seeing (UK), 1973
Royal Schools of Music, *Rudiments and Theory of Music*, Associated Board of the Royal Schools of Music, 1958
Rubin, Williams (Ed), *Cézanne: The Late Work*, Thames & Hudson, 1978
Ruskin, John, *Modern Painting* (5 vols), reprinted in Library Edition, George Allen, 1903–1905
Russell, John, *Braque*, Phaidon Press, 1959
Sandler, Irving, *Abstract Expressionism*, Pall Mall Press, 1970
Schmied, Wieland, *Mark Tobey*, Thames & Hudson, 1967
Scholes, Percy, (Ed: J. O. Ward), *Oxford Companion to Music*, Oxford University Press, 1970
Scuphor, Michel, *A Dictionary of Abstract Painting*, Methuen, 1958
Stravinsky, Igor, *The Poetics of Music in the Form of Six Lessons*, Harvard University Press (USA), 1970
Suzoki, Juzo, *Sharaku*, Ward Lock, 1968
Swift, Emerson H., *Roman Sources of Christian Art*, Columbia University Press (USA), 1951
Tate Gallery, London, *Turner 1775–1851* (exhibition catalogue), Tate Gallery, Publications Department, 1974
Trier, Edward, *Jean Arp*, Thames & Hudson, 1968
Urban, Martin, *Emil Nolde: Landscapes*, Pall Mall Press, 1970
Vachtova, Ludmila, *Frank Kupka*, Thames & Hudson, 1968
Vollard, Ambroise, *Cézanne: His Life and Art*, Crown Publishers (USA), 1937
Wijsenbeck, L. J. F., *Mondrian*, Studio Vista, 1969
Walberg, Patrick, *Surrealism*, Thames & Hudson, 1965
Werner, Alfred, *Modigliani*, Thames & Hudson, 1967
Whitford, Frank, *Expressionism*, Hamlyn, 1970
Wingler, Hans, *The Bauhaus*, MIT Press (USA), 1969

Mathematics

Ayres, Frank, *Projective Geometry*, Schaum Outline Series, McGraw–Hill (USA), 1967
Boyer, C. B., *A History of Mathematics*, John Wiley & Sons (USA), 1968
Clarke, L. Harwood, *Ordinary Level Mathematics*, Heinemann Educational, 1969
Crowder & Martin, *Trigonometry – A First Course*, English Universities Press, 1962
Cundy and Rollett, *Mathematical Models*, Oxford University Press, 1973
Dedron and Itard, *Mathematics and Mathematicians*, Transworld (USA), 1974
Gardner, Martin, *Mathematical Puzzles and Diversions*, Penguin Books, 1975
Geary, Lowry and Hayden, *Technical Mathematics (General Course)*, Longman
Gordon, Charles K., *Introduction to Mathematical Structures*, Dickenson Publishing Co (USA), 1968
Hawk, Minor C., *Descriptive Geometry*, Schaum Outline Series, McGraw–Hill (USA), 1962
Horner, H. A., *ONC Mathematics* Vols 1 and 2, Heinemann Educational, 1966, 1967

Jacobs, Harold R., *Mathematics: A Human Endeavour*, W. H. Freeman (USA), 1971
Kline, Morris, *Mathematics in Western Culture*, Penguin Books, 1972
Land, F., *The Language of Mathematics*, John Murray, 1960
Lockwood, E. H., *A Book of Curves*, Cambridge University Press, 1961
Mandelbrot, B. B., *Fractals, Form, Chance and Dimension*, W. H. Freeman (USA), 1977
Matthews, W. H., *Mazes and Labyrinths: Their History and Development*, Dover Publications (USA), 1970
Northrop, Eugene P., *Riddles in Mathematics*, Penguin Books, 1967
Pascoe, L. C., *New Mathematics*, Hodder & Stoughton, 1970, 1971
Pedoe, Dan, *Geometry and the Liberal Arts*, Penguin Books, 1976
Pedoe, J., *Advanced National Certificate Mathematics*, English Universities Press, 1955
Penney, David, *Perspectives in Mathematics*, Benjamin (USA), 1972
Pierce, J. R., *Almost all About Waves*, MIT Press (USA), 1974
Polya, George, *Mathematical Discovery* Vols 1 and 2, John Wiley & Sons (USA), 1962, 1965
Protter and Morrey, *College Calculus with Analytic Geometry*, Addison-Wesley (USA), 1970
Sawyer, W. W., *Mathematician's Delight*, Penguin Books, 1973
Sawyer, W. W., *Prelude to Mathematics*, Penguin Books, 1971
Sawyer, W. W., *A Path to Modern Mathematics*, Penguin Books, 1971
Sawyer, W. W., *The Search for Pattern*, Penguin Books, 1970
Scanes, W. A., *A Survey of Graphs*, Allman & Son, 1967
Skemp, Richard R., *The Psychology of Learning Mathematics*, Penguin Books, 1971
Slaby, S. M., *Fundamentals of Three Dimensional Descriptive Geometry*, Harcourt Brace Jovanovich (USA), 1966
Spencer, D. D., *Gameplaying with Computers*, Spartan Books (USA), 1969
Sperry, *Short Course in Spherical Trigonometry*, Johnson Publishing Co (USA), 1928
Stein, Shermann K., *Mathematics: The Manmade Universe*, W. H. Freeman (USA), 1975
Steinhaus, H., *Mathematical Snapshots*, Oxford University Press (USA), 1969
Stephenson, G., *An Introduction to Matrices, Sets and Groups*, Longman, 1965
Swaine, K. B., *An Introductory Course to Pure Mathematics*, Harrap, 1958
Wilder, R. L., *The Evolution of Mathematical Concepts*, Transworld (USA), 1974

Science and technology
Anderson, J. C., and Leaver, K. D., *Materials Science*, Nelson, 1974
Bachelard, Gaston, *The Poetics of Space*, Beacon Press (USA), 1964
Bizony, M. T. (Ed), *The New Space Encyclopedia*, Artemis Press, 1969, 1973
Boys, C. V., *Soap Bubbles and the Forces which Mould Them*, Heinemann Educational, 1960
Bucksbaum, R., *Animals Without Backbones*, Penguin Books, 1955
Callahan, J. J., 'Curvature of Space in a Finite Universe', *Scientific American*, Vol 238/2, 1976
Case and Chilver, *Strength of Materials*, Arnold, 1962
Chaplin, John, *Wings and Space*, Ian Allen, 1970
Cruise and Newman, *Photographic Techniques in Scientific Research*, Academic Press, 1973
Einstein and Infield, *The Evolution of Physics*, Cambridge University Press, 1971
Eiseley, Loren, *The Unexpected Universe*, Penguin Books, 1973
Fairweather and Sliwa, *AJ Metric Handbook*, Architectural Press, 1970
Fellows, D. K., *The Environment of Man*, Hamilton Publishing Co (USA), 1975
Gingervich, Owen (Ed), *Cosmology + 1*, Scientific American and W. H. Freeman & Co.
Hopkins, H. J., *A Span of Bridges*, David & Charles, 1970
Hoyle, Fred, *Encounter with the Future*, Trident Press, 1965
Kubic Bubbles, Advance Educational Toys, 1977
King, Ivan R., *The Universe Unfolding*, W. H. Freeman (USA), 1976
Krick, Edward V., *Engineering and Engineering Design*, John Wiley & Sons (USA), 1968
Loeb, Arthur L., *Color and Symmetry in Crystallography*, John Wiley & Sons (USA), 1971
Milne, L. and M., *The Arena of Life*, Allen & Unwin, 1972
Moore, Patrick, *The Observer's Book of Astronomy*, Frederick Warne, 1974
Morgan, W., *The Elements of Structure*, Pitman, 1964
Mudie, R. and C., *The Story of the Sailing Ship*, Marshall Cavendish, 1975
Phillips, F. C., *An Introduction to Crystallography*, Oliver & Boyd, 1971

Postle, Dennis, *Fabric of the Universe*, Macmillan, 1976
Pough, Frederick, H., *A Field Guide to Rocks and Minerals*, Constable, 1970
Radford, G. D., *Mechanical Engineering Design*, Macmillan, 1966
Rosenauer, N., *Kinematics of Machines*, Dover Publications (USA), 1967
Satterthwaite, G. E., *Encyclopaedia of Astronomy*, Hamlyn, 1966
Scheludko, A., *Colloid Chemistry*, Elsevier, 1966
Shigley, J., *Mechanical Engineering Design*, McGraw-Hill (USA), 1972
Singer, Charles, *A Short History of Scientific Ideas*, Oxford University Press, 1962
Smith, Geoff, *Wealth Creation*, Institute of Management Services, 1978
Wallace and Fenster, *Mechanics*, Holt, Rinehart & Winston (USA), 1969
Weaver, K. F., 'The Incredible Universe', *National Geographic Magazine*, Vol 145, No 5, 1974
Wells, A. F., *The Third Dimension in Chemistry*, Oxford University Press, 1968
Went, F. W., and Editors of *Life*, *The Plants*, Time Inc (USA), 1965
Wick, Gerald L., *Elementary Particles*, Geoffrey Chapman, 1972

Technical drawing and graphic design

Abbott, W., *Technical Drawing*, Blackie, 1970
Bayliss, R., *Geometry and Drawing*, Hutchinson Educational, 1970
Biegeleisen, J. I., *Book of One Hundred Type Face Alphabets*, Signs of the Times Publishing Co (USA), 1974
Biggs, J. R., *Letter Forms and Lettering*, Blandford Press, 1977
Bourgoin, J., *Arabic Geometrical Pattern and Design*, Dover Publications (USA), 1973
Capelle, Friedrick, *Professional Perspective Drawing for Architects and Engineers*, McGraw-Hill (USA), 1969
Ching, Frank, *Architectural Graphics*, Architectural Press, 1976
Clutterbuck, C. K., *3-D Scale Drawing*, English Universities Press, 1966
Fetter, W. A., *Computer Graphics in Communication*, McGraw-Hill (USA), 1965
Franke, Herbert W., *Computer Graphics: Computer Art*, Phaidon Press, 1971
French, Thomas E., and Vierck, Charles J., *Engineering Drawing and Graphic Technology*, McGraw-Hill (USA) 1978
Fripp, A. D., and Thompson, A. R., *Human Anatomy for Art Students*, New Art Library, 1946
Hamilton, Edward A., *Graphic Design for the Computer Age*, Van Nostrand-Reinhold (USA), 1970
Hofmann, Armin, *Graphic Design Manual*, Tiranti, 1965
Holmes, John M., *Applied Perspective*, Pitman, 1967
Horton, W. G., *Data Display Systems*, Business Books, 1969
Hutt, Allen, *Newspaper Design*, Oxford University Press, 1967
Kelsey, W. Eric, *Geometrical and Building Drawing*, Crosby Lockwood, 1970
Knight, S. A., *Understanding Graphs*, Blackie, 1966
Levens, A. S., *Graphics*, John Wiley & Sons (USA), 1968
Lockwood, Arthur, *Diagrams*, Studio Vista, 1969
Luzadder, W. L., *Fundamentals of Engineering Drawing*, Prentice-Hall (USA), 1971
'Massin', *Letter and Image*, Studio Vista, 1970
Reekie, R. Fraser, *Draughtsmanship*, Arnold, 1969
Rose, T. G., *Business Charts*, Pitman, 1957
Thomson, R., *Principles of Graphic Communication for Engineers*, Nelson, 1978, 1979
Weidemann, Kurt, *Book Jackets and Record Sleeves*, Thames & Hudson and Andre Deutsch, 1969
Wickham, Geoffrey, *Rapid Perspective*, Tiranti, 1967
Wingler, Hans M., *Graphic Work from the Bauhaus*, Lund Humphries, 1969

Index

Purism 16, 26, 204, 295
psychology 3, 48, 49
pyramid 237, 240, 264
Pythagorean harmony 84,
116–117, 141, 255
Pythagoras' Theorem 21, 105,
154, 224, 262
psychology 23, 63, 115, 195

quadratic equations 73, 211
quadrilaterals 24, 166, 174
quality 81, 124, 205
quark 7, 54
quartz crystals 243
quasar 97

radar 97, 206, 215, 256
radian 65, 219
radiate 97–100, 163, 189, 246,
269, 273, 277
radius curve 153, 204
ragtime 260
railway line effects 153, 231
random 26, 32, 36, 168, 191, 200,
281, 284, 290
rate of change 32, 63, 74, 93, 123,
255, 268
ratio 21, 72, 75, 103, 122, 199,
287
Ray, Man 294
Read, Herbert 295
realizing sensations 16–17, 123,
230
recession 81, 177, 194
reciprocity 59, 86, 96, 117, 143,
151–164, 170, 182, 273
reciprocating pump 182
recode 49, 103
recognition 8, 9, 27, 58, 274
recording 13, 186
rectangle 41, 46, 56, 88, 90, 104,
138, 154, 165, 254, 281, 288
rectangular hyperbola 214
red shift 273
reflection 22, 34, 142, 146, 208,
238
reflex angle 23
regimentation 28
regular polygons 23, 66, 158, 174,
239–241, 255, 267
relative, relativity 14, 16, 25, 37,
98, 128, 177
religion 15, 52
Rembrandt, van Rijn 47, 98
Renaissance 95, 106, 156, 203,
232
repeat, repeat patterns 15, 38, 66
repetition 9, 18, 28, 38, 123, 140,
283, 291, 299
replica 125, 158
repulsion 248
resonance 7, 15, 40, 118, 120

retaliation 178
retreat 180
reverse curve 201
revolution, rev 19, 20, 63, 151,
219
rhombic 221
rhythm 38, 39, 46, 51, 57, 123,
130, 143, 187, 202, 253, 298
Riemann, Bernhard 1, 98
right angled triangle 21–22, 106,
114, 158, 228
right hand 7, 31, 175–176, 178
Riley, Bridget 45
ripple 216
rivalry 283, 292
rocket 269
Rodin, Auguste 180, 186
rods 222, 240
roller and slab 152
rollers, rolling 54, 152, 153, 217
romantic 108, 201, 286, 304
roof plan 228
root series 104, 108, 113
root three rectangle 106
root two rectangle 105
rotating rectangles 103, 104
rotation 34, 48, 53, 62, 72, 103,
146, 158, 183, 189, 240, 269,
276
Rothko, Mark 255, 287
roulettes 217
royals, playing cards 28
Rubaiyat 165
Rubens, Peter Paul 195, 201
Ruskin, John 201
Russell, Bertrand 72
Ryan, Christopher 207

sail 4
Salisbury Cathedral 187
same and similar 9, 13, 14, 18,
251
sameness 12, 16, 17, 251
Sander parallelogram 275
sandwich effect 259
satire 283
Saturn 149
scale 38, 55, 100, 122, 131, 139,
193, 256, 259, 261
scaling noise 168
scanning 28, 97, 165, 281
Schwitters, Kurt 294
sciagraphy 239
science fiction 292
scientific method 37, 262
screw, see helix
sculpture 125, 177, 186, 212
  see also individual artists
sea 170, 258, 304
secant 219
security 55, 190, 251, 292
section 228
sedimentary weighting 258

segment 174
self-expression 11, 16
semi-regular solids 225, 241
semi-tone scale 118
sensitivity 3, 36, 80, 187
sensory communications 80, 251
sensory form 267, 278
sensory scale, structure 27, 124,
129, 136, 255, 278
sentimental 200
septagon 23, 160
sequence, sequential order 8–9,
28–29, 32, 134, 289
series, see structure or progression
serration 24, 75, 279
set 33, 133
Seurat, Georges 287
seven note scale 117
Severini, Gino 227
sex 38, 181
shadows 239
Shakespeare, William 186, 300
shape 14, 120, 123, 261, 268, 281
shear 243
shell 210, 221, 241
Sierpinski, W. 167
signals 13
silhouette 186, 280
silica glass 246
silicon 240
similar polygons 19–22, 90, 105,
114, 149, 234, 288
similarity 12, 14, 18, 23, 72, 90,
123, 140, 246, 287, 298
simple curve 200
simple harmonic motion 63
simple interest 74
simple oscillatory structure 142,
182
simplicity 4, 288
simply supported beam 210, 277
simultaneity 8
simultaneous 13, 37, 55, 70
simultaneous contrast of
colour 204
sine, sin x 149, 219
sine curve 63–65, 120
Singier, Gustave 207
singularity 9, 40, 56, 249
sinh x 219–220
skeleton 186, 276
skill 4, 11, 36
skin 268, 280, 281
slenderness ratio 277
sliding, slip plane 267, 278
slope 75, 191, 208, 279
small whole numbers, Law of 118
snow crystals 158, 168, 260
soap bubbles 272, 273
sodium 245
solar system 7, 149, 172, 246, 297
solid and void 57, 89
solitude 40, 46
solution of problems 287, 302

space 16, 17, 56, 70, 97, 99, 171,
183, 204, 240, 281, 304
space grids 32, 123, 193, 264
Spanier, Muggsy 53
spectrum 239
spin, spinner 7, 169
spiral 46, 94, 97, 104, 114, 115,
168, 175, 185, 220
spiral of Archimedes 54
spirit 291
splitting 52, 76, 81
square 21–22, 40, 46, 88, 186,
192, 240, 250, 267, 278, 289
squaring the circle 121
St Peter's, Rome 280
stability 191, 251
standing waves 291
star 97, 149, 177, 248
status 130, 246, 286
stereographic drawings 226
still life 17
Stijl, de 57, 204
stochastic music 169
straight line 2, 98, 108, 165, 171,
200, 231, 262, 267
straight line graphs 74, 208
strain 260, 266–269
Stravinsky, Igor 291
street furniture 129
stressed skin 272
stressing 171, 187, 251, 260, 266,
272
stretching and squeezing 268, 298
string 64, 117, 186, 268
stroboscopic 227
strong nuclear force 246
structure, see number, sensory,
visual
strut 276
subconscious 302
subliminal response 72
subordination 124, 130, 195
sum of an AP 73
sum of a GP 76, 86
sum to infinity 86
sun 97, 149, 177, 213, 297
sunflower 110
Sung dynasty 67
superconscious order 285, 302
superelevation 153
superellipse 154, 267
superimposition 123, 158, 160,
194, 264, 277
supernova 248
superstition 33
superpolyhedra 32, 270
Suprematism 16, 47
surface tension 170, 272
Surrealism 17, 261, 294
survival 12, 124, 178, 290
suspension bridge, cable 210, 277
symbiosis 164
symbol 3, 171, 286
symbolism 5, 204